Understanding Strength and Conditioning as Sport Coaching

Contemporary strength and conditioning coaching is, for the most part, informed by the exercise sciences, with little engagement being made with sociocultural and pedagogical perspectives which have emerged in sports coaching research over the last two decades. In *Understanding Strength and Conditioning as Sport Coaching: Bridging the Biophysical, Pedagogical and Sociocultural Foundations of Practice*, the authors – whose expertise in strength and conditioning, sports coaching and pedagogy – help students and coaches to integrate perspectives from these disciplines to enhance their strength and conditioning coaching practice.

The book encourages readers to add moral, ethical and political considerations to the technical aspects of their coaching practice. It discusses and applies concepts to a full range of strength and conditioning settings, including elite performance, young athletes, ageing athletes and returning to play following injury.

Featuring an eResource, and structured around rich, narrative pedagogical cases reflecting the issues faced by practising strength and conditioning coaches, the book offers a thoroughly engaging introduction to pedagogical and sociocultural concepts and literature in a strength and conditioning context. This is a vital book for students of strength and conditioning, and an important resource for practising strength and conditioning coaches and sport science staff.

Tania Cassidy is Associate Professor in Sport Pedagogy at the School of Physical Education, Sport and Exercise Sciences, University of Otago, New Zealand.

Phil Handcock is Lecturer in the Prescription of Physical Activity and Exercise, Athletic Training and Conditioning at the Institute of Sport, Exercise and Health, Otago Polytechnic, Dunedin, New Zealand.

Brian Gearity is Assistant Professor and Director of Online Graduate Programs in Sport, Strength and Conditioning, and Psychology of Coaching at the Graduate School of Professional Psychology, University of Denver, USA.

Lisette Burrows is Professor of Community Health at Te Huataki Waiora School of Health, University of Waikato, New Zealand.

We are only ever uncovering 'truths for now'. *Understanding Strength and Conditioning as Sport Coaching* challenges these truths, challenges our everyday practices and asks us to actively engage in our own critical thinking. Participating in these processes are integral to growth and mastery. Worthy ambitions.

Jason Cowman, *Head of Athletic Performance,*
National Team, Irish Rugby Football Union

Until now, the role of the coach in strength and conditioning has been overlooked. This book looks at strength and conditioning from a coaching perspective, covering the key interdisciplinary knowledge that a successful coach requires. This type of thinking will change our perspective of strength and conditioning and help develop the coach of the future.

Ian Jeffreys, *NSCA board member, Professor,*
University of South Wales, Strength
and Conditioning Coach

Understanding Strength and Conditioning as Sport Coaching is unlike any other book in the field of strength and conditioning. The authors take their approach from pedagogy, sport coaching and strength and conditioning coaching to provide a comprehensive look inside what it takes to improve athletes' physical development and preparation.

Scott Caulfield, *Director of Strength and Conditioning,*
Colorado College, and Former Head Strength
and Conditioning Coach, NSCA

Understanding Strength and Conditioning as Sport Coaching

Bridging the Biophysical, Pedagogical and Sociocultural Foundations of Practice

Tania Cassidy, Phil Handcock, Brian Gearity and Lisette Burrows

LONDON AND NEW YORK

First published 2020
by Routledge
2 Park Square, Milton Park, Abingdon, Oxon, OX14 4RN

and by Routledge
52 Vanderbilt Avenue, New York, NY 10017

Routledge is an imprint of the Taylor & Francis Group, an informa business

© 2020 Tania Cassidy, Phil Handcock, Brian Gearity and Lisette Burrows

The right of Tania Cassidy, Phil Handcock, Brian Gearity and Lisette Burrows to be identified as authors of this work has been asserted by them in accordance with sections 77 and 78 of the Copyright, Designs and Patents Act 1988.

All rights reserved. No part of this book may be reprinted or reproduced or utilised in any form or by any electronic, mechanical, or other means, now known or hereafter invented, including photocopying and recording, or in any information storage or retrieval system, without permission in writing from the publishers.

Trademark notice: Product or corporate names may be trademarks or registered trademarks, and are used only for identification and explanation without intent to infringe.

Library of Congress Cataloging-in-Publication Data
Names: Cassidy, Tania, 1964- author. | Handcock, Phil, author. | Burrows, Lisette, 1963– author. | Gearity, Brian, author.
Title: Understanding strength and conditioning as sport coaching : bridging the biophysical, pedagogical and sociocultural foundations of practice / Tania Cassidy, Phil Handcock, Lisette Burrows, and Brian Gearity.
Description: New York, NY : Routledge, 2020. | Includes bibliographical references and index.
Identifiers: LCCN 2019058557 (print) | LCCN 2019058558 (ebook) | ISBN 9781138301818 (hardback) | ISBN 9781138301825 (paperback) | ISBN 9780203732243 (ebook)
Subjects: LCSH: Physical education and training. | Athletes—Training of. | Weight training. | Coaching (Athletics)
Classification: LCC GV711.5 .C386 2020 (print) | LCC GV711.5 (ebook) | DDC 613.7/1—dc23
LC record available at https://lccn.loc.gov/2019058557
LC ebook record available at https://lccn.loc.gov/2019058558

ISBN: 978-1-138-30181-8 (hbk)
ISBN: 978-1-138-30182-5 (pbk)
ISBN: 978-0-203-73224-3 (ebk)

Typeset in Times New Roman
by Apex CoVantage, LLC

Visit the eResource: www.routledge.com/9781138301825

Contents

List of tables vii
Acknowledgements viii

PART 1
Setting the scene 1

1 Introduction 3
2 Mapping the construction of strength and conditioning knowledge 18
3 Concepts and frameworks – putting strength and conditioning under the microscope 29

PART 2
Elite sport performance 47

4 Measurement, assessment and testing – what does it all mean? 49
5 Training volume – fear of missing out (FOMO) 57
6 'Helicopter' strength and conditioning: questioning the role of monitoring 67

PART 3
Developing as a strength and conditioning professional 79

7 Developing as a competent strength and conditioning professional 81
8 Women and strength and conditioning coaching 91
9 Finding a professional voice and collaborating 103

PART 4
Conditioning across the lifespan 115

10 Healthy development of youth for sport 117

| 11 | Talent identification and development and creating an environment for success | 128 |
| 12 | Older and wiser? | 140 |

PART 5
Health, injury and wellbeing — 151

13	Conditioning for protection?	153
14	Return to play following injury	166
15	Looking after yourself as a strength and conditioning coach	177

Index — 188

Tables

2.1	Strength and conditioning organisation mission statements	23
2.2	Strength and conditioning organisation codes of ethics summary	24
2.3	Categorisation of articles published in strength and conditioning professional journals (last four issues)	25
2.4	Categorisation of national conference podium presentations	26

Acknowledgements

We extend our sincere thanks to all those who have willingly shared their ideas and experiences with us over the years and as such have, knowingly or not, contributed to the ideas presented in this book.

TC: To my family and friends, a very big thank you for your constant love and support. I wouldn't 'work' without you. A special thank you to Georgia, Jake, Toby, Zach, Lewis, Greta, Annabella and Rosa for your love, making me laugh and giving me reasons to play.

PH: For Dad. My heartfelt thanks to Deb who helped immensely by not hindering – love you. Thanks to family, friends and colleagues who constantly encouraged this. A huge thanks to my students – your puzzled looks were all I needed to constantly reconsider what I thought I knew – I owe you all.

BG: I would like to thank everybody who supported my development in strength and conditioning including: Dad – John Gearity (always), Coach Barona at Beachwood High School (1993–1997), Don McPhillips at John Carroll University (1997–2001), the S&C staffs with the Cleveland Indians baseball team (1999–2001) and the University of Tennessee (2001–2009), Jump N' Gymnastics and Tumbling (2013–2014), the Purvis High School Tornadoes (2012–2014), everybody with the National Strength and Conditioning Association and *Strength & Conditioning Journal*, and so many others.

Part 1
Setting the scene

1 Introduction

Introduction
How it all started

    Tania
    Phil
    Brian
    Lisette
    The authorship team as brokers

The aims of this book
What is meant by sociocultural, pedagogical and biophysical concepts?
Why is this book needed?
Who is this book for?
How is it organised?
References

Introduction

Contemporary strength and conditioning coaches (SCCs) primarily draw on the exercise sciences to inform their practice (Gearity & Henderson Metzger, 2017; Kuklick & Gearity, in press; Mills & Gearity, 2016; Mills et al., 2018; Mills & Gearity, 2018). While research from these disciplines undoubtedly adds value to practice, we contend that strength and conditioning (S&C) practices could be further enhanced, theoretically and practically, by also drawing on research emanating from the sociocultural and pedagogical disciplines. It is our intention in this book to start a conversation with SCCs, and the S&C field in general, by making cases for the benefits of interpreting S&C practices using pedagogical and sociocultural informed research. This has precedence with Cassidy et al. (2004) identifying a similar gap in sports coaching and subsequently volumes of research in this area has started to fill this gap and show the utility of thinking socioculturally and pedagogically.

There continues to be relatively little available literature that questions some of the taken-for-granted practices in coaching and acknowledges the complex reality within which coaches work (Bowes & Jones, 2006; Côté et al., 1995). The significance of this book lies partly in response to Knudson and Morrison's (2002) call for a reality-based integrative approach to human movement. It is a position rooted in the belief that a sociocultural pedagogical approach is imperative for understanding such a complex and dynamic activity as coaching, where, invariably the whole is considerably greater than the sum of the constituent parts (pp. 7–8).

4 *Setting the scene*

We recognise that because historically S&C education and professional development have been informed by the exercise science disciplines, many SCCs may not see the value in a book that draws *only* on pedagogical and sociocultural literature. For this reason, we have designed this book to act as a 'bridge' to support conversations relating to S&C practice, and to draw on the biophysical *as well as* sociocultural and pedagogical literature. If we fail to acknowledge the historical importance exercise science has played, and continues to play, in informing SSC's practices, we will also fail to acknowledge how many SSCs currently understand their role. We recognise that as some SCCs will feel comfortable with their existing knowledge and practices, they may find some of the discussion in this book to be unsettling, disrespectful and possibly confrontational. It is not our intention for it to be so; rather we acknowledge that care needs to be taken when challenging the status quo.

To achieve this, we have adopted Tinning's (2002) concept of 'modest pedagogy', which we understand to mean that when questioning the status quo, it is important to be mindful of the history, personal investments and nuanced environments in which we all work. Further, modest pedagogy was not viewed as a prescription of what to do; rather it sought to encourage practitioners to understand their place in a complex world. Tinning goes on to assert that by adopting a modest pedagogy, we become aware of the limitations of 'rationality as a catalyst for change' (p. 236). Hence our use of a narrative in the form of realist fiction (aka pedagogical cases) at the beginning of the chapters in sections 2–5, to stimulate an engaged and emotive response from the reader. Narratives are considered a 'powerful professional development' tool (Clandinin, 2001, p. viii) that can demonstrate the complexities of practice and provide an opportunity to reveal and explore the emotions of practice (Potrac et al., 2013). The narratives in this text come in various forms and have been written as 'pedagogical cases', which Armour (2014) describes as a professional development tool, or in other words a 'mechanism', for incorporating ideas from multiple (sub)disciplines and using the personal voice to reflect the emotions of practice as well as potentially 'developing an integrative science of learning and a shared language in human movement fields' (p. 12). What follows is the opening narrative for the book which situates this work.

How it all started

Tania

On 29 November 2011, I received a 'cold call' email from Brian Gearity. He was emailing in his capacity as Guest Editor of 'the *Strength and Conditioning Journal (SCJ)*, a peer-reviewed publication of the National Strength & Conditioning Association [which] focused on connecting scholarship and practical concerns in strength and conditioning'. He informed me that he was compiling a 'Special Topic Issue on Strength and Conditioning Coach Education', and he invited me to 'submit an application/translating research-to-practice paper'. He went on to say that I had been 'identified' because of my 'achievements and abilities as a practitioner or as a scholar in coach education or sport science'. The business-like email concluded with 'P.S. Hey Tania. I have admired your work (e.g. *Understanding Sports Coaching*, which I used for a course I taught) over the years and I thought you may be interested in this special issue'.

Despite not having any background in S&C, Brian's personalised postscript had stroked my ego, so I promptly responded to him.

> Dear Brian, Thank you for the invitation and your kind words at the end of the invitation. I am glad that my work has been of some use to you. As you may be aware strength and

conditioning is not really an area in which I have much, if any, expertise but I have a colleague who teaches strength and conditioning in our programme and I wonder if you would permit me to investigate the possibilities of him and I doing a joint article.

From Brian's response to my email it was clear flattery had been a deliberate strategy of his because he said, 'I figured if I sent this proposal to quality coaching ed. scholars then they would either (a) pass it on to directly interested parties or (b) bring on a collaborator'.

In the intervening months, Phil and I worked together in an effort to meet the brief of the Special Edition before submitting the manuscript. At the end of October 2012 we received the reviewer's less-than-complimentary responses. Brian, in his role as Associate Editor, summarised them, some of which are reflected in the following.

The two reviewers thought that the manuscript identified important concerns and described the complexity and changing nature of strength and conditioning coaching. However, they also had significant concerns regarding this manuscript. One of the challenges of writing this kind of scholarship is it presents a new discourse and needs to be carefully worded and deftly argued in order to convince reviewers that a strong case has been made. I encourage the authors to revise their submission as a piece on this important issue would help add to our understanding of strength and conditioning coaching and coach education. Brian went on to say:

> one of the reviewers identified that after critiquing some aspects of S&C, the authors failed to provide a better approach. Is the implication that coaches should continuously engage in critique and critical thinking of every aspect of athletic performance and coaching?

The reviewers' comments were not what we were expecting, so it took a few weeks (read months) to pick ourselves off the floor and respond. In March 2013 we sent the following to Brian:

> As you would have seen from the first reviewer's comments the manuscript needs a rethink rather than a tweak but we consider that the comments were fair. . . . While we are making slow process your invitation has certainly provided us the opportunity to work together and (re)think the strength and conditioning space, so thank you.

In August 2013, nearly two years after the initial invitation to submit an article in a 'Special Topic Issue on Strength and Conditioning Coach Education', we finally submitted the revised manuscript, and it has subsequently appeared as: Handcock, P., & Cassidy, T. (2014). Reflective practice for rugby union strength and conditioning coaches, *Strength and Conditioning Journal*, 36(1), 41–45.

That might have been the end of my foray into the world of S&C had it not been for me dislocating my knee and rupturing my ACL while trialling for a place in the New Zealand 50+ field hockey team in November 2015. After the initial shock (and pain), and subsequent surgery, I was determined to make a comeback; after all, the next Masters World Championship was scheduled for 2018 in Barcelona, and who does not want to visit Barcelona? During the rehabilitating period, I was unexpectedly sent a complimentary S&C book from Routledge. Out of curiosity, I looked at the contents page and a chapter caught my attention because it specifically focused on strength and conditioning for field hockey. How serendipitous was that? However, upon reading it, I became acutely aware that the content of the chapter was not aimed at a mature female athlete returning from injury. It was then that I took a closer look at the contents page. What I saw was a contemporary S&C book, several hundred pages in length, with no obvious engagement with pedagogical or sociocultural issues. To be fair, that was not the focus of the book. I then went online and looked at other contemporary S&C books, and I found a similar trend across them all, i.e. an absence of discussions that were informed by sociocultural and pedagogical research. That is when I phoned Phil and said, 'I've got an idea.'

Phil

Well, a textbook certainly wasn't really something that I had on my list of projects, but the seed for this idea was planted with the collaborative manuscript that Tania has just described. On graduating, I had enjoyed a brief eight-year career as an exercise professional. That work included stints in corporate fitness, athletic injury rehabilitation and strength and conditioning. Fresh out from my Master's degree, I thought I was well prepared and well ahead of the game in terms of my knowledge and scientific understanding of exercise. I soon discovered two things about being an exercise professional: I might have known 'stuff', but I didn't know the right stuff; and secondly, that being an exercise professional was a fairly isolated and lonely experience.

In reality, I lacked the practical skills or experience that I felt was needed for those roles. While I thoroughly enjoyed my work, I had many frustrations and made many mistakes along the way, some of which I learned from and some of which I am still learning from. In those roles, I'd encountered various challenges and issues, yet when I discussed these with colleagues, it seemed that they weren't having similar experiences. So, I eventually convinced myself that the problem had to be me, or the problem was the athletes that I was working with; probably both! It wasn't until I moved into academia that I had the opportunity, motivation and support to reflect more on our profession.

In my first few years as a university lecturer I persisted with my strongly biophysical approach to teaching exercise prescription and strength and conditioning; it seemed obvious and my students appreciated the content and that approach. It was only when I developed practicum courses, where the students engaged in supervised community practice, that I noticed that these students were all having similar problems to the ones that I had encountered back in my exercise professional career. As we reflected together, it seemed that the discrepancies between theory and practice were almost everywhere if you really bothered to look for them. We also learned together about the importance of relationships, understanding each individual, being able to teach, coach and communicate effectively and being able to understand the importance of personal and professional values, and ethical professional behaviour.

I also had the additional benefit of a steady stream of graduates who were now out working as exercise professionals and facing similar challenges on a daily basis. They were only too happy to discuss those problems and allow me to mentor their ongoing professional development – and for that I'm very grateful. Suddenly, we had the basis for an exciting new strength and conditioning curriculum that thrived on exploring the fusion between sociocultural, biophysical and pedagogical principles. This approach appealed immensely to some students, was tolerated by others and was offensive to still another group of students. And right there I think you have a microcosm of the challenges facing strength and conditioning professionals: some athletes want to be told what to do, some want guidance, some want significant independence, some want clarity; some want new, some want old. Successful strength and conditioning demands professional competence in many areas.

I'm excited to be contributing to this book and to work alongside wise heads like Tania, Brian and Lisette who have rich and disparate backgrounds and can offer the theoretical understandings and language to explore some of the professional issues that are presented in each chapter. I value an approach that recognises different levels of knowledge, expectations and comfort, and seeks to question and explore rather than to discredit and undermine.

Brian

As Tania wrote, I can come across as a real charmer. But only on email to people who don't know me! I've been told by colleagues outside the United States that I'm 'quite American' and I do embody stereotypes associated with S&C and sport. I'm a former collegiate (American) football player and teenage champion powerlifter. I started lifting weights when I was about 12 and have continued to do so three to six days per week ever since. I'm 5'10", nearly 100 kilos (215 lbs), and I have a goatee and shaved head. So, yes, I'm pretty much what's expected when we think of S&C, and I was an SCC at the high school, collegiate and professional levels.

In college, at John Carroll University, I majored in physical education and exercise science with dual concentrations in athletic training and exercise specialist. I was steeped in the traditional curriculum of anatomy, physiology, biomechanics – the biophysical aspects of human living and athletic performance. But the physical education piece came into play when we also learned lesson planning, organising students and doing things in everyday life, not merely recalling our knowledge on exams about science. Fast forward many years later and I was coaching at the University of Tennessee whilst going to graduate school; first my master's, then straight on for my PhD. I always enjoyed the biophysical aspects of sport, but the social and behavioural aspects, complex people situated in a history of time and all the forces affecting them, captured my intellectual curiosity. It also helped provide the critical thinking and theory or research concepts to understand what I saw as an SCC. Why don't athletes always do what I tell them? Why do I want them to do what I tell them? Why isn't that athlete listening to that coach? How come there aren't more women SCCs? Why do we continue to organise and implement these practices, and how come we don't ever think what we're doing is a problem? Does anybody else share my concerns or observations?

Again, fast forward many years, and I had sent another 'cold email' to Dr. Jeffrey Chandler, Editor in Chief (EIC) of *SCJ*, to lead a special issue on coach education; for his exceptional efforts as EIC and mentoring, amongst other achievements, Dr. Chandler was awarded the NSCA's highest honour in 2019: the Boyd Epley Award for Lifetime Achievement. As a new professor at the time, I wanted to draw more attention to how we prepare SCCs and to broaden our thinking through the social and behavioural sciences, as well as philosophy. Even the biophysical aspects of life, training and performance occur in a dynamic, complex social environment, and the relatively young field of S&C hadn't yet done much about that in its journals. Fortunately for me, and for our field, Dr. Chandler was receptive to the idea and supported me throughout the process, including handling quite critical and constructive feedback from reviewers. More recently, also with *SCJ*, in 2018 and 2019 we published two special issues, one on the sociology of S&C (Mills & Gearity, 2018) and the other on psychology (Moore & Gearity, 2019).

As guest editor, I tried to solicit scholar-practitioners from mostly my contacts in sociology and psychology of sport coaching (Gearity, 2014). I needed good writers with a command of theory, research and practice. Yes, I sent Tania an intentionally flattering email, but as I hoped, she was able to contribute an article, with the assistance of Phil. Subsequently,

Phil came to Denver, Colorado, US, where I had moved to in 2014 to start a new Master's of Arts degree in Sport Coaching, with a certificate programme in S&C, at the University of Denver. Phil and I were able to chat a bit in person, and then about a year later the idea for the book germinated. Phil had also offered an interesting idea to analyse NSCA conference presentations to systematically show what we already knew – a lack of sociocultural and pedagogical aspects (Handcock et al., 2017).

Tania had already co-written a book in the general sports coaching field, so I figured following her lead would be a good idea. Little did I know what a laborious task we'd set ourselves! We used our knowledge of theory and practice to problematise, or flesh out, topics and issues that could be included. Unfortunately, the field of S&C is fairly new and small, so we couldn't benefit from a wider sociocultural pedagogical analysis. Thus, taken-for-granted assumptions and new ways of seeing things can cause some dissonance, or disjuncture, and take some time to work through. Quite frankly, I think that's terrific and exactly what scholar-practitioners should be doing. When I think about how much biophysical research basically does the same studies over and over with little novelty or insight, I can't help but think our S&C field, and our individual lives and society, would be better with greater focus on sociocultural pedagogical research. Not only is our work as authors and researchers in this area just getting started, we hope others will jump into the scholarly conversation. Like those special issues with *SCJ*, our thinking and research will change, as will our observations about social issues and discourses and practices to be critiqued – which just goes to show why we need to nurture this sociocultural pedagogical thinking.

Lisette

When we started this writing project, Tania had been in the office next door to me for 25 years. We studied at the same institution (albeit a year apart), both taught health and PE in high schools, both eventually returning to work at the place we got our undergraduate degrees, and both have relished the ways sociocultural knowledge has enhanced our practice. Twenty-five years amounts to a lot of conversations, a lot of 'connection', and a lot of opportunity to share our world views. We have always enjoyed trading stories about how we teach, what we teach, and why we do it like we do. We have also always relished opportunities to share our stumbling efforts to use theory in ways that enliven our practice. When Tania asked whether I'd be interested in working with her, Phil and Brian on this book I worried I'd have next to nothing to add, knowing next to nothing of strength and conditioning, but she and Phil thought otherwise. They reckoned having someone out of the field, yet familiar with sociocultural resources, would be useful. Phil's deep knowledge of the SCC professional field, his capacity to wonder, his openness to fresh ideas and humour were unquestioned. Tania's capacity to bring sociocultural concepts alive in a 'lived' way was obvious, and I'd heard good things about Brian's work. Opportunities to engage with thoughtful colleagues who are passionate about learning, the profession and ready, willing and able to hear different perspectives on these are rare, so I leapt at the chance.

Having worked at an institution that attracted many students with backgrounds and aspirations in sport performance, I have heard plenty about what matters to athletes. Students talk about parents, partners and children. They talk about critical incidents that shaped their engagement in sport. Coaches' dispositions and behaviours clearly shape their experience of, and commitment to, sporting excellence. Amongst family and friend groups, I have witnessed the relentless search for the latest, most 'cutting edge' expertise, about how to prepare for a range of sporting activities. More often than not the latter is discovered via Google or social media. Further, strength and conditioning information garnered from these sources is often predominantly biophysical in orientation. While it is, of course, important to understand the physiology, biomechanics and other biomedical markers of performance, the lived experience of trying to achieve what science suggests is the right way to train is invariably shaped by a whole bunch of contextual things. A desire to shed further light on these things fuelled my motivation to join the writing team. While my background is largely working with students who wish to become health and/or physical education teachers, I see the pedagogical and sociocultural resources they need and use as being similar to those required in an SCC setting. Like Phil, I have no interest in undermining existing practice. Rather, prompting a reflexive stance to what must always be an imperfect practice (at least in my case!), asking 'Why do I do what I do and with what effect for those I work with?' seems a modest, yet important question for all in the field of SCC and beyond.

The authorship team as brokers

In 2017 when we submitted a book proposal to Routledge, the sub-title was: *Bridging the Biophysical, Pedagogical and Sociocultural Foundations of Practice*. At that time, we were not aware of Wenger's (1998) concept of brokering. Any mention of brokering would have conjured up images of financial, or mortgage, brokers who act as 'go-betweens' for clients and lenders. Yet, recently we have become aware of how the concepts of broker and brokering, and their links to the process of bridging, have been used in discussions around the building of learning capability. Wenger (2012, p. 14) described brokers as people who see a 'boundary to be bridged . . . and a need for a community', and use their memberships of, and legitimacy within, multiple communities to establish productive links across (i.e. to bridge) these boundaries.

It is evident from the narratives in this section that this authorship team are members of multiple, and potentially disparate, communities. Yet, all of us could, and still can, see the possibilities of developing learning capabilities in people, as well as ourselves, by establishing links across the boundaries of our various communities. Furthermore, we are well placed (i.e. have legitimacy) in these communities to become brokers and act as 'go-betweens'. While having vision and legitimacy enables some brokering to occur, Wenger (1998) suggested brokers also need to use tools and encounters to facilitate the building of bridges. Some of the members of this authorship team have been having encounters for decades, while others are more recent. The conversations that have occurred in our encounters have also enhanced our learning as we endeavour to develop learning opportunities for others. This book, which can be thought of as a boundary crossing tool, would have been quite different in structure and content had we not intuitively been brokers. Yet the process of becoming brokers has not always been straightforward, as alluded to in these narratives. As an authorship team, we too had to work through difficulties, establish bridges across the boundaries of our respective communities and develop a shared understanding of issues and challenges. This had to occur without having the luxury of common artefacts such as language (even though we all spoke English), routines and practices (Engeström et al., 1995). Now that the book has been completed, it should not be seen as 'The End'. Bridging communities requires ongoing work if relationships and understandings are to be sustained, and collaborations to occur. Our desire is that this book will contribute to, and stimulate, new conversations amongst everyone, who is interested in, and committed to, exploring and examining the status quo in S&C, or any profession for that matter regardless of the communities in which they reside.

The aims of this book

The broad aim is to contribute to the burgeoning conversations occurring amongst some SCCs on the merits of examining their practices using pedagogical and sociocultural theoretical concepts. More specifically, the aim of the book is to act as a 'bridge' and/or 'scaffold' to help support SCCs to have conversations that are informed by the biophysical *as well as* pedagogical and sociocultural literature. We use these two words thoughtfully, to recognise that many SCCs are already integrating, or have thought deeply about, many of the concepts that we discuss in this book; thus we are 'bridging' across to those understandings and experiences. Others may be comfortable in their S&C spaces, and for them the book could act as a 'scaffold' to build and support new ways of thinking and acting. Our overall purpose of encouraging these conversations is to enable SCCs to gain further insights into, and understandings of, their practice and by doing so increase the chances that they will offer more educative and developmental opportunities for athletes with whom they work. While we recognise the importance of acknowledging the historical importance exercise science has played, and continues to play, in informing SCC's practices, we consider it to be equally important for SCCs to explore and examine the status quo by questioning the technical, cultural, ethical, professional and political practices and issues that occur in S&C contexts.

What is meant by sociocultural, pedagogical and biophysical concepts?

Throughout the book we use the terms sociocultural, pedagogical and biophysical, so it is important to explain how we understand and use these terms. At a dictionary level, 'sociocultural' means 'relating to, or involving a combination of social and cultural factors' (www.merriam-webster.com/dictionary/sociocultural). Yet, when Kirk and colleagues (1996) discussed the sociocultural foundations of human movement, they explained that in the context of human movement studies, sociocultural is a name given to one of the two major groups of sub-disciplines, which include social-psychology, pedagogy, philosophy, sociology and history. They, and others e.g. Sage (1992), acknowledged that the composition of the group nested under the umbrella of sociocultural is continually changing as other sociocultural sub-disciplines emerge. In the years since these scholars made their observations, other sub-disciplines, such as gender studies, economics, law and social work, could now just as easily be incorporated under the sociocultural heading. The primary focus of those working in the S&C community is on improving human performance, and as a consequence they may find it difficult to immediately see the relevance of sociocultural sub-disciplines to S&C. We recognise that sociocultural sub-disciplines will make varying levels of contribution to the study of S&C; nonetheless it is our hope that the discussion and examples we provide in this book will enable SCCs to gain further insights into, and understandings of, their practice.

As noted earlier, pedagogy is a sub-discipline of a sociocultural perspective. But as Cassidy et al. (2016) have previously done, we discuss pedagogy and sociocultural independently, mainly to 'emphasize the importance of each component within the totality of coaching' (p. 8). We are not claiming to be the first to discuss pedagogy in S&C, as others have called for SCCs to embrace coaching pedagogical practices (e.g. Dorgo, 2009). Pedagogy is a word that has multiple interpretations, because it is often informed by the educational traditions of the particular society in which the term is being used. It is not a word in common use in S&C communities and if it is, it is likely to be done so to describe the 'art or science of teaching' (www.merriam-webster.com/dictionary/pedagogy). In this book we draw on a more scholarly definition of pedagogy, one that has been influenced by continental Europeans and discussed in the context of sports coaching. Drawing on the work of Lusted (1986), Cassidy et al. (2004, 2009, 2016) views pedagogy as a process of knowledge production that occurs in the interactions between the coach (teacher), the athlete (learner) and content, within a particular context (Cassidy, 2000, 2004). Similarly, Armour (2011) defined sport pedagogy as comprising three complex and interactive dimensions, namely; 'knowledge in context . . . learners and learning . . . [and] teacher/teaching and coaches/coaching' (p. 3).

Not only are there multiple interpretations of pedagogy, there have also been calls for coach educators to employ 'teaching strategies suitable for adults', an approach known as andragogy (Lauder, 1993, p. 2). Arguably Lauder's call for andragogy was because he viewed pedagogy to be synonymous with the teaching, or instruction, of children. We suggest this as an explanation because of the claim made by Jones et al. (2004) that the association the term pedagogy has to working with children is a possible reason as to why, at that time, the term pedagogy was not widely used in the sport coaching literature. In response to Lauder's (1993) position, Cassidy (2004) argued that the problem is not with the term pedagogy per se, but rather with the way the term is constructed and interpreted. When pedagogy is viewed more broadly, as it is in this book (see the previous paragraph), and viewed as a process, which is culturally bound and relational, then it is inclusive of all ages and stages of development. Moreover, by viewing pedagogy as a process, it provides opportunities for us to move away from viewing coaching predominantly as a 'craft', where the emphasis is placed on technical skills and strategies, and privileging the 'expert' practitioner.

So, while the term pedagogy may not often be explicitly discussed in the S&C community, pedagogical practices occur out of necessity as SCCs work with athletes, with specifically designed programmes, and with the goal of changing athlete behaviour. In this book, by explicitly discussing pedagogical literature and making links to S&C practices, we aim to demonstrate the relevance of pedagogical concepts to the S&C community. One device that we have used to make these links is to introduce pedagogical cases, which are richly described narratives (Armour, 2014; Cronin & Armour, 2019). In this book the pedagogical cases include basic demographics of SCCs, the contexts in which they are working, the relationships that they have with various stakeholders, the critical incidents which they face and their educational and sporting backgrounds. The cases are a composite of experience and anecdotal evidence in the S&C context, presented in the form of a realist tale (Sparkes, 2002) with the aim of making them accessible and relatable to members of the S&C community.

In a companion text to Kirk et al. (1996), Abernethy and colleagues (2013) described the biophysical foundations of human movement and in doing so incorporated the following sub-disciplines in their scope; functional anatomy, biomechanics, exercise physiology, motor control and sport and exercise psychology. They acknowledged that the latter sub-discipline could equally be located under a sociocultural heading. Historically S&C education and professional development has been informed by the biophysical sub-disciplines. Consequently, it has often been viewed as 'common sense' to draw upon these sub-disciplines when trying to enable SCCs to gain further insights into, and understandings of, their strength and conditioning practices. While we agree with the merits of using biophysical sub-discipline knowledge to improve practice and performance, we differ from some others in the S&C community because we value drawing on biophysical sub-disciplines in conjunction with sociocultural disciplines and pedagogical concepts.

Why is this book needed?

The pioneering SCCs primarily came from a tradition of weightlifting. Consequently, strength and conditioning education has traditionally been grounded in the exercise sciences. Thus, the traditions, rituals and routines of S&C communities and SCCs respectively, and the historical grounding of S&C education in exercise sciences, has encouraged many SCCs to predominantly focus on the 'what' and the 'how'. This book is significant for the field because as Quinn et al. (1996) have suggested, professional intellect operates on four levels; 'knowing what', 'knowing how', as well as 'knowing why' and 'caring why'. Contemporary SCCs face challenges that extend well beyond knowing 'what' and knowing 'how', which is one reason why we believe this book is needed. Another motive is that there is some merit in S&C coaches becoming more critically reflective, because that ability provides a mechanism by which they can further engage with some of the moral, ethical and societal issues intertwined within their practice. This is always topical as evident with the 2017 Oregon football controversy that resulted in the head strength and conditioning coach being suspended for one month. Three Oregon players were hospitalised following an intense preseason workout that included extending the session as punishment for incorrect exercise execution and for not following directions. The incident sparked national conversations about player safety and the level of care in college football.

With the evolving challenges associated with athlete preparation, calls have been made for SCCs to take one arm out of their white coats and begin to think and act a 'little more like coaches' and become more critically reflective practitioners (Handcock & Cassidy, 2014; Kuklick & Gearity, 2015; Mills & Gearity, 2016). Despite these recent appeals, there is limited S&C literature to support the development of SCCs to become reflective, to encourage them to think critically about their practice, or see the merits of exploring pedagogical, and sociocultural ideas in the context of S&C coaching. This may be linked to the professional status of the S&C community. We consider the S&C community to be in a similar position regarding professional status as the physical education community was over 30 years ago, and where the general sports coaching community was 15 years ago (Cassidy et al., 2004). Consequently, we consider it important for the S&C community to take heed of Kirk's (1986) observation that those 'who lack the capacity for reflective thought and informed critical judgement may be in danger not only of confirming their lowly professional status, but also of leaving themselves open to political manipulation and the subtle influence of propaganda' (pp. 155–156). Yet becoming a reflective SCC is not without its issues. As Cushion (2018) correctly points out, albeit in the context of the general sports coaching community, the concept of reflection has itself become a taken-for-granted routine and ritual of many coaches and those working in coach education. To examine what this has meant, Cushion conducted a critical analysis of reflection and reflective practice discourses in coaching. In the process of doing so he observed, and subsequently discussed, the 'unintended consequences of reflection as a form of surveillance that normalizes coaches' practices through the act of confession' (p. 82). Any pressure to conform under scrutiny may negate the intentions of reflective practice to have coaches encouraged to learn and develop their individual practices.

A further claim as to why a book like this is needed was highlighted by Cassidy et al. (2016) when they argued for producing a third edition of their book. At that point they stated their book was not about giving

> 'handy hints' for coaches to neatly dip into when the perceived need arises. On the contrary, we present social and pedagogical notions which themselves should be viewed as pedagogic; in the sense of assisting readers for what is required of them, 'to learn what only be implied, and never as direct advice' (Flyvbjerg et al., 2012, p. 4). By insisting that we only give readers ideas to think with, as opposed to exact and 'correct' practical prescriptions, we hope to privilege the quality of communicative interaction over any

preciseness of instruction (Pineau, 1994); the concepts here still need to be thought about hard, with imagination, and not just taken as a priori knowledge (Jones et al., 2011). The point is to continue to develop a 'quality of mind' in coaches to explore such questions as: do I understand why I act and coach in certain ways? Why do I espouse certain values and ideas and reject others? Can I explore ideas with which I do not normally conform? Am I able to see situations from others' points of view? Are my coaching methods congruent with my principles? And, can I devise alternative pedagogies that may be more educative? (Fernandez-Balboa, 2000). Those hoping for a list of 'effective' coaching behaviours, then, will inevitably be disappointed; a dissatisfaction for which we offer no apology

Quoted in Cassidy et al., 2016

Yet, we need to be mindful that when attempting to facilitate SCC's engagement in educative conversations about their practice, it may not be enough to highlight the findings in the literature, make compelling and logical arguments, or argue the benefits of SCCs becoming reflective practitioners (Handcock & Cassidy, 2014; Kuklick & Gearity, 2015). Decades ago Tinning (1995) said that 'if becoming reflective were simply a rational process, then it would be easy to train teachers [read, SCCs] to be reflective' (p. 21). Changing behaviours and practices that have developed over time requires a degree of emotional commitment because a coach's identity or subjectivity is often 'embedded' within these behaviours and practices (Tinning, 1995).

Who is this book for?

This book will appeal to a range of people, from undergraduate students studying S&C, to key certifying organisations (i.e. ASCA, NSCA, UKSCA) who support the professional development of SCCs, as well as to coaches, teachers and practicing strength and conditioning coaches. While many of the narratives and discussions in this book are focused around sport, and often elite sport, the authors acknowledge that S&C is a rapidly evolving profession (Bishop et al., 2019). For example, S&C methods and principles have been embraced by the private sector (Bishop et al., 2019) and have implications for related areas such as fitness (general and employee), health and/or rehabilitation. We believe that the conversations prompted by this book will help S&C professionals working in these areas.

For undergraduate and beginning postgraduate students, this book can serve as an introductory illustration of the interconnectedness of the biophysical, sociocultural and pedagogical components of S&C. By making links between the theoretical concepts and the pedagogical cases presented at the beginning of each chapter, readers will gain insight into the complexity and interrelatedness of S&C practice. The ideas expressed in the text will hopefully encourage S&C certifying organisations to expand their professional development offerings to support SCCs in having discussions about their practice. These conversations will be informed by biophysical *as well as* pedagogical and sociocultural literature and will explore and examine the status quo as well as question the technical, moral, ethical and political practices and issues that occur in the S&C context. Currently these discussions are largely absent from the key S&C certifying organisations (Handcock & Cassidy, 2017). Two Special Topic Issues in the *Strength and Conditioning Journal* (2014, 2018) that have focused on Coach Education and Sport Sociology respectively indicate a growing appetite for discussions that are informed by pedagogical and sociocultural topics and concepts. Moreover, the content of the book provides all readers with opportunities to reflect on how they understand S&C practices and to gain insight into how engaging with biophysical, pedagogical and sociocultural concepts could stimulate them to further enhance their own S&C practices.

14 *Setting the scene*

How is it organised?

In our role as brokers we have organised this book with the aim of 'exchanging information and supporting co-workers in finding innovative solutions by recombining old ideas into new solutions' (Gustavsson & Säfsten, 2017, p.239). Moreover, the organisation of the book is influenced by two underlying beliefs. It is informed by our belief that S&C is a complex, relational and inter-disciplinary[1] practice and that by engaging with the biophysical *as well as* pedagogical and sociocultural literature, we can better enhance our understanding, and enactment, of S&C practice. This belief influenced our decision to organise the chapters so that *each* commentary does not follow the customary practice of having discipline-specific sections. By weaving the potentially more familiar biophysical literature with the less familiar pedagogical and sociocultural literature, readers will be introduced to new ways of examining current S&C practices. By structuring the chapters thus, the book is intended to act as a 'bridge' and/or scaffolding to support members of the S&C community to engage with what may be unfamiliar literature. It is hoped that subsequently this may enable members of the S&C community to gain better insights into, and understandings of, their own practice, and subsequently develop more sociocultural and pedagogical informed practices to enhance athlete development.

The second belief that influenced the organisation of the book is that any discussions about S&C should be grounded in practice. This belief influenced our decision to begin each chapter within sections 2–5 with a pedagogical case. The reason why we incorporate a pedagogical case that relates to S&C practice at the beginning of each chapter is to provide readers with a 'hook', to whet their appetite and encourage them to continue reading the chapter. Moreover, we hope to support and contribute to the growing number of people having conversations about the merits of examining SCC practices using pedagogical and sociocultural theoretical concepts.

While the intent of the pedagogical cases remains consistent across chapters, the style of each case has purposefully been designed to reflect specific aspects of the SCC practices and highlight the complex nature of working as an individual, affiliated to a profession, whilst interacting within organisational and cultural contexts. The pedagogical cases have been written by the authorship team, who bring different disciplinary and cultural perspectives as well as varied sporting experiences. We have enjoyed the freedom to 'create' pedagogical cases based on the expertise (applied and theoretical) that we 'bring to the table'.

Chapters 4–15 have a consistent structure with two core elements. First is a description of SCC coach(es) via the pedagogical case, which highlights the issues they face and/or conquer within their daily practice. Second is the exploration of the case from an issues-based approach, which we describe as a commentary. We chose to take an issues-based approach to move the discussion away from the typical 'siloed' biophysical and sociocultural perspectives, or smaller (sub-)disciplinary discussion units. Had we adopted a siloed approach, we would inevitably place the onus of making connections between the disciplines and practice, on those working in the S&C field. Instead, in an issue-based discussion we draw on our disciplinary perspectives and make a coordinated and coherent interdisciplinary contribution to the discussion of the respective issues.

The second section of the chapters (in the commentary) is where the bridging or scaffolding occurs. Here we make links between the practices and critical incidences described in the narrative and the literature. Having identified topical issues from the narrative, we draw on biophysical, sociocultural and pedagogical literature to discuss possible implications for S&C practices. Chapters 2–15 conclude with 'End of chapter tasks' that encourage readers to: make links with the ideas expressed in the chapter and their own practice; think reflectively and critically about their work, what and who shapes what they do, and why they do it; and engage with diverse theoretical and practical resources. The tasks are 'multi-level/ mixed ability', in acknowledgement that members of the S&C community will have a range of experiences when it comes to challenging the status quo, as well as with the pedagogical and sociocultural literature. In each chapter the narrative and the end of chapter tasks act as 'bookends' linking the theoretical discussion to practice.

The book is physically organised into five parts. Specifically, the first three chapters – 'Introduction' (Chapter 1), 'Mapping the construction of strength and conditioning knowledge' (Chapter 2) and 'Concepts and frameworks (Chapter 3) are located under the part heading 'Setting the scene'. This is followed by four topical parts dealing respectively with 'Elite sport performance', 'Developing as a strength and conditioning professional', 'Conditioning across the lifespan' and 'Health, injury and wellbeing'. Each of these parts contains three relevant chapters, with each chapter concluding with a set of tasks/questions and suggested readings. Specifically, Part 2 explores the issues that an S&C may face in the context of working in elite sport, particularly 'Measurement, assessment and testing – what does it all mean?' (Chapter 4), 'Training volume – fear of missing out (FOMO)' (Chapter 5) and 'Helicopter' strength and conditioning – questioning the role of monitoring' (Chapter 6). Part 3 focuses on the process of developing as an S&C professional. Here we discuss 'Developing as a competent strength and conditioning professional' (Chapter 7), 'Women and strength and conditioning coaching' (Chapter 8) and 'Finding a professional voice and collaborating' (Chapter 9). Part 4 tackles issues many SCCs may face when working in different developmental spaces, including 'Healthy development of youth in sport' (Chapter 10), 'Talent identification and development' (Chapter 11) and 'Older and wiser' (Chapter 12). Finally, Part 5 incorporates chapters that focus on 'Conditioning for protection' (Chapter 13), 'Returning to play following injury' (Chapter 14) and 'Looking after yourself as a strength and conditioning coach' (Chapter 15). We do not envisage this book will be read chronologically from Chapter 1 to 15. Rather, we encourage readers to read Chapter 1 to gain a 'flavour' of the book before 'dipping their toes' into the ideas discussed in the subsequent chapters as they desire. This way readers can develop their own pathway of understanding and make their own connections. Chapters 2 and 3 still 'set the scene', and therefore we do suggest readers engage with this material, specifically Chapter 3, which focuses on the concepts that permeate the discussion throughout Chapters 4–15.

Note

1 Newell (1998) states that 'Interdisciplinary studies may be defined as a process of answering a question, solving a problem, or addressing a topic that is too broad or complex to be dealt with adequately by a single discipline or profession . . . IDS draws on the disciplinary perspectives and integrates their insights through construction of a more comprehensive perspective' (p. 245).

References

Abernethy, B., Kipper, V., Hanrahan, S., Pandy, M., McManus, A., & MacKinnon, L. (2013). *Biophysical Foundations of Human Movement* (3rd ed.), Champaign, IL: Human Kinetics.

Armour, K.M. (2011). Introduction. In K.M. Armour (ed.), *Sport Pedagogy: An Introduction for Teaching and Coaching*, Harlow: Pearson.

Armour, K.M. (ed.). (2014). *Pedagogical Cases in Sport, Exercise and Physical Activity. Volume 1: Physical Education and Youth Sport*, London: Routledge.

Bishop, C., Mundy, P., Hunwicks, R., Paxton, K., Crofton, A., Tombs, C., & Cleather, D. (2019). The future development pathway of strength and conditioning: A proposed model from the UKSCA, *Professional Strength & Conditioning*, 52: 30–34.

Bowes, I., & Jones, R.L. (2006). Working at the edge of chaos: Understanding coaching as a complex, interpersonal system, *The Sport Psychologist*, 20(2): 235–245.

Cassidy, T. (2000). Investigating the pedagogical process in physical education teacher education, unpublished doctoral dissertation, Deakin University, Australia.

Cassidy, T. (2004). Revisiting coach education (and coaching) in the twenty first century, *Modern Athlete and Coach*, 42(2): 12–16.

Cassidy, T., Jones, R., & Potrac, P. (2004). *Understanding Sports Coaching: The Social, Cultural and Pedagogical Foundations of Coaching Practice*, London: Routledge.

Cassidy, T., Jones, R., & Potrac, P. (2009). *Understanding Sports Coaching: The Social, Cultural and Pedagogical Foundations of Coaching Practice* (2nd ed.), London: Routledge.

Cassidy, T., Jones, R., & Potrac, P. (2016). *Understanding Sports Coaching: The Pedagogical, Social, and Cultural Foundations of Coaching Practice* (3rd ed.), London: Routledge.

Clandinin, D. (2001). Foreword. In C.M. Clarke (ed.), *Talking Shop*, New York: Teachers College, p. viii.

Côté, J., Salmela, J., Trudel, P., Baria, A., & Russell, S. (1995). The coaching model: A grounded assessment of expert gymnastic coaches' knowledge, *Journal of Sport and Exercise Psychology*, 17(1): 1–17.

Cronin, C., & Armour, K. (eds.). (2019). *Care in Sport Coaching: Pedagogical Cases*, London: Routledge.

Cushion, C. (2018). Reflection and reflective practice discourses in coaching: A critical analysis, *Sport, Education and Society*, 23(1): 82–94.

Dorgo, S. (2009). Unfolding the practical knowledge of an expert strength and conditioning coach, *International Journal of Sports Science & Coaching*, 4(1): 17–30.

Engeström, Y., Engeström, R., & Kärkkäinen, M. (1995). Polycontextuality and boundary crossing in expert cognition: Learning and problem solving in complex work activities, *Learning and Instruction*, 5(4): 319–336.

Fernandez-Balboa, J-M. (2000). Discrimination: What do we know and what can we do about it? In R.L. Jones & K.M. Armour (eds.), *Sociology of Sport: Theory and Practice*, London: Longman.

Flyvbjerg, B., Landman, T., & Schram, S. (2012). Introduction: New directions in social science. In B. Flyvbjerg, T. Landman, & S. Schram (eds.), *Real Social Science: Applied Phronesis*, Cambridge: Cambridge University Press.

Gearity, B.T. (2014). Guest editorial: Special topic issue, coach education, *Strength and Conditioning Journal*, 36(1): 1.

Gearity, B.T., & Henderson Metzger, L. (2017). Intersectionality, microaggressions, and microaffirmations: Towards a cultural praxis of sport coaching, *Sociology of Sport Journal*, 34: 160–175.

Gustavsson, M., & Säfsten, K. (2017). The learning potential of boundary crossing in the context of product introduction, *Vocations and Learning*, 10(2): 1–18.

Handcock, P., & Cassidy, T. (2014). Reflective practice for rugby union strength and conditioning coaches, *Strength and Conditioning Journal*, 36(1): 41–45.

Handcock, P., & Cassidy, T. (2017). Rugby: A conspiracy of pain. Paper presented at World in Union conference, Palmerston North, New Zealand, 28 June–1 July.

Handcock, P., Gearity, B., Cassidy, T., & Burrows, L. (2017). When the student is ready, the teacher will appear: The conflicted strength and conditioning coach? Paper presented at International Council for Coaching Excellence, Liverpool, UK, 29 July–2 Aug.

Jones, R., Armour, K., & Potrac, P. (2004). *Sports Coaching Cultures: From Practice to Theory*, London: Routledge.

Jones, R., Potrac, P., Cushion, C., & Ronglan, L.T. (eds.). (2011). *The Sociology of Sports Coaching*, London: Routledge.

Kirk, D. (1986). Beyond the limits of theoretical discourse in teacher education: Towards a critical pedagogy, *Teaching and Teacher Education*, 2(2): 155–167.

Kirk, D., Nauright, J., Hanrahan, S., Macdonald, D., & Jobling, I. (1996). *The Sociocultural Foundations of Human Movement*, Melbourne: Macmillan.

Knudson, D., & Morrison, C. (2002). *Qualitative Analysis of Human Movement* (2nd ed.), Champaign, IL: Human Kinetics.

Kuklick, C., & Gearity, B. (2015). A review of reflective practice and its application for the football strength and conditioning coach, *Strength and Conditioning Journal*, 37(6): 43–51.

Kuklick, C., & Gearity, B.T. (in press). New movement practices: A Foucauldian learning community to disrupt technologies of discipline, *Sociology of Sport Journal*.

Lauder, A. (1993). Coach education for the twenty first century, *Sports Coach*, Jan.–Mar.: 2.

Lusted, D. (1986). Why pedagogy? *Screen*, 27(5): 2–14.

Mills, J.P., Caulfield, S., Fox, D., Baker, K., & Woolverton, L. (2018). Social construction of strength and conditioning coach knowledge and practice, *Strength and Conditioning Journal*, 40(6): 21–28.

Mills, J.P., & Gearity, B.T. (2016). Towards a sociology of strength and conditioning, *Strength and Conditioning Journal*, 38(3): 102–105.

Mills, J.P., & Gearity, B.T. (2018). Guest editorial: Special topic issue, sport sociology, *Strength and Conditioning Journal*, 40(6): 1–2.

Moore, W., & Gearity, B.T. (2019). Guest editorial: Special topic issue, sport psychology, *Strength and Conditioning Journal*, 41(2): 1–2.

Newell, W. (1998). Professionalizing interdisciplinarity. In W. Newell (ed.), *Interdisciplinarity: Essays from the Literature*, New York: College Board, pp. 529–563.

Pineau, E. (1994). Teaching is performance: Reconceptualising a problematic metaphor, *American Educational Research Journal*, 31(1): 3–25.

Potrac, P.W., Gilbert, W., & Denison, J. (eds.). (2013). *Routledge Handbook of Sports Coaching*, London: Routledge.

Quinn, J., Anderson, P., & Finkelstein, S. (1996). Managing the professional intellect: Making the most of the best, *Harvard Business Review*, Mar.–Apr.: 71–80.

Sage, G. (1992). Enhancing human performance in sport: Toward empowerment and transformation. In *American Academy of Physical Education Papers, No. 25*, Champaign, IL: Human Kinetics.

Sparkes, A. (2002). *Telling Tales in Sport and Physical Activity*, Champaign, IL: Human Kinetics.

Tinning, R. (1995). We have ways of making you think, or do we? Reflections on 'training' in reflective teaching. In C. Pare (ed.), *Training of Teachers in Reflective Practice of Physical Education*, Trois-Rivieres, Quebec: Université du Quebec a Trois-Rivieres.

Tinning, R. (2002). Engaging Siedentopian perspectives on content knowledge for physical education, *Quest*, 21: 378–391.

Wenger, E. (1998). *Communities of Practice: Learning, Meaning and Identity*, Cambridge: Cambridge University Press.

Wenger, E. (2012). Communities of practice and social learning systems: The career of a concept. https://wenger-trayner.com/wp-content/uploads/2012/01/09-10-27-CoPs-and-systems-v2.01.pdf (accessed 10 Dec. 2019).

2 Mapping the construction of strength and conditioning knowledge

Introduction
What is a profession?
Signature pedagogies
Professional competence
Strength and conditioning's signature pedagogies

    Mission statements
    Codes of Ethics
    Education and certification practices
    Continuing education
    Publications
    Workshops
    Conferences

Summary
End of chapter tasks
References

Introduction

As we explained in Chapter 1, the specific aim of this book is to encourage strength and conditioning coaches (SCCs) to continue to be, or become, increasingly competent, reflective and critical professionals who view strength and conditioning (S&C) coaching as a relational practice. In this chapter, we discuss what it means to be a professional and describe conceptualisations of professional knowledge and competence. We then examine the conventional construction of S&C professional knowledge by examining the 'signature pedagogies' of the profession.

    The freedom and privilege of calling oneself a professional is often taken for granted and is, under most circumstances, seldom subject to close scrutiny. SCCs often consider themselves to be professionals and would likely contend that they were very competent professionals. Such assumptions and assertions highlight important considerations as to what characterises a professional, and by what criteria one establishes professional competence. These questions are explored in this chapter and should be important to SCCs, and of interest to those who educate and 'train' SCCs, those who administer S&C professional bodies and systems of certification, and those who engage the services of SCCs.

What is a profession?

Professions are typically characterised by mastery of specialist and complex knowledge and skills that would normally be acquired through formal education and training (Cruess et al., 2004; Lorenz, 2012). Cruess et al. (2004) chose to define professions by emphasising the professional behaviours and societal obligations of a profession. In their view, professionals are accountable to society and are governed by a code of ethics that commits them to ongoing competence, integrity and ethical and altruistic behaviours. There is a tacit contract between a profession and society that acknowledges these expected behaviours and, in return, the professionals are granted the exclusive rights to use their knowledge to practice as they see fit (Cruess et al., 2004; Lorenz, 2012). These rights are often fiercely defended by professions. In this respect, Lawson (1984) suggests that professions control some of their professional 'power' through the process of problem setting. By describing and defining the nature of problems and suggesting an optimal process for the profession to solve them, a profession can gain some primacy over their domain of work and minimise any threats to that dominance.

Having a collective sense of the profession and a shared commitment to the profession are also important parts of being a professional (Kirk, 2007). Cruess et al. (2016) captured some of the 'other' elements of being a professional in their revision of Miller's pyramid of professional competence and identity. Miller's (1990) original pyramid of assessing professional competence progressed from examining a base of knowledge (knowing that), to competence (knowing how), to performance (showing how), to doing (acting and behaving as expected). Part of becoming a professional involves developing a professional identity, and Cruess et al. (2016) submit that individuals come to a profession with existing values, attitudes and beliefs. As those characteristics are likely to have influenced that individual's choice of professional pathway, they are likely complementary and of value. Cruess et al. (2016) argue that when constructing professional identity, the 'self' must be permitted to persist and coexist with one's emerging professional identity. In that respect, these authors amended Miller's professional competence pyramid to add 'identity' as the new apex level. The notion of 'identity' they characterised as 'consistently demonstrates the attitudes, values, and behaviours expected of one who has come to "think, act, and feel like a [professional]"' (Cruess et al., 2016, p. 181). As a largely subjective and tacit notion, the 'is' would be difficult to assess for professional certification purposes. However, it could be formatively assessed and should be highlighted for budding professionals for their continuing self-assessment.

While professional organisations may direct the expected behaviours of its members through certifications and codes of conduct, a professional body should also be defined by its professionals, to ensure a mutually beneficial and synergistic relationship. A professional's identity is linked to their profession through professional collegiality, commitment and a sense of responsibility to colleagues (Lorenz, 2012). Moreover, deeper insight into a profession can also be obtained by examining how professionals are taught and acquire their specialist knowledge (Shulman, 2005a). For Shulman, a profession can be distinguished by its methods of professional education and how that profession socialises emerging practitioners. Shulman described these as the 'signature pedagogies' of a profession.

Signature pedagogies

Signature pedagogies describe the teaching that occurs in professional preparation forums with the aim of organising 'fundamental ways in which future practitioners are educated for their new professions' (Shulman, 2005a, p. 52). This can result in novices to the profession being instructed 'to *think*, to *perform*, and to *act with integrity*' (p. 52). Indications of a profession's signature pedagogies can be gleaned from various sources including that profession's public domain presence (Shulman, 2005b). For example, a professional organisation's mission statement is an articulation of its fundamental purpose and values, is usually publicised for the benefit of members, and seeks to educate those who may pursue that organisation's services. A more explicit expression of a profession's norms is generally reflected in its code of ethics (Frankel, 1989), which describes how members of the profession are expected to act.

There is an implicit and moral dimension to a signature pedagogy that is driven by a set of beliefs about appropriate professional attitudes, values and behaviours. Also implicit is how a profession structures its professional teaching, learning and assessment, as well as how learners are guided and encouraged to engage with their disciplinary knowledge (Shulman, 2005b). Moreover, Shulman suggested that signature pedagogies are reliant on sets of assumptions about the best way to teach content-specific knowledge. Professional educational structures and assessments are often based on a summative assessment of the knowledge, skills and attributes considered to be the minimal requirement for safe and effective practice. Through certification, professional organisations endorse and encourage those educational structures, by acting gatekeepers of, continuing education programmes and materials, professional journals, conferences and workshops.

A lay observer can appreciate that each profession requires specific content knowledge, but may not consider or appreciate how a professional learns to practise. With the plethora of available medical dramas on television, most people can relate to the example of signature pedagogies of medical training. As with many professions, the challenge of medical training is to integrate vast formal explicit knowledge with clinical experiences and encourage the development of more tacit practices of enquiry and problem solving. Historically, medical education has involved lecture and tutorial style delivery of content knowledge, scaffolding to clinical placements with clinicians leading students through a 'master and apprentice' style of learning. Medical training culminates with residency training, where graduates further develop their clinical and professional skills under progressively reduced supervision. The signature pedagogies of medicine demonstrate what this profession considers important in terms of knowledge, skills and attitudes.

While medical training has been developing and progressing for centuries, S&C has a much briefer history. The signature pedagogies of SCC are therefore, understandably, less evolved in the sense that they are not as clearly defined, or as familiar, as they would be for many professions. The route to a career in S&C is ordinarily through an undergraduate university education in exercise sciences, kinesiology or physical education. From there, graduates will often seek internships with the dual objectives of learning how to practise, and often as foot-in-the-door entrées to employment. Other graduates will seek to extend their knowledge base with postgraduate study, often linked to internship placements. Before exploring our interpretation of the signature pedagogies of S&C (which appears later in this chapter), it is worthwhile to consider the dimensions of professional competence.

Professional competence

Who and what constitutes a professional is hotly contested (Evetts, 2009; Foss Lindblad & Lindblad, 2009; Frelin, 2013; Hargreaves, 2000). Debates focus on the difference between 'being professional (behaving professionally) and being *a* professional (belonging to a profession)' and whether a profession is 'something to be *enacted* or something to be *achieved*' (Frelin, 2013, p. 6, *emphasis in original*). According to Frelin, professionalism is a term that captures collective practices, which occur within a profession, while professionality involves concrete evidence of professional behaviour by an individual. Differentiating between professionalism and professionality highlights the importance of acknowledging the way in which 'human relationships' (p. 12) are vaguely linked to professional practices, which has implications when developing, or utilising, competence models or frameworks, a point to which we return later in this chapter.

Adding to the debate around who is, and what constitutes, a professional is the contentious interpretations of competence. According to Teodorescu (2006), a competence model focuses on the 'definition of measurable, specific, and objective milestones describing what people have to accomplish to consistently achieve or exceed the goals for their role, team, division, and the whole organization' (p. 28). This view of competence has been questioned. Frelin (2013) draws on the work of Biesta (2011) to describe competence as the 'ability to do things' (p. 6), but suggested that, in an educational context at least, having ability is not enough. What is required by a practitioner is competence, as well as 'educational judgement', aka 'professionality' (Frelin, 2013). As Biesta (2011) pointed out, 'a teacher who possesses all the competences teachers need but who is unable to judge which competence needs to be deployed when, is a useless teacher' (p. 10). While we agree with this sentiment, we find the use of the terms competence and competences confusing. We interpret competences (and we prefer the term competencies) to be sub-sets of competence. In this book we understand professional competence to mean more than a collection of competencies. Instead we view competence to be relational and situational. Failure to do so ignores the nuanced understanding needed when working in '*interpersonal professions*', such as SCCs, because a focus on gathering competencies can erode or discourage 'integrated perspectives' (Frelin, 2013, p. 7, *emphasis in original*). This position is particularly relevant in S&C where novice SCCs often seek to demonstrate competence by collecting competencies through micro-credentialing and other continuing education opportunities. Throughout this book, we hold the position that S&C coaching is a relational and situated practice (Frelin, 2013).

A challenge for the emerging S&C profession is to elucidate the knowledge, skills, and attitudes of a competent professional (Gearity, 2009). One means of doing this is to employ a professional competence framework to: describe the attributes of a competent professional, determine areas of strength and possible areas of omission in professional preparation, and describe the signature pedagogies of strength and conditioning. Various models of professional competence have been proposed (e.g. Cheetham & Chivers, 1996; Cruess et al., 2016; Epstein & Hundert, 2002; Miller, 1990; Quinn et al., 1996), but none specifically for strength and conditioning (Szedlak et al., 2019; Till et al., 2019). Cheetham and Chivers (1996) described a holistic model of professional competence as comprising four key components: (1) knowledge/cognitive competence; (2) functional competence; (3) personal/behavioural competence and (4) values/ethical competence. These components have been unpacked and are expanded upon in this section. The Cheetham and Chivers (1996) framework appears to be a useful starting point for SCCs who wish to act as a professional and find that they require deeper knowledge to interrogate the suggested cause-and-effect relationships that often underpin a discipline (Quinn et al., 1996). We argue that the framework encourages SCCs to develop a level of cognitive competence to enable them to anticipate and contemplate some of the potentially problematic and subtle interactions, as well as the unintended consequences of exercise and training. For instance, individuals may respond differently to workload modes, intensities and volumes in terms of responses like adaptation and recovery. While fundamental knowledge may predict specific patterns of adaptation, a cognitively competent professional might be better able to anticipate and plan for unexpected adaptations. To help map S&C professional competence, we have adapted the Cheetham and Chivers (1996) framework to include six areas of competence:

1. mastery of discipline-specific *professional knowledge* that could be described by Quinn et al.'s (1996) categorisation of 'knowing that'.
2. *functional competence* which we have interpreted to be knowing 'how' to effectively complete tasks.
3. *cognitive competence* which we describe as the ability to understand how to apply knowledge in different ways to accommodate different circumstances and individuals, such as youth (Chapter 10), older (Chapter 12) or injured (Chapter 14) athletes.
4. *personal and behavioural competence* which covers the ability to adapt personal and professional behaviours and to interact effectively and collegially with others in professional settings.
5. *values and ethical competence* which might include caring about the benefits and potential consequences of S&C for individuals and groups training under the SCC's care.
6. *cultural competence* which would depend on knowledge of community dynamics and understanding the challenges and opportunities of living with a community that may be influenced by factors like family structures, socioeconomic, ethnic, religious and linguistic backgrounds.

While there is value in SCCs utilising an existing, albeit adapted, competence framework to guide their practice, in subsequent chapters we discuss what is missing in the Cheetham and Chivers (1996) model; and the possibilities of identifying desirable S&C-specific professional competence. Attending to these oversights may assist in the development of an S&C-specific professional competence framework. All the pedagogical cases in the book have elements from this competence framework and, while these may not be discussed explicitly, we hope readers will make the connections to, and see the relevance for, S&C practice.

Strength and conditioning's signature pedagogies

To ascertain the signature pedagogies of S&C, we explored the public 'footprint' of three respected strength and conditioning professional organisations, specifically the National [USA] Strength and Conditioning Association (NSCA), the United Kingdom Strength and Conditioning Association (UKSCA) and the Australian Strength and Conditioning Association (ASCA). The NSCA was founded in 1978 and is the most established and widely respected professional body within the international S&C communities. This organisation's systems of education and certification have been widely adopted internationally. The NSCA has liaison relationships with the UKSCA (founded in 2004) and the ASCA (founded in 1992). To gain insight into the signature pedagogies of these organisations, we examined documents from their websites, specifically the mission statements, codes of ethics, education and certification practices, publications, workshops and conference material.

Mission statements

A mission statement is a brief description of an organisation's fundamental purpose for existence, its values, and generally indicates what the organisation will do for its members and customers. The mission statements of all three S&C organisations (see Table 2.1) appear similar, although they represent slightly different professional paradigms and values. The NSCA mission statement focuses on research-based knowledge and practical application, and thus emphasises a knowledge as well as technical and functional competence. The UKSCA also acknowledges the need for research-based knowledge, but their mission statement also includes references to good practice and professional standards, along with valuing communication within the profession and competent professionals. The ASCA focuses on quality, assuring SCCs for the protection and benefit of society. While the omission of a particular value from a mission statement does not mean that the organisation does not hold that value as important, it does highlight explicit priorities for an organisation.

Codes of ethics

A code of professional ethics provides guidance and sets common standards for the profession. Frankel (1989) cautions that not all codes of ethics are necessarily authentic. By this he means that although some of the listed elements indicate serious intent, others will be tactical (for the profession) or have been included to impress others. Some will represent philosophical stances that are not necessarily universally accepted, and some will be included to control 'deviant' ideas or practices from within the profession. His point is that codes of ethics may be functional, but they will also inevitably have political undertones.

A summary of the codes of ethics from the three S&C organisations (see Table 2.2) highlights key areas of inclusion/exclusion. It is worth noting that that there are only five domains where all three organisations concur. While non-discriminatory practices should be considered universal, the other four domains could be considered as predominantly self-serving for the organisations. The inclusion of misrepresenting credentials, respecting professional boundaries, and referring clients to other professionals could be construed as mechanisms to improve reciprocity and encourage other professionals to follow a similar code.

Education and certification practices

Each organisation offers different levels and forms of certification. The NSCA certification for Certified Strength and Conditioning Specialists (CSCS) is considered the industry standard

Table 2.1 Strength and conditioning organisation mission statements

Organisation	Statement
NSCA	As the world-wide authority on strength and conditioning, we support and disseminate research-based knowledge and its practical application, to improve athletic performance and fitness.
UKSCA	To establish and maintain high professional standards for UK strength and conditioning practitioners and facilities; promote and disseminate good practice, knowledge and research in strength and conditioning; facilitate communication among members; represent the interests of the membership of the UKSCA, ensure that world class coaching in strength and conditioning is available to athletes at all levels in the UK, facilitate communication among UKSCA members.
ASCA	As the peak industry body, ensure and enhance quality-assured strength and conditioning coaches for sports and the sporting community.

Table 2.2 Strength and conditioning organisation codes of ethics summary

Principle	Organisation		
	NSCA (2015)	UKSCA (undated)	ASCA (2013)
1 Be non-discriminatory	✓	✓	✓
2 Be fair & equitable	✓		✓
3 Respect confidentiality	✓		✓
4 Ensure institutional compliance	✓		✓
5 Observe copyright	✓		✓
6 Comply with organisational bylaws	✓		✓
7 Refrain from illegal/unethical behaviour	✓		✓
8 Never misrepresent credentials	✓	✓	✓
9 Adhere to the defined scope of practice	✓	✓	✓
10 Referral to other professionals	✓	✓	✓
11 Conduct only ethical research	✓		✓
12 Pursue continuing education/improvement	✓	✓	✓
13 Never reflect adversely on the organisation	✓	✓	
14 Never engage in financial exploitation	✓		
15 No personal substance abuse	✓		
16 Obey local and government laws			✓
17 Observe applicable sport body laws		✓	✓
18 Be knowledgeable about drugs in sport laws		✓	✓
19 Have a duty to advise the organisation of any disciplinary/legal proceedings faced		✓	
20 Client centred/interests are primary purpose		✓	
21 Respect the client/S&C relationship		✓	
22 Be insured		✓	

for SCCs. Equivalent certifications in liaison organisations are the UKSCA's Accredited Strength and Conditioning Coach (ASCC) and the ASCA's Level 2 accredited coach. While the key prerequisite for NSCA certification as a CSCS is a relevant tertiary education, neither of the liaison organisations mandates prior tertiary study. The NSCA has an accreditation process for programmes of study and lists accredited university/college programmes that offer approved strength and conditioning programmes of study. Those programmes are predominantly kinesiology or exercise science based.

An analysis of the competency documentation of the three S&C organisations reveals an almost exclusive emphasis on knowledge, particularly exercise science and nutritional knowledge, and the functional competencies associated with practically applying this knowledge. The only notable exceptions to this techno/rational emphasis are the NSCA's inclusion of a brief section relating to motor learning and sports psychology, and the UKSCA's inclusion of a section on communication skills and confidentiality. In summary, S&C certification criteria emphasise professional scientific knowledge and functional competence as the required competencies for entry into the profession.

Continuing education

The value placed on continuing professional development is clear from the codes of ethics of the three S&C organisations. Each has specific criteria for members to maintain their certification that includes time spent practicing as an SCC, contributions to the discipline through presentations or publications, participation in conferences, workshops and symposia, as well as other forms of formal and relevant study. Each organisation contributes to its members' professional development by publishing professional publications and organising annual conferences and regular workshops. It can be assumed that these offerings are all specifically developed to meet the continuing education needs of members, while remaining consistent with the values of the professional body.

Publications

Professional journals are typically produced for the benefit of members. The NSCA produces two professional journals, the *Strength and Conditioning Journal* (*SCJ*) and the *Journal of Strength and Conditioning Research* (*JSCR*), and three online, NSCA member-only journals. *SCJ* places an emphasis on application and delivering practical evidence-based information, while *JSCR* endeavours to improve knowledge-based strength and conditioning practices, with more of an emphasis on improved understanding and integration of sport sciences. The UKSCA and ASCA also publish journals, *Professional Strength and Conditioning* and *Journal of Australian Strength and Conditioning* respectively, that aim to provide up-to-date information pertinent to S&C professionals. A stocktake of the table of contents from the last four issues from each organisation's journal (see Table 2.3) demonstrates that all publications present information on exercise science and practical application. The *JSCR*, as per its mission statement, has an emphasis on knowledge competence, while the other three publications place greater emphasis on functional competence. The other elements of professional competence, as viewed in the previously described adaptation of Cheetham and Chivers (1996) model, account for between 5% and 20% of the content of each journal.

Workshops

The continuing education offered, advertised or endorsed by the three S&C organisations provides further insight into the signature pedagogies of the profession. The main focus of NSCA continuing education workshops was how to programme, organise, and instruct S&C programmes. Of the 62 workshop sessions scheduled, only 6 (~10%) did not emphasise this

Table 2.3 Categorisation of articles published in strength and conditioning professional journals (last four issues)

	Organisation publications			
	NSCA		UKSCA	ASCA
	SCJ	JSCR	Professional Strength and Conditioning	Journal of Australian Strength and Conditioning
# of articles	47	120	12	31
Professional knowledge	21 (~47%)	102 (~85%)	3 (~25%)	18 (~58%)
Functional competence	24 (~51%)	15 (~12%)	5 (~42%)	11 (~35%)
Cognitive competence	2 (~4%)	2 (~2%)	1 (~8%)	–
Personal and behavioural competence	–	–	2 (~17%)	2 (~6%)
Values and ethical competence	–	–	1 (~8%)	–
Cultural competence	–	1 (<1%)	–	–

Table 2.4 Categorisation of national conference podium presentations

	Organisation		
	NSCA (2018)	UKSCA (2019)	ASCA (2019)
Professional knowledge	29 (~71%)	23 (~59%)	14 (~42%)
Functional competence	12 (~29%)	12 (~31%)	15 (~45%)
Cognitive competence	–	1 (~2.5%)	4 (~12%)
Personal and behavioural competence	–	1 (~2.5%)	–
Values and ethical competence	–	1 (~2.5%)	–
Cultural competence	–	1 (~2.5%)	–

functional competence. The ASCA listed only one functional competence workshop, and the UKSCA offered five day-long workshops, with one based on communication and behavioural skills and reflective practice. With the exception of the latter workshop, no organisation promoted continuing education that addressed any of the other areas of professional competence highlighted earlier in this chapter.

Conferences

National conferences are a significant part of a professional organisation's business. They are a way of demonstrating valued member services and are a proxy measure of an organisation's popularity and success. Given that conferences are primarily for members and for others working in or allied to the profession, the content of conferences is instructive when attempting to understand a profession's signature pedagogies. The themes of podium presentations from each association's most recent annual conferences (see Table 2.4) illustrate that these typically favour techno-rational content. The NSCA conference has a particular emphasis on pure science. In contrast, the UKSCA and the ASCA have a greater emphasis on how science has been applied in practical settings and also feature limited content from other elements of the modified Cheetham and Chivers (1996) professional competence framework. But as with the NSCA, it is evident that these organisations also privilege biophysical knowledge and practical competence.

Summary

There have been numerous descriptions of the knowledge, skills and attitudes required of a successful SCC (e.g. Dorgo, 2009; Gilbert & Baldis, 2014; Kontor, 1989; Szedlak et al., 2019; Till et al., 2019), each emphasising areas of professional competences, beyond biophysical knowledge, are in need of equal or greater attention. The common pathway to becoming an effective SCC through an exercise sciences education is in reality rather limited. While biophysical knowledge is certainly an essential requirement for professional competence in S&C, we contend that SCCs need also to be competent in the other domains described in the modified professional framework (Cheetham & Chivers, 1996). This chapter has demonstrated that professional S&C organisations reflect and reinforce that dominant pathway, through privileging an exercise science knowledge base and parallel functional competencies.

We note that professional S&C organisations are making progress in this respect by including consideration of other aspects of professional competence. For example, NSCA's *Strength and Conditioning Journal* has recently published two Special Topic Issues, one on Sport Sociology for S&C (December 2018) and one on Sport Psychology for S&C (April 2019). Increasingly, papers are being published that reflect non-biophysical areas of S&C professional competence (e.g. Mills & Gearity, 2018; Szedlak et al., 2019; Till et al., 2019). The intent of this book is to encourage conversations about some of these other areas of professional competence that may not have been included in traditional educational preparation or certification. The remaining chapters in this book will introduce topics relevant to the development of cognitive competence, personal and behavioural competence, values and ethical competence, as well as cultural competence. Our hope is that these discussions will resonate with the experiences and aspirations of the S&C communities.

In acknowledging all of the good emanating from S&C professional associations and their educational and certification programmes, it is important to recognise that there can be a 'flip side' to such organisations. Buchanan (1991), writing about the medical profession, cautions that professions are not always about professional freedom and can and do exert forms of social control. He points out that professions are often 'granted powers to control the education and training of members and have considerable power over admission to and expulsion from the group' (p 104). Our mapping exercise of S&C knowledge highlights that organisations add emphasis to and privilege specific areas of professional competence, and intentionally or not are therefore exerting some level of control over the profession.

End of chapter tasks

1. Using the numerous criteria offered in this chapter, argue for, or against, S&C meeting these criteria to be considered a profession.
2. Design a curriculum (i.e. courses, desired outcomes, signature pedagogies) to prepare entry-level SCCs for practice. What knowledges are dominant or marginalised in this curriculum? Why, and what went into your thought process?
3. Review the code of ethics provided in the chapter and discuss instances where you experienced, or observed, what you consider a violation of these ethics; you could search the internet for cases too. What are the implications of this for the field of S&C and its consideration as a profession?
4. Clearly values and ethical competence, as well as personal and behavioural and cognitive competence, have been marginalised in S&C. Describe some of the reasons why this has occurred. What are some implications of this situation for the preparation of SCCs and the advancement of S&C in general?

References

Australian Strength and Conditioning Association. www.strengthandconditioning.org/images/about/strategic-plan/strategic-plan-draft-2017-2020.pdf (accessed 8 Nov. 2019).

Biesta, G. (2011). Disciplines and theory in the academic study of education: A comparative analysis of the Anglo-American and continental construction of the field, *Pedagogy, Culture & Society*, 19(2): 175–192.

Buchanan, A. (1991). The physician's knowledge and the patient's best interest. In E. Pellegrino, R. Veatch, & J. Langan (eds.), *Ethics, Trust, and the Professions: Philosophical and Cultural Aspects*, Georgetown: Georgetown University Press.

Cheetham, G., & Chivers, G. (1996). Towards a holistic model of professional competence, *Journal of European Industrial Training*, 20(5): 20–30.

Cruess, R.L., Cruess, S.R., & Steinert, Y. (2016). Amending Miller's pyramid to include professional identity formation, *Academic Medicine*, 91(2): 180–185.

Cruess, S.R., Johnston, S., & Cruess, R.L. (2004). Profession: A working definition for medical educators, *Teaching and Learning in Medicine*, 16: 74–76.

Dorgo, S. (2009). Unfolding the practical knowledge of an expert strength and conditioning coach, *International Journal of Sports Science & Coaching*, 4(1): 17–30.

Epstein, R.M., & Hundert, E.M. (2002). Defining and assessing professional competence, *JAMA*, 287(2): 226–235.

Evetts, J. (2009). New professionalism and new public management: Changes, continuities and consequences, *Comparative Sociology*, 8(2): 247–266.

Foss Lindblad, R., & Lindblad, S. (2009). The politics of professionalising talk on teaching. In M. Simons, M. Olssen, & M. Peters (eds.), *Re-Reading Education Policies: Studying the Policy Agenda of the 21st Century*, Rotterdam: Sense Publishers.

Frankel, M.S. (1989). Professional codes: Why, how, and with what impact? *Journal of Business Ethics*, 8(2–3): 109–115.

Frelin, A. (2013). *Exploring Relational Professionalism in Schools*, Rotterdam: Sense Publishers.

Gearity, B. (2009). Effective collegiate baseball strength coaching, *Strength & Conditioning Journal*, 31: 74–78.

Gilbert, W.D., & Baldis, M.W. (2014). Becoming an effective strength and conditioning coach, *Strength & Conditioning Journal*, 36: 28–34.

Hargreaves, A. (2000). Four ages of professionalism and professional learning, *Teachers and Teaching: Theory and Practice*, 6(2): 151–182.

Kirk, L.M. (2007). Professionalism in medicine: Definitions and considerations for teaching, *Proceedings: Baylor University Medical Centre*, 20: 13–16.

Kontor, K. (1989). Defining a profession, *NSCA Journal*, 11(4): 75.

Lawson, H.A. (1984). Problem-setting for physical education and sport, *Quest*, 36: 48–60.

Lorenz, C. (2012). If you're so smart, why are you under surveillance? Universities, neoliberalism, and new public management, *Critical Inquiry*, 38(3): 599–629.

Miller, G.E. (1990). The assessment of clinical skills/competence/performance, *Academic Medicine*, 65(9 suppl): S63–S67.

Mills, J.P., & Gearity, B.T. (2018). Guest editorial, special topic issue, sport sociology, *Strength & Conditioning Journal*, 40(6): 1–2.

National Strength and Conditioning Association. www.nsca.com/globalassets/about/nsca-strategic-plan-summary.pdf (accessed 8 Nov. 2019).

Quinn, J.B., Anderson, P., & Finkelstein, S. (1996). Managing professional intellect: Making the most of the best, *Harvard Business Review*, Mar.–Apr.: 71–80.

Shulman, L.S. (2005a). Pedagogies of uncertainty, *Liberal Education*, 91(2): 18–25.

Shulman, L.S. (2005b). Signature pedagogies in the professions, *Daedalus, on Professions & Professionals*, 134(3): 52–59.

Szedlak, C., Callary, B., & Smith, M.J. (2019). Exploring the influence and practical development of coaches' psychosocial behaviors in strength and conditioning, *Strength and Conditioning Journal*, 41(2): 8–17.

Teodorescu, T. (2006). Competence versus competency. What is the difference? *Performance Improvement*, 45(10). DOI:10.1002/pfi.027.

Till, K., Muir, B., Abraham, A., Piggott, D., & Tee, J. (2019). A framework for decision-making within strength & conditioning coaching, *Strength and Conditioning Journal*, 41(1): 14–26.

United Kingdom Strength and Conditioning Association. www.uksca.org.uk/assets/pdfs/ASCCdocs/AccMemAppPackMar14.pdf (accessed 8 Nov. 2019).

3 Concepts and frameworks – putting strength and conditioning under the microscope

Introduction
Critical thinking
Praxis
Reflection and reflexivity
Problem setting

    Naming and framing

Relational and situated
Working and learning in groups
Ethical frameworks

    Normative ethics

        Critique of normative ethics

Cultural competence
Summary
End of chapter tasks
References

Introduction

The stated aim of this book is to stimulate SCCs to engage in conversations, particularly conversations that are illuminated by the pedagogical and sociocultural literature. In this chapter we introduce some of the terms, language and conceptual lenses (frames of reference), that we will use in our discussions in later chapters. Some of these will be familiar and some will be less so. In this chapter we specifically describe critical thinking, praxis, the concepts of reflection, reflexivity and problem setting, and we frame S&C coaching as a relational and situated practice. We also discuss the value of professional support through groups, ethics and ethical concepts, and conclude with consideration of the importance of cultural competence for S&C.

Critical thinking

A common assumption held by many is that 'thinking critically' means an individual is judging something, or someone, in a negative fashion – criticising! But as Sage (1992) has pointed out, '[c]ritical social thought applied to sport is not critical simply in the sense of expressing disapproval of contemporary sport forms and practices' (p. 93). Instead, he argued that the intent of critical social thought is to encourage sport scientists, and we would add SCCs, to expand their work 'beyond understanding, predicting and controlling to consider the ways in which the social formations of sport can be improved, made more democratic, socially just, and humane' (p. 93). What he was calling on sport scientists to do nearly 30 years ago, we are calling on SCCs to do now, and that is to think critically *and* to act (or practice) critically.

A challenge faced by practitioners, such as SCCs, when they are asked to think critically is that they are being asked to critique practices that they might consider to be 'natural' or 'normal' and 'acceptable', practices which they may have learned early in their coach development and possess competence in, and may even be evaluated or rewarded for. Therefore, it is important to recognise the emotional attachments and embodied nature of practice, because if these aspects are not considered, then there is a distinct possibility that there will be a lack of commitment to social critique and social change (Cassidy & Tinning, 2004). Moreover, trying to 'think critically' can also be difficult as too much critique can be perceived as counterproductive, particularly as many of the exchanges and criticisms may 'operate at a level of abstraction' (Lincoln & Denzin, 2000, p. 1050). The trick therefore is to try to achieve balance and to temper finding gaps and identifying questions with generating ideas for alternate ways of practicing and possible solutions. Despite these challenges, if those working in the S&C community do not think critically about practice, they may suffer the same fate that Kirk (1986) suggested would happen to physical educators if they did not become more reflective and develop a capacity for 'informed critical judgement'. That is, they may confirm 'their low professional status' and leave 'themselves open to political manipulation' (p. 156). We argue that in order for S&C to be respected as a profession, it must be reflective and open to critical appraisal.

Praxis

Part of the attraction of S&C as a profession is the opportunity to apply exercise science theories through practice, usually within sporting contexts. With the dominant signature pedagogies in the profession identified in Chapter 2, there may be some temptation to assume that practice progresses predominantly via advances in theory. While that may be so in some cases, the term 'praxis' connotes that the relationship between theory and practice is inevitably shaped by other influences. Praxis is practice, but it also embeds a form of critical thinking and comprises the combination of reflection and action. An ancient view of praxis contended that the ability to think critically cannot be separated from acting critically. Praxis can therefore be viewed as a progression of cognitive and physical actions. It not only involves actions but also considers the effects of those actions so that the observed results can be contemplated and used to revise and refine further actions. The ancient Greeks considered the concept of praxis to be embodied in 'the wise man [*sic*]' who always aimed 'to act appropriately, truly and justly in a social-political situation' and 'allowed ends as well as means to be problematic, and to be a matter of choice' (Carr & Kemmis, 1986, p. 17). From this quote we can see that theory and practice may interact constantly and are influenced by other factors. Carr and Kemmis (1986) claim that the only fixed element in praxis is phronesis, which has been described as practical wisdom (Hardman & Jones, 2011), and it is this that fosters the inclination to act truly and virtuously. The reflexivity of praxis is a significant part of what distinguishes professional practice from expert service provision (George, 2008).

Reflection and reflexivity

Many professional education programmes and models emphasise that professional practice is not merely a matter of learning theory and then applying it. Reflection is one pedagogical strategy that has been embraced as a method of extending and encouraging ongoing learning in, and through, practice (Lay & McGuire, 2010). As a method of thinking and acting, reflection is not new but has been described and defined in various ways to suit different purposes and within different professional contexts. Over a century ago, John Dewey (1910, p. 6) described reflective thought as the '[a]ctive, persistent, and careful consideration of any belief or supposed form of knowledge in the light of the grounds that support it, and the further conclusions to which it tends'. His discussion on reflection emphasises rational analysis and as such, reflection is often described as 'an in-depth consideration of events or situations outside of oneself: solitarily, or with critical support where the person doing the reflecting assesses "who said and did what, how, when, where, and why"' (Bolton, 2010, p. 13). If we pause to unpack those statements, it can be seen that reflection is a habit that provides a means of logically contemplating one's practice and some of the consequences of that practice.

Other interpretations of reflection abound. Boyd and Fales (1983, p. 100) defined reflection as a process of personally 'exploring an issue of concern, triggered by an experience, which creates and clarifies meaning in terms of self and results in changed conceptual perspective'. In Mezirow's (1990) work the different scopes for reflection become more prominent. He described reflective action as being an inherent part of decision making and has suggested differentiated contexts for reflection. Specifically, he identified 'content reflection' to query the assumptions of one's knowledge base, 'process reflection' to examine the methods and strategies being used, and, 'premise reflection' to 'trouble' many of the things that we presuppose with practice (Mezirow, 1990; Williams, 2001). Schön (1987) used the analogy of topography to illustrate the need for reflection. He characterised the 'high ground' as being home to the more manageable problems typically encountered that can often be solved with evidence-based techno-rational solutions, whereas he described the 'swampy lowlands' as being messy and confusing and generally resistant to similar solutions. Schön (1987) suggested using reflection to build greater tacit and inferred understanding of those 'swampy challenges', where objectivity is nigh on impossible and where learnings will often occur via trial and error. For a profession like S&C where many of the human behaviours and individual differences can have marked affects on outcomes, Schön's recommended pathway for reflection seems both attractive and necessary.

Reflection has been a concept that has been discussed and applied in the context of sport coaching for nearly two decades, with various models of reflection being discussed, utilised, and critiqued (Cushion, 2018). The discussion of reflection and reflective practice in the context of S&C has less of a history (e.g. Handcock & Cassidy, 2014; Kuklick & Gearity, 2015; Mills & Gearity, 2016), arguably because of the historical reliance of SCCs on the biophysical literature and a 'modernist desire for certainty and for getting things "right"' (Cassidy & Tinning, 2004, p. 187). This desire can be seen in those SCCs who have a very strong preference for making sure that programmes are 'set in stone' at the beginning of the season and who are reluctant to raise questions about taken-for-granted practices with fellow SCCs or the wider coaching group. Before making the case for SCCs to embrace reflection, it is worth considering Cushion's (2018) concerns regarding the widespread use of reflection and reflective practice in the sports coaching literature. He argues that the concepts of reflection have been 'taken-for-granted' and the underlying assumptions have not been rigorously scrutinised. Cushion (2018) contends that while reflection has much to offer coaches, 'there is a lack of reflexivity on the part of coaching practitioners and researchers to distinguish reflective practices that are transformative from those complicit with existing power hierarchies' (p. 87).

The point Cushion (2018) is making here is that many coaches may only be 'name checking' reflection and perhaps unwittingly complying with the dominant thinking within their sports and coaching. By doing so they are likely missing the broader value that is available with reflection. In introducing the word 'reflexivity' into the conversation, Cushion points towards some of that overlooked value. The distinction between reflective and reflexive may seem largely semantic, trivial and confusing, but reflexive practice is more complex and adds value to reflective practices. Reflexive contemplation involves 'looking in on oneself', understanding relationships and how the practices of these relationships can shape the shared practices of organisations. Bolton (2010) explains that the reflexive process requires an individual to pay

> close attention upon *one's own* actions, thoughts, feelings, values, identity, and their effect upon others, situations, and professional and social structures. The reflexive thinker has to stand back from belief and value systems, habitual ways of thinking and relating to others, structures of understanding themselves and their relationship to the world, and their assumptions about the way that the world impinges upon them.
> (Bolton, 2010, p. 14, *emphasis added*)

Reflexive practice therefore requires individuals to contemplate not only what they do but also their values and beliefs and how they identify as a professional, and to consider some of the ingrained ways of thinking and behaving that they have adopted. To overcome this perceived lack, or mis-use of reflexivity, we suggest SCCs could examine, and become more aware of, the limitations of what they know, question how their behaviour informs and mirrors organisational practices as well as explore how and why these practices marginalise and/or exclude groups and individuals.

To shift from being reflective practitioners to becoming reflexive practitioners, Gorli et al. (2015) promoted the notion of 'reflection as practical reflexivity', which examines:

> the habitual ways of seeing the world and the norms of thought and behaviour acquired from authoritative sources and taken for granted. . . . [Also to] evaluate consolidated habits of perceiving, thinking, remembering, resolving problems and feeling. Reflection as practical reflexivity consists of a constant process of interrogation whereby we reconstruct shared meanings with others.
> (p. 1351)

The notion of practical reflexivity reinforces the view that thinking critically cannot be separated from acting critically (Carr & Kemmis, 1986). Moreover, the earlier examination and evaluation process of our habitual world can produce 'aha' or 'arresting moments' that can assist practitioners to understand that they are actually agents and architects of their organisations (Gorli et al., 2015). By way of example, Byrne and Cassidy (2017) illustrated how 'aha' or 'arresting moments', which they described as 'interruptions' (Biesta, 2006), were used by a head coach after he was dismissed from his position. The coach recalled how he learned from those 'arresting problematic coaching situations' and subsequently enjoyed a high level of success as a head coach. Learning from 'a reaction to a disturbance, as an attempt to reorganize and reintegrate as a result of disintegration' (Biesta, 2006, p. 27) can be a strategy for personal professional development (see Chapter 7) and caring for oneself (see Chapter 15).

Problem setting

In the previous sections, we suggested there is merit to SCCs developing a capacity for 'informed critical judgement' and becoming reflexive practitioners. In this section, we carry on in this vein by suggesting that if SCCs desire to be recognised as professionals, then there is some benefit in their understanding the process of problem setting, with its associated processes of naming and framing. Lawson (1984) argued that many professionals fail to understand the importance of the problem setting process. Instead, they allocate too much time trying to demonstrate and justify a problem, and eagerly trying to solve that perceived problem (Lawson, 1984). Similarly, Schön (2001) argued that because most professional education and training programmes privilege problem solving and problem finding, emerging professionals are likely to carry those learned perspectives into their practices. Therefore, a potential bias exists in professional practice; practitioners will try to identify problems and apply research-based knowledge to solve these problems. The point Lawson (1984) and Schön (2001) make is that professionals can often get carried along on a wave of enthusiasm with the aim of finding and solving problems, problems that may have been poorly defined to begin with.

If SCCs were to shift their attention away from problem solving and focus initially on problem setting, this would likely present opportunities to develop a deeper understanding as to why some S&C practices are promoted and others are not. For example, an SCC may adopt a functional screening method to identify movement imbalances for future attention. It may be, however, that imbalances are not problematic and do not impair performance or predispose to injury. According to Lawson (1984), there are multiple stimuli for problem setting, including: a desire to become, or develop as, a professional; social and technological change; client demands and the threat of deprofessionalisation. The process of problem setting is value laden, so there are no universally appropriate responses to these stimuli. This in turn presents a key challenge for problem setting because personal biases and external pressures are difficult to negate (see Chapter 4).

Importantly, S&C is a profession that tends to idealise innovation, and often new methods and technologies are accelerated to market with little testing, rigour or robust scientific (biophysical and/or psychosocial) evaluation. There is a sense of self-imposed pressure for many S&C professionals to be early adopters of new methods and technologies, at times experimenting with new methods before athletes or clients are able to source alternate information from non-professional sources. Consequently, an S&C professional may be using a technology or conditioning technique primarily because it is available, is seen to be cutting edge and promises to solve problems. A further attraction is that early uptake can help position SCCs as being ground-breaking leaders in their field rather than merely followers. Furthermore, Coutts (2014) pointed out that there is a tendency in sport sciences to yield to the temptation to over-utilise the available technologies and their data before proof of concept, and before appropriate validity and reliability trials have been completed. Subsequently, many SCCs use new technologies to measure, or monitor, athletes without really being certain about *what* they are measuring, *how* they are measuring 'it' and what problem has been set (see Chapter 4).

34 *Setting the scene*

Naming and framing

Socialisation plays a significant role in how we *frame* problems because we interpret new experiences based on our previous experiences (Lawson, 1984). The term 'frame' can be understood as how a problem has been outlined or defined. The process of framing (identifying or defining) is an 'editing', which can result in some issues being viewed as problems while others are not. It is worth noting that much of the framing process may occur at a tacit level and is informed by key influences. In the case of SCCs, potential key influences include socialisation as a former athlete, a university S&C graduate, a member of a sports club and being part of the wider S&C community and local community. Moreover, these influences will undeniably, and tacitly, inform and edit what becomes framed as a problem in an attempt to 'transform the unfamiliar into the familiar' (Lawson, 1984, p. 52).

Lawson (1984) contends the *names* given to problems generally fall into two categories: 'technical efficiency' and 'morality'. The former focuses on fixing problems, while the latter is concerned more with privileges, needs and rights. A focus on technical efficiency in the S&C context is evident:

1   in the mapping exercise of the content of professional journals and national conferences (see Chapter 2) where the emphasis is on knowledge and functional competence.
2   in the practices of aspiring SCCs who desire to collect and use a greater repertoire of techniques such as movement screening, rating of perceived exertion (RPE) and to adopt new technologies and techniques that utilise global positioning systems.
3   in the questions explored like 'How do we prevent injury?' or 'What can be done to reduce fatigue?'

While professionals certainly need to master techniques in order to fix technical issues that arise in practice, there is a danger that 'knowing that' and 'knowing how' (Quinn et al., 1996) are assumed to be the most important attributes of a competent professional. As discussed in Chapter 1, professional competence also requires professionals to be concerned about 'knowing why' and 'caring why' (Quinn et al., 1996).

In terms of 'caring why', a focus on what Lawson (1984) has labelled morality is less obvious in S&C contexts, but examples can still be found. For example:

1   in the practices of SCCs who do not immediately rush in to fix things, but instead conduct a preliminary analysis to confirm whether the perceived problem does indeed require attention. For example, when an SCC examines the squad statistics from previous seasons to explore trends in injury prevalence and finds that only a particular group of players experienced injury and that it was a specific type of injury. It may have been non-contact hamstring strains and groin/adductor strains occurring mainly in football wingers. Therefore, the decision is to care for the wingers, and not that we need a prehabilitation programme for all to prevent hamstring injuries.
2   in questions like 'How do we negotiate the tensions when a player is eager to return to play after injury (conforming to the sporting ethic) and delaying that player's return until they can demonstrate fitness close to their pre-injury state?' This common dilemma requires a coach to focus on athlete wellbeing rather than team performance (see Chapter 14).
3   in questions like 'What is happening in the lives of the athlete, outside of the sport, that may be contributing to a feeling of fatigue?' By asking this question, the focus moves away from constantly surveilling the athletes to caring about them.

These three examples illustrate the way in which the names that we use to describe a problem 'betray' our values, and how the naming of a problem provides not only a basis for action, but also legitimacy for particular actions to occur (Lawson, 1984). As was pointed out in Chapter 2, 'knowing why' and 'caring why' are just as important as 'knowing that' and 'knowing how' when developing professional competency (Quinn et al., 1996).

Relational and situated

As stated in the introduction to this chapter, we view SCC to be a relational practice. According to Zou (2016), the concept of relational practice focuses on understanding the ways in which personal, interpersonal and social structural factors shape an individual's experiences. While many would agree, in theory, that it is desirable for S&C coaching to be a relational practice, we suggest that the current practices of many SCCs do not reflect this desired outcome. The reasons why this may be the case are reflected in the following quote. While this quote is lengthy and focuses on nursing education, its description of the way in which functional knowledge is privileged, and relational practices are undervalued in the nursing community, is, we believe, similar to that prevailing in many S&C environments.

> Teaching and learning in nursing education often focus on mechanical skills and technical interventions. . . . Education curricula frequently emphasize scientific, measurable technical knowledge, ignoring interpersonal aspects of nursing care. Students are taught to assess physical needs of patients, while psychosocial needs are very often ignored. Interpersonal aspects of nursing are often reduced to a set of communication behavioral skills [3, 5]. Thus, in clinical practice, novice nurse students are pushed to focus on learning nursing skills. The junior status of students leads to their powerless position and impairs their ability to advocate for the needs of patients and act for their best interests. Their relational capacity, such as authenticity, responsiveness, mutuality and engagement, is not recognized; their contribution to relational nursing practice is not valued [6].
> (Zou, 2016, p. 2)

It may be that SCCs do not place emphasis on promoting relational practices because relational work, and the associated attributes needed to conduct relational work, like caring for others, have not been viewed as strengths and have been stereotyped as 'feminine' work and 'traits associated with women's greater emotional needs' (Fletcher, 2001, p. 9). In the broader sports coaching contexts, a small number of researchers are beginning to explore and advocate for considering the important role emotions play in coaching practices (see Potrac & Marshall, 2011; Potrac et al., 2017). In Chapters 14 and 15 we introduce the notion of care, exploring how it can be played out in the sports coaching context (see Cronin & Armour, 2019) and in the SCC context (see Peterson, 2019).

Working and learning in groups

Successful relational practices rely on practitioners to have good interpersonal skills (Zou, 2016). One way to facilitate, and develop, interpersonal skills is to work with, and in, groups. Groups can be organised to meet formally or informally, and it has been suggested that as groups spend more time together, their members become bound by the value in learning together, developing satisfaction through shared understanding, developing common knowledge about practices and approaches to problems and perhaps developing a sense of identity (Wenger et al., 2002). When exploring the way in which learning occurs in groups, Lave and Wenger (1991) theorised the concept of 'situatedness'. In explaining situatedness, they argued that learning is inseparable from the social practice, and that situated learning is 'more encompassing in intent than conventional notions of "learning *in situ*" or "learning by doing"' (p. 31). Moreover, situated learning involves the whole person, rather than an individual passively receiving information on, or about, the world.

To describe 'engagement in social practice that entails learning as an integral constituent' Lave and Wenger (1991, p. 35) introduced the concept of 'legitimate peripheral participation' (LPP), which they suggested as also a 'way to speak about the relations between newcomers and old-timers, and about activities, identities, artefacts, and communities of knowledge and practice' (p. 29). Specifically, LPP describes how newcomers become part of a 'community of practice' (CoP) and how in doing so they become a full participant (or at least as full as possible) in a sociocultural practice. Wenger et al. (2002) argued that CoPs require similar structural elements, which include a *domain* of knowledge, a *community* of people and shared *practices*. The *domain* includes common knowledge and a common identity and becomes legitimised through the shared practices of the membership. The *community* is the social fabric of learning, where learning is viewed as a social process and demands trust, respect and commitment. The shared *practices* are the frameworks, tools, mechanisms, even language that the members use to further develop, implement and evaluate their domain. According to Wenger et al., these three elements enable CoPs to form *knowledge structures*. Given the above explanation, it is important to recognise that not all groups are CoPs, nor are all CoPs identical.

Building on these ideas, Wenger (1998) contended that the process of learning in a community is a 'vehicle for the evolution of practices and the inclusion of newcomers while also (and through the same process) the vehicle for the development and transformation of identities' (p. 13). However, for learning to be the vehicle, the community has to have some coherence, and here Wenger suggests that a CoP requires the presence of three dimensions, namely the participants have to be *mutually engaged* in *a joint enterprise* in which they have a *shared repertoire*. The discussion of CoPs in sports coaching contexts has grown dramatically in the past 15 years, so much so that the term Coaching Communities of Practice (CCoPs) was coined (Culver & Trudel, 2006). However, not all the discussions of CoPs in the sports coaching context have rigorously engaged with the work of Lave and Wenger (1991) and Wenger (1998). Consequently, calls were made to clarify the use of the concept of CoP in sport (Cassidy, 2008; Culver & Trudel, 2008). When research was conducted with sport coaching groups that did reflect Wenger's (1998) suggested dimensions of a CoP (see Cassidy et al., 2006; Culver & Trudel, 2006), it was noted that the coaches voiced the need for the facilitators to exert some control over the direction and length of the discussions that occur in the group if they were to be of optimal value. The observations of the coaches reflected the position of Wenger et al. (2002) who contended, 'the most important factor in a community's success is the vitality of its leadership' (p. 80). Cassidy and Rossi (2006) drew on the work of Wenger (1998) when discussing the implications of using CoP to energise coach education. This work may have some merit when designing professional development opportunities for SCCs. According to Wenger (1998), learning can be designed *for*; that is, learning can be brought about by facilitating the conditions in which it can occur. Such facilitation requires future learning opportunities to be organised around plans, procedures, schedules and curricula; yet Wenger also considers that less is more, because learning is more about the response to design rather than the result of it.

Noted limitations of CoPs are that they can be restricting and may not reflect the complex relationships that surround practitioners (Mallett et al., 2008; Wenger-Trayner &

Wenger-Trayner, 2015). In response to these limitations, Wenger-Trayner and Wenger-Trayner (2015) proposed that the boundaries of the communities, with their potential for tension, can be viewed as opportunities for learning to occur. Explicitly acknowledging that boundaries are potentially problematic, as well as sites for learning, is consistent with the earlier discussion in this chapter about how the notion of 'interruption' can facilitate learning (Biesta, 2006). Given that work drawing on the notion of interruption already exists in sports coaching literature (Byrne & Cassidy, 2017; Cassidy et al., 2017), we contend there would be some value in SCCs beginning to: (1) think critically *and* to act (or practice) critically; (2) examine, and become more aware of, the limitations of what they know, question how their behaviour informs and mirrors organisational practices as well as explore how and why these practices marginalise and/or exclude groups and individuals; and (3) understand the processes associated with problem setting as well as the naming and framing of problems.

Ethical frameworks

Normative ethics

A dominant way of thinking about ethics in the Western world is via a normative ethical framework. This normative approach has also been adopted by those interested in ethics and sports coaching (e.g. Cassidy et al., 2016; Hardman & Jones, 2011; Jones, 2008; McNamee, 2008). Interestingly, in the recently published *Routledge Handbook of Strength and Conditioning* (Turner, 2018), ethics was not a topic that warranted an index entry. Given the context in which SCCs work, we consider this to be a considerable oversight.

According to Morgan (2007), normative ethics pose questions, arguments and reason with the aim of prescribing 'how we should act in certain circumstances' (p. xiii), particularly when we find ourselves having to make an ethical, rather than a prudent, response. An ethical situation has been described by Shogan (2007) as one that involves fairness and welfare of sentient beings. She describes a sentient being as one who 'can physically or psychically suffer, whose welfare or fair treatment can be harmed, and who, therefore, can be assisted on some way' (p. 2). Normative ethics have been categorised under four normative ethical perspectives (contractarian, deontological, utilitarian and virtues) (Morgan, 2007). For centuries debates have raged around the assumptions of these ethical perspectives, and it is not within the scope of this book to contribute further to this debate. Instead, the purpose of the following section is to introduce one framework that SCCs can draw upon when they find themselves in an ethical situation and have to make an ethical, rather than a prudent, response.

In Morgan's (2007) *Ethics in Sport* tome, he discusses the four normative ethics in more detail. He posits that a *contractarian* perspective of ethics is based on the assumptions that 'human agents cannot achieve what they want in life without the cooperation of others', that 'moral decisions must be impartial', and any decision would focus on 'considerations of fairness and justice rather than self interest' (pp. xxix–xxxi). A *utilitarian* perspective of ethics focuses on the consequences of the decision or act and is based on the assumptions that the 'only good worth pursuing is pleasure or happiness', the correct actions would be those 'that produce the greatest benefits' as long as the actions were 'practical and useful' (DeSensi & Rosenburg, 1996, p. 59) and would produce good as opposed to evil (Robinson & Garratt, 1996). This perspective is reflected in the common saying 'the greatest good for the greatest number'. There are two forms of the utilitarian perspective, act- and rule-utilitarianism, with the former focusing on what act(s) have the greatest benefit, with the latter focusing on what rule(s) have the most utility (Morgan, 2007). A *deontological* ethical perspective assumes that a person will act in ways that they assume is the right thing to do, regardless of the consequences, even if that action caused harm. Not surprisingly, this perspective is viewed as non-consequential. Yet, what is considered the 'right thing to do' may be informed by 'rules' (e.g. codes of conduct, or return-to-play protocols), which is described as 'rule-deontology'; or by moral obligations, which can change depending on circumstances and has been described as act-deontology (Morgan, 2007). The fourth normative ethical perspective discussed by Morgan (2007) is the *virtuous* ethical perspective which focuses on being good rather than simply doing right, and it requires people to make a conscious choice to act with moral intent. Actions are judged to be virtuous if it is 'what a virtuous agent [i.e. someone of good character] would, characteristically, do in the circumstances' (Driver, 2007, p. 138). Since virtues can be viewed as lived values, it is not surprising that advocates of the virtues perspective assume that when making an ethical decision, or acting ethically, consideration needs to be given to developing excellence and placing a premium on values, such as 'courage, justice, honesty and integrity in our dealings with one another' (Morgan, 2007, p. xxxii). Gaining an understanding of normative ethics is useful for all because they can 'guide, instruct, recommend, advise, and evaluate how human beings should behave' (p. xiii). Yet it is important to note that normative ethics is only one framework for understanding ethics, and it is not without its critics.

Critique of normative ethics

Normative ethical frameworks, which are largely premised on philosophies originating with the ancient Greeks, have been a focus of Western philosophers for centuries. Crane and Matten (2007) contend that normative ethical theories are limited because by privileging rules, rights and duties, they take limited account of the complexities of the 'real world' and push to one side the importance that relationships and the affective domain play in any ethical situation. Moreover, recommending the 'principled' approach to resolving ethical situations ignores the context in which the decision-makers are located. Normative ethics have also been challenged by those who argue for the importance of acknowledging culture when discussing ethics (Miller, 2005). The importance of culture on ethical practice is reflected in the 4th edition of Crane and Matten's (2016) book on business ethics in the age of globalisation, where they discuss topics including world religions, whistle blowing, feminist ethics and the ethical challenges presented by social media. While these discussions are contextualised in business, the issues they raise are equally relevant to those working in the SCC and broader sports coaching contexts. Moreover, Crane and Matten draw on examples from Asia, Arabia, Latin America and Africa to provide insight into the ethical debates and dilemmas faced by businesses in these regions. Given the increasing cultural diversity in many sports teams and clubs, it highlights the importance of SCCs not only understanding the assumptions that inform their own ethical perspectives and subsequent behaviours, but also understanding how ethical perspectives are influenced by culture (which includes their own culture) and what this means for practice and decision making.

Other critics of normative and universalist approaches to ethics contend that such approaches do not acknowledge the constantly changing moral standards of cultures and societies (Rorty, 1999). Chattopadhyay and De Vries (2013) contend that 'respect for cultural and moral diversity is an ethical imperative' (p. 644) and demonstrate how 'the application of "universal" principles does not promote respect and justice . . . [but] can, in fact, cause real harm to persons' (p. 640). They go on to make a case for reflecting on what is considered 'normal' ethical perspectives because often the 'vantage points' from which judgements are made are rarely questioned. Chattopadhyay and De Vries (2013) illustrated this when they described the practices of a researcher, who they claim did not reflect on his own cultural perspective when he raised questions about family and individual autonomy. When the researcher asked 'which element should have more weight in our decision-making: collective (family) or individual decision-making?' Chattopadhyay and De Vries (2013) point out that the researcher does not notice his 'own cultural perspective', which results in his prioritising 'one over the other' and not being able to conceive that 'an ethical decision can hold these two in tension when rendering a decision' (p. 642). They go on to point out that if the researcher held a Hindu-Sikh religio-cultural point of view, then the question would not be about either the family or the individual; instead it would be 'about how to find the points of convergence, if not harmony, between the individual and the collective' (p. 642).

It is not only the Hindu-Sikh community, or researchers, who challenge the individual-collective dichotomy; many other cultural groups also do so, and this has implications for the globalised coaching world. For example, in New Zealand there would be some value in the SCCs of the All Black Sevens team reflecting on how their practices reinforce, or not, the individual-collective dichotomy. This was highlighted by the attention 18-year-old Niko Jones, son of ex-All Black La'auli Sir Michael Jones, received upon his selection into the team. In a recent interview Sir Michael was asked to describe the secret of Niko's success, at which point he explained Niko was proud of his Samoan heritage, was involved in the church and was surrounded by the ethos that it takes a village to raise a child. He said these factors played a

> 'big part in shaping' Niko, and a big part of the support structures and scaffolding that's been central to where he is now. . . . He'll never lose that appreciation and recognition that he is a by-product of this loving village, and I can't see him disconnecting himself from it, and that includes the role of his faith. We have always stressed it and he understand the fact that he's been given a gift and he has to protect it . . . a big part of using it well is how he can use it to give back to his community' Sir Michael said.
>
> (Hunia, 2019)

Other critiques of normative ethics come from proponents of care ethics, who contend that deontological and utilitarian ethical perspectives emphasise generalisable standards and impartiality. Critics claim that normative ethics fail to acknowledge what has traditionally been viewed as feminised values and virtues (Gilligan, 1982), with Cronin et al. (2019) pointing out that many women continue to undertake 'nurturing caring work', which is often 'undervalued' and/or 'taken for granted'. Drawing on Norman's (2010) work, the latter group suggests this situation has implications for sports coaching generally and, we contend, S&C more specifically, because women coaches are so underrepresented in these fields. Despite the critiques of normative ethics, the ethics of care is nonetheless a normative ethical perspective because moral action focuses on interpersonal relationships and on benevolence or care as a virtue as well as emphasising the importance of the individual response. The difference between the individual and the general is illustrated by the moral questions that are asked; for example, 'what is just' versus 'how to respond' (Bailey & Cuomo, 2008).

Noddings (2002) is one who attempts to disrupt the links between the discussion of care and normative ethical perspectives. She does this by interrogating virtues. When Cronin et al. (2019) discuss care theory and sports coaching, they drew attention to the way Noddings firmly distinguishes between care as a virtue and care as a relation. When discussing care as a virtue, Cronin et al. (2019) noted that this can be illustrated by an accountant who is 'diligently concerned with accuracy and "carefully" completes a spread sheet' (p. 16). In contrast, they explain that when discussing care as a relation, the emphasis is on the affective domain which requires 'trust, dialogue and empathy between both individuals' (p. 16). Noddings (2002) distinguishes between 'caring for' and 'caring about' and also makes the distinction between 'natural caring', which 'does not require an ethical effort to motivate it' (p. 11), and 'ethical caring', which requires an individual to make a conscious decision to care for someone.

Cultural competence

A challenge facing SCCs is the need to be prepared to relate to clients from an increasingly diverse world. It is unlikely that an SCC will interact only with clients who look, think and behave like them, so there is a need for SCCs to become more culturally competent. We believe that the S&C professional competence framework (see Chapter 2) could be improved by adding culture competence as a key competency. The term cultural competence evolved from terms such as cultural sensitivity and cultural awareness and has been described as the ability to 'apply knowledge and skill appropriately in interactions with clients' (Srivastava, 2007, p. 9). This requires recognition, and understanding of, foundational notions such as culture, race, diversity and marginalisation (Srivastava, 2007). Therefore, a culturally competent professional values and respects cultural diversity as well as having the willingness and ability to adopt, and adapt, practices in ways that support all people with whom they are working.

One potential starting point for SCCs, and their associated organisations, as they work towards becoming culturally competent is to engage with those who advocate for adopting culturally relevant pedagogies. This suggestion is not new (see Howard, 2003; Legge, 1997; Salter, 2000). Recently, Flory and McCaughtry (2011) developed a three-step 'cultural relevance cycle' that is broad enough in scope to support all willing practitioners to develop culturally relevant pedagogies. The three steps are: (1) knowledge of community dynamics; (2) knowing how community dynamics influence educational processes; and (3) implementing strategies that reflect cultural knowledge.

According to Flory and McCaughtry (2011), a practitioner who is engaging in a culturally relevant pedagogy has knowledge of the community dynamics. That is, they know about things like: the family structures in which participants live; the socioeconomic, ethnic, religious and linguistic backgrounds, learning styles, as well as the challenges and opportunities of living in the community. They also know how the community dynamics can influence educational processes; for example, the support participants receive outside of, in this case, the S&C environment. Important to the third step in the 'cultural relevance cycle' is the notion of cultural distance. Flory and McCaughtry describe cultural distance as the 'discrepancy between world-views, values, and backgrounds that shape individuals' and groups' explanations for how the world operates' (p. 50). Empirical research illustrates the considerable cultural distance that exists between teachers and students in many urban educational contexts in Western countries (Flory, 2017). We contend that the anecdotal, and observational, evidence suggests there is also considerable cultural distance between the membership of the S&C community and elite athletes in countries such as the UK and USA, especially for those residing in urban areas. So what strategies could an SCC, who wishes to engage in a culturally relevant pedagogy, adopt?

Working in the context of Aotearoa/New Zealand, McDowell (2017) seized the opportunity to develop cultural competence in practitioners, in her case non-Māori teachers who were teaching Māori students. Here McDowell adopted a strategy of asking the teachers questions that encouraged them to reflect on how their practices reflected five cultural competencies, which were informed by a Māori world view. More recently, and building upon her earlier work, McDowell (2019) adapted the reflective questions with the aim of making them relevant to those working in a sports coaching context. While we recognise that the Māori world view informing the questions may not directly translate to other cultural contexts, it is possible that McDowell's questions (see the following list) can provide those SCCs wishing to develop culturally relevant pedagogies with a framework, or stimulus, to think about what questions they could ask themselves, and their peers, as they try to practice in ways that are more culturally responsive to the context in which they work. The questions that reflect five cultural competencies are:

1 Who are your participants? How do you know? How do you connect tangata whenuatanga[1] in your practice?
2 What opportunities do you provide/facilitate for learning relationships to be developed across, and within, all parties?
3 How do you develop a collaborative, inclusive and supportive learning environment? How is giving and receiving enacted in ways that uphold the mana[2] of people and the environment?
4 What range of active learning strategies, tools and resources do you use?
5 What opportunities do you provide to enable/encourage all people to communicate confidently?

Summary

In this chapter we set out to provide background and convey our understanding of the different theoretical lenses that we use in this book to examine S&C practice. We have clarified our interpretation of 'critical thinking' and discuss how 'praxis' embodies theory, practice and critical thought. We attempt to distinguish between reflection and reflexivity and emphasise how important introspection is for the latter. In this chapter we also explained the methods of 'problem setting' and 'naming' and 'framing' the professional issues that we encounter in our practices. One of the central arguments for the professional competence framework presented in Chapter 2 is that S&C coaching is 'relational' and 'situated' and therefore requires competence in a broad range of areas. This chapter also introduces 'communities of practice' and the importance of mutual professional support through groups. Introductory information on ethical frameworks was presented with some critique to lay a foundation for the ethical discussions found in other chapters of this book. We close out this chapter with discussion of the observation that clients are likely to be different from us, reinforcing the need for SCCs to also be culturally aware and competent.

End of chapter tasks

1 Several key concepts were introduced in this chapter, such as critical thinking, reflection, reflexivity, problem setting, relational and situated, naming and framing. On a piece of paper or with notecards, define these concepts and give an example of it specific to S&C.

2 Are there any theories or practices in S&C that are set in stone and should be left unchallenged? Reflect on what's informing your decision making and why you may, or may not, hold such a view.
3 Much of the biophysical science that informs S&C seeks to predict, control and be reproducible, in usually sterile and controlled settings. Discuss this reductionist view of science and its effects on the field, and judge its worth.
4 Identify some things you have reflected on in S&C. With a peer or small group, or perhaps through reaching out to an experienced SCC, compare your reflections with theirs. What explains the similarities and differences in your reflections?
5 Create a concept map that identifies a problem in S&C. Write down why it's a problem. Then, add to the map by drawing a line and a word bubble; inside the bubble, extend the problem setting process by writing in an important feature of this problem – perhaps what values are expressed, who is implicated by the problem, etc. Create more bubbles and lines, and when doing so, you can use arrows to show the directionality of how things affect one another and their corresponding (un)known outcomes.

Notes

1 *Tangata Whenuatanga* can be understood as 'people and places' (New Zealand Ministry of Education, 2011).
2 *Mana* can be understood as 'prestige, authority, control, power, influence, status, spiritual power, charisma' (https://maoridictionary.co.nz/word/3424).

References

Bailey, A., & Cuomo, C. (2008). *The Feminist Philosophy Reader*, Boston: McGraw-Hill.
Biesta, G.J.J. (2006). *Beyond Learning: Democratic Education for a Human Future*, Boulder, CO: Paradigm.
Bolton, G. (2010). *Reflective Practice. Writing and Professional Development* (3rd ed.), London: Sage Publications.
Boyd, E.M., & Fales, A.W. (1983). Reflective learning: Key to learning from experience, *Journal of Humanistic Psychology*, 23(2): 99–117.
Byrne, G., & Cassidy, T. (2017). 'Pleased to be sacked': Coach Pat Lam's 'learnings' and the evolution of a professional rugby union organisation, *International Sport Coaching Journal*, 4(3): 326–334.
Carr, W., & Kemmis, S. (1986). *Becoming Critical: Education, Knowledge and Action Research*, London: Falmer.
Cassidy, T. (2008). Clarifying the concept of communities of practice in sport: A commentary, *International Journal of Sports Science and Coaching*, 3(1): 19–21.
Cassidy, T., Burrows, L., Bates, R., & Merriless, J. (2017). 'Just doing it': A strength based approach to coaching athletes. In G. Kohe & D. Peters (eds.), *High Performance Disability Sport Coaching*, London: Routledge, pp. 60–76.
Cassidy, T., Jones, R., & Potrac, P. (2016). *Understanding Sports Coaching: The Pedagogical, Social, and Cultural Foundations of Coaching Practice* (3rd ed.), London: Routledge.
Cassidy, T., Potrac, P., & McKenzie, A. (2006). Evaluating and reflecting upon a coach education initiative: The CoDe of rugby, *The Sport Psychologist*, 20(2): 145–161.
Cassidy, T., & Rossi, T. (2006). Situating learning: (Re)examining the notion of apprenticeship in coach education, *International Journal of Sports Science and Coaching*, 1(3): 235–246.
Cassidy, T., & Tinning, R. (2004). 'Slippage' is not a dirty word: Considering the usefulness of Giddens' notion of knowledgeability in understanding the possibilities for teacher education, *Journal of Teaching Education*, 15(2): 175–188.
Chattopadhyay, S., & De Vries, R. (2013). Respect for cultural diversity in bioethics is an ethical imperative, *Medicine, Health Care and Philosophy*, 16(4): 639–645.

Coutts, A. (2014). In the age of technology, Occam's razor still applies, *International Journal of Sports Physiology and Performance*, 9(5): 741.

Crane, A., & Matten, D. (2007). *Business Ethics: Managing Corporate Citizenship and Sustainability in the Age of Globalization* (2nd ed.), Oxford: Oxford University Press.

Crane, A., & Matten, D. (2016). *Business Ethics: Managing Corporate Citizenship and Sustainability in the Age of Globalization* (4th ed.), Oxford: Oxford University Press.

Cronin, C., & Armour, K. (eds.). (2019). *Care in Sport Coaching: Pedagogical Cases*, London: Routledge.

Cronin, C., Armour, K., & Gano-Overway, L. (2019). Care theory and sport coaching. In C. Cronin & K. Armour (eds.), *Care in Sport Coaching*, London: Routledge, pp. 15–29.

Culver, D., & Trudel, P. (2006). Cultivating coaches' communities of practice: Developing the potential for learning through interactions. In R. Jones (ed.), *The Sports Coach as Educator: Re-Conceptualising Sports Coaching*, London: Routledge.

Culver, D., & Trudel, P. (2008). Clarifying the concept of communities of practice in sport, *International Journal of Sports Science & Coaching*, 3(1): 1–10.

Cushion, C. (2018). Reflection and reflective practice discourses in coaching: A critical analysis, *Sport, Education and Society*, 23(1): 82–94.

DeSensi, J., & Rosenberg, D. (1996). *Ethics and morality in sport management*, Morgantown, WV, USA: Fitness Information Technology Inc.

Dewey, J. (1910). *How We Think*, Boston: Heath.

Driver, J. (2007). *Ethics: The Fundamentals*, Malden, MA: Blackwell.

Fletcher, J. (2001). *Disappearing Acts: Gender, Power, and Relational Practice at Work*, Cambridge, MA: MIT Press.

Flory, S.B. (2017). Culturally responsive pedagogy and teacher socialization. In K. Andrew, R. Richards, & K. Lux Gaudreault (eds.), *Teacher Socialization in Physical Education: New Perspectives*, London: Routledge, pp. 162–175.

Flory, S.B., & McCaughtry, N. (2011). Culturally relevant physical education in urban schools: Reflecting cultural knowledge, *Research Quarterly for Exercise and Sport*, 82(1): 49–60.

George, M. (2008). Interactions in expert service work: Demonstrating professionalism in personal training, *Journal of Contemporary Ethnography*, 37(1): 108–131.

Gilligan, C. (1982). *In a Different Voice*, Boston: Harvard University Press.

Gorli, M., Nicolini, D., & Scaratti, G. (2015). Reflexivity in practice: Tools and conditions for developing organizational authorship, *Human Relations*, 68(8): 1347–1375.

Handcock, P., & Cassidy, T. (2014). Reflective practice for rugby union strength and conditioning coaches, *Strength and Conditioning Journal*, 36(1): 41–45.

Hardman, A., & Jones, C. (2011). *The Ethics of Sports Coaching*, London: Routledge.

Howard, T. (2003). Culturally relevant pedagogy: Ingredients for critical teacher reflection, *Theory into Practice*, 42(3): 195–202.

Hunia, R. (2019). RNZ second generation sport stars: Blessing or a curse? www.rnz.co.nz/news/sport/379659/second-generation-sports-stars-blessing-or-a-curse (accessed 14 Dec. 2019).

Jones, C. (2008). Teaching virtue through physical education: Some comments and reflections, *Sport, Education and Society*, 13(3): 337–349.

Kirk, D. (1986). Beyond the limits of theoretical discourse in teacher education: Towards a critical pedagogy, *Teaching and Teacher Education*, 2(2): 155–167.

Kuklick, C., & Gearity, B. (2015). A review of reflective practice and its application for the football strength and conditioning coach, *Strength and Conditioning Journal*, 37(6): 43–51.

Lave, J., & Wenger, E. (1991). *Situated Learning: Legitimate Peripheral Participation*, Cambridge: Cambridge University Press.

Lawson, H.A. (1984). Problem-setting for physical education and sport, *Quest*, 36: 48–60.

Lay, K., & McGuire, L. (2010). Building a lens for critical reflection and reflexivity in social work education, *Social Work Education*, 29(5): 539–550.

Legge, M. (1997). Developing a bicultural pedagogy to teach Te Reo Kori: An inquiry into my own teaching. Paper presented at the New Zealand conference on Health and Physical Education. Te Waiora me Te Reo Kori Hui o Aotearoa, July, Auckland, New Zealand.

Lincoln, Y., & Denzin, N. (2000). The seventh moment: Out of the past. In N. Denzin & Y. Lincoln (eds.), *Handbook of Qualitative Research* (2nd ed.), Thousand Oaks: CA: Sage.

Mallett, C., Rossi, T., & Tinning, R. (2008). Relational interdependence between individual agency and affordances in how high performance coaches learn. In T. Rossi, P. Hay, L. McCuaig, R. Tinning, & D. Macdonald (eds.), *Sport Pedagogy Research, Policy and Practice: International Perspectives in Physical Education and Sports Coaching: North Meets South; East Meets West*, AIESEP World Congress, Proceedings.

McDowell, G. (2017). Te Ao Māori learning journeys of teacher educators, unpublished Master's thesis, University of Otago, Dunedin, New Zealand.

McDowell, G. (2019). Te Ao Māori learning in sports coaching. Personal communication, 30 Apr.

McNamee, M. (2008). *Sports, Virtues and Vices: Morality Plays*, London: Routledge.

Mezirow, J. (1990). How critical reflection triggers transformative learning. In J. Mezirow & Associates (eds.), *Fostering Critical Reflection in Adulthood: A Guide to Transformative and Emancipatory Learning*, San Francisco, CA: Jossey-Bass, pp. 1–20.

Miller, R. (2005). On making a cultural turn in religious ethics, *The Journal of Religious Ethics*, 33(3): 409–443.

Mills, J., & Gearity, B.T. (2016). Towards a sociology of strength and conditioning, *Strength and Conditioning Journal*, 38(3): 102–105.

Morgan, W. (2007). *Ethics in Sport,* Champaign, IL: Human Kinetics.

New Zealand Ministry of Education. (2011). *Tātaiako: Cultural Competencies for Teachers of Māori Learners*, Wellington: Ministry of Education.

Noddings, N. (2002). *Starting at Home: Caring and Social Policy*, London: University of California Press.

Norman, L. (2010). Feeling second best: Elite women coaches' experiences', *Sociology of Sport Journal*, 27(1): 89–104.

Peterson, G. (2019). Developing and awareness of emotion management strategies to support athlete success, *Strength and Conditioning Journal*, 41(2): 3–7.

Potrac, P., & Marshall, P. (2011). Arlie Russell Hochschild: The managed heart, feeling rules, and emotional labour: Coaching as an emotional Endeavour. In R. Jones, P. Potrac, C. Cushion, & L.T. Ronglan (eds.), *The Sociology of Sports Coaching*, London: Routledge.

Potrac, P., Smith, A., & Nelson, L. (2017). Emotions in sport coaching: An introductory essay, *Sports Coaching Review*, 6(2): 129–141.

Quinn, J., Anderson, P., & Finkelstein, S. (1996). Managing the professional intellect: Making the most of the best, *Harvard Business Review*, Mar.–Apr.: 71–80.

Robinson, D., & Garratt, C. (1996). *Introducing Ethics*, Cambridge: Icon Books.

Rorty, R. (1999). *Philosophy and Social Hope*, New York: Penguin Books.

Sage, G. (1992). Enhancing human performance in sport: Toward empowerment and transformation. In *American Academy of Physical Education Papers, No. 25*, Champaign, IL: Human Kinetics.

Salter, G. (2000). Deciding between cultural identity or 'success' in physical education: Describing attitudes and values', *Journal of Physical Education New Zealand*, 33(3): 67–83.

Schön, D.A. (1987). *Educating the Reflective Practitioner*, San Francisco, CA: Jossey-Bass.

Schön, D.A. (2001). The crisis of professional knowledge and the pursuit of an epistemology of practice. In J. Raven & J. Stephenson (eds.), *Competence in the Learning Society*, New York: Peter Lang, pp. 183–207.

Shogan, D. (2007). *Sport Ethics in Context*, Toronto: Canadian Scholars' Press.

Srivastava, R. (2007). Understanding cultural competence in healthcare. In R. Srivastava (ed.), *The Healthcare Professional's Guide to Cultural Clinical Competence*, Toronto: Elsevier Health Sciences.

Turner, A. (2018). *Routledge Handbook of Strength and Conditioning: Sport-Specific Programming for High Performance*, London: Routledge.

Wenger, E. (1998). *Communities of Practice: Learning, Meaning and Identity*, Cambridge: Cambridge University Press.
Wenger, E., McDermott, R., & Snyder, W. (2002). *Cultivating Communities of Practice: A Guide to Managing Knowledge*, Boston: Harvard University Press.
Wenger-Trayner, E., & Wenger-Trayner, B. (2015). Learning in a landscape of practice: A framework. In E. Wenger-Trayner, M. Fenton-O'Creevy, S. Hutchinson, C. Kubiak, & B. Wenger-Trayner (eds.), *Learning in Landscapes of Practice: Boundaries, Identity, and Knowledgeability in Practice-Based Learning*, London: Routledge.
Williams, B. (2001). Developing critical reflection for professional practice through problem-based learning, *Journal of Advanced Nursing*, 34(1): 27–34.
Zou, P. (2016). Relational practice in nursing: A case analysis, *Nursing and Health Care*, 1(1): 1–5.

Part 2
Elite sport performance

4 Measurement, assessment and testing – what does it all mean?

Introduction
Part 1: pedagogical case
Part 2: commentary

    Problem setting
    What are the stimuli for Mau to undertake problem setting?

Summary
End of chapter tasks
References

Introduction

This chapter explores the predilection in S&C for making already complex work even more complex. With pressures to excel, SCCs can start seeing signals where there may be only noise, adopt prototypical technologies and methods of analysis without really 'road-testing' those methods, accumulate copious data on their athletes' fitness and training, and attempt to 'diagnose' problems that may not actually be problematic. In this chapter we argue that pedagogical and sociocultural perspectives can help SCCs avoid the tendency to overanalyse and overcomplicate their work. Furthermore, we question the value of SCCs becoming preoccupied with 'problem solving' when oftentimes inadequate attention is paid to how those problems are 'set'.

Part 1: pedagogical case

When Mau graduated from university with a Bachelor of Science (majoring in Strength and Conditioning; S&C) he initially volunteered as a strength and conditioning coach (SCC) with a local football (soccer) team, whilst working full-time as a personal trainer at a local fitness centre. His long-term goal was to become a full-time, and paid, SCC. In an effort to achieve his goal, Mau became a member of the National Strength and Conditioning Association (NSCA), attended its annual conference, vociferously scanned the professional journal they produced and followed the blogs and social media posts of a couple of popular and high-profile SCCs. Mau experimented with some of the ideas he gleaned from these sources and introduced several of the new exercises and drills into football practices and with selected clients at the gym. He regularly received positive feedback on his innovative practices from the athletes and coaches, as well as from clients at the gym. He was gratified by this but often wondered, if he could be this successful working part-time, with limited resources, how effective could he be if he was to become a well-resourced, full-time SCC? This goal was achieved when Mau was appointed by the local professional football club as a full-time and paid SCC, working with the men's, women's and academy (youth) teams. At the time he was delighted to be offered the job, but now two years into his tenure with the club, Mau was a little disappointed that he did not appear to be achieving the results he had expected with the athletes.

Once a week Mau met a group of friends at a popular bar. Members of this group included his former S&C university lecturer and an old school friend who had recently enrolled for a PhD in the area of S&C. When this group gathered, the topic of conversation inevitably turned to football. Initially all of Mau's work stories were 'good-news' stories, particularly how much he was enjoying having a budget to invest in technology, how he was using the technology with the athletes, and also having the opportunity to individualise functional movement training for athletes. One of the first things he had purchased was a set of heart rate monitors, and he excitedly told his friends that he required all athletes to wear these during all training sessions. These monitors sent real-time data on athlete work-rate directly to his computer. At the time Mau said it was like 'magic' to have all of this data immediately at his fingertips. He had also got the club to purchase a set of GPS units for athletes to wear during trainings and games. Mau thought that these units were even more amazing than the heart rate monitors as he was able to analyse, off-line, the distances covered by individuals, the speeds attained, and their accelerations and decelerations. Moreover, the GPS units could identify periods of intense play and different activity profiles by position, and he could then use all of this information to assist him in individualising an athlete's training programme, as well as a check to ensure that individual athletes were not becoming too fatigued and possibly becoming prone to injury.

Technology was not the only benefit Mau enjoyed as a full-time paid SCC. He was also provided with opportunities to undertake professional development courses. In the recent off-season he had enrolled in a movement screening course. He knew from his university days that athlete screening was a part of any 'needs analysis' and was something that was required before an SCC could 'plan and design training programmes'. Mau was energised after completing the movement screen course and had since elected to screen all of the athletes in the training group. He believed that the movement screen complemented the standard fitness testing battery he had been using. Based on his findings from the screens, Mau had since introduced prehabilitation and functional exercises into the conditioning routines of most of the athletes.

Initially Mau had only shared his positive experiences, but as he entered his third year as the SCC, he felt that he could trust the group enough to begin sharing some of his concerns and frustrations. By doing so, he was hopeful that they would become his 'critical friends' and gently challenge him on why he was doing things the way he was, as well as make suggestions as to why they thought things were not quite going to plan. He found that as he began to confide in his friends, they were more willing to take the opportunity to ask questions that they had obviously been eager to ask. One asked; 'What are you doing with all of the heart rate and GPS data that you are collecting? I don't see how you could possibly have enough time to make sense of all of that' and 'What do the coaches and athletes think of the data?' Mau had to confess that once the season got under way, he really didn't have time to look at the data in any great detail; in fact he was only really looking at the total distances that each athlete covered. He used these values as rudimentary measures of individual training load. In response to this answer, his lecturer friend asked, 'How can you be sure of the thresholds for training load for each athlete? Surely each athlete must be different.' Another friend was interested in the ethics of collecting all of this data on the athletes, especially when those athletes knew that the coaches may be looking at the data. Somewhat defensively, Mau countered that they were not 'spying' on the athletes, merely measuring and monitoring them for their own good. He argued that requiring athletes to wear heart monitors and GPS units was an important part of ensuring that the athletes were not doing too little training or, in the case of some athletes, making sure they were not doing too much. The latter reason was how he 'sold' technologies to the athletes, coaches and club. He also pointed out that the data provided him with an opportunity to track the athlete's welfare so they did not get injured.

His friends' questions had, however, planted seeds of doubt for Mau. For example, what was he really doing with that massive amount of data, and what did the process of collecting the data do to his relationship and level of trust with the athletes? Were athletes concerned about being monitored all of the time? Were they now simply training in order to 'satisfy' the technology? What were the risks? If pressed, how was Mau going to communicate and rationalise his analysis, or provide meaningful feedback to the athletes and coaches?

Mau's friends were also interested in his thoughts on the movement screening course and how he was finding it when applied practically to screen footballers. The PhD student friend was openly highly sceptical of movement screens. He had read most of the research on movement screening and, while some of the research showed moderate reliability, their validity and usefulness were being strongly critiqued in the research literature. According to him, the evidence supporting movement screens as injury screens was ambiguous, and scores on the screens did not appear to have any relationship to athletic potential or performance. Once again, these questions raised further doubts in Mau's mind. What seemed like great ideas were now looking less helpful. He had convinced the club to invest in these technologies, so he felt obligated to make use of them. These doubts provided an opportunity for him to question why all of the athletes in the training group appeared to have functional movement issues, even those that he considered to be very good athletes. Were these false positives? What's more, several of the athletes who had sustained major injuries in previous seasons had still scored well on the movement screen. How could this be?

Part 2: commentary

Problem setting

Mau's experiences are poignant illustrations of the challenges that many SCCs face when they consider or implement different technologies or techniques into their practice, particularly if they do not have a strategic plan for their use and are unaware of related sociocultural issues. The adoption of any conditioning plan will likely be informed by personal ideologies and experiences of conditioning, and will ideally be based on clearly identified strength and conditioning needs of the athletes. However, as we argue in this section, it should also be designed after clearly understanding how the so-called problem has been set.

Mau's experiences of not obtaining the results he'd expected could be explained as being a consequence of his failing to adequately 'problem set'. Lawson (1984) argued that many professionals fail to understand the importance of the problem setting process; instead they allocate too much time trying to demonstrate and justify a problem, and are eager to try and solve a perceived problem. Similarly, Schön (2001) argued that because most professional education and training programmes privilege problem solving and problem finding, emerging professionals are likely to carry this learned approach into their practice. Therefore, a potential bias exists in professional practice; namely, practitioners will often actively try to identify problems and apply research-based knowledge to solve these problems. The point that both Lawson (1984) and Schön (2001) make is that professionals can often get carried along on a wave of enthusiasm with the aim of finding and solving problems, problems that have in fact been poorly defined and that may not actually exist. How does this happen, and how can SCCs avoid this trap?

In the pedagogical case in the previous section, Mau utilised a newly learned movement screen and introduced GPS technology and heart rate monitors for various reasons. The techniques and technologies were considered to be new, innovative and 'cutting-edge'. They were readily available and Mau had the budget to purchase these items. In Lawson's (1984) terminology, these would be categorised as 'technical efficiency' challenges. Mau believed that these tools would assist him in his duty as a competent SCC, contribute to the athletes' health and wellbeing, and help the athletes to optimally develop their physical capabilities. If he was honest with himself, this innovation was also Mau's way of demonstrating his value to the club. For some reason, these ideas from the business and technology world guided, or more strongly controlled, his thinking and practices. He had assumed being an effective coach required him to buy, consume and implement these products (Jones & Denison, 2018). In the highly competitive domain of elite sport S&C, successful self-presentation is considered a key influence in securing paid employment (Bolino et al., 2016) and suitably impressing coaches and athletes to remain a contributor to an organisation. Being innovative and cutting-edge is one way for an SCC to create a point of professional difference and be favourably noticed.

In his football S&C role, Mau had observed two key problems that are common issues in elite sport; the challenge of preventing injury, and the uncertainty around athletes' low frequency (or background) fatigue, both of which are considered to ultimately influence on-field performance. If athletes are not available for selection due to injury, they are of little help to the team, and any benefit of their conditioning becomes temporarily moot. If athletes are available for selection but are not 'jumping out of their skin' and ready to play, then they are not likely to be as effective in game settings. Furthermore, their undesired 'background' fatigue may in turn expose them to greater injury risk. Despite all of this technology, injuries are still occurring – while technology isn't solving the problem, it is neither producing the problem nor causing SCCs to be unthinking.

In his enthusiasm, Mau had arguably overlooked two important considerations; he had failed to identify whether those factors were in fact a problem within the club and teams that he worked with, and to define the exact nature and extent of any detected problems. He also needed to understand how the information and data generated from using the technology and techniques would help prevent or solve such problems. There is also the consideration of how technology changes coach-athlete relationships and organisational dynamics. If the technology is to be used to help decide who to cut, or to coerce athletes, then who can be honest in such situations? A key point is that we're trying to help better prepare SCCs for some of these sociocultural realities and to continue to think about these issues from numerous perspectives – this means we won't necessarily find a 'tidy' fix or answer.

If SCCs seek to be considered professionals, then we contend that there is some benefit in their recognising that 'the products of problem-setting (missions, goals, objectives) are central to the process of professionalization' (Lawson, 1984, p. 48) as well as understanding the process of problem setting, with its associated processes of how the nature and dimensions of a problem are defined and explained (see naming and framing in Chapter 3). We are not trying to suggest here that being objectives driven describes a particular view of what it means to be a professional, and it must be recognised that there are other notions of professionalism such as ethics and virtue, or behavioural models (Irby, 2017).

Gaining a deeper understanding of an issue can facilitate professional development. So if SCCs were to shift their attention away from problem solving and focus initially on problem setting, this would likely present opportunities to develop a deeper understanding as to why some S&C practices are promoted and favoured, and others are not. According to Lawson (1984), there are multiple stimuli for problem setting, including; a desire to become or develop as a professional, social and technological change, client demands, and the threat of deprofessionalisation. Because the process of problem setting is value laden, there are no universally appropriate responses to these stimuli. This in turn presents a key challenge for problem setting as personal biases, and dominant discourses are difficult to critique or negate.

Lawson (1984) suggests that our socialisation plays a significant role in how we describe and explain perceived problems (Chapter 3) because we interpret new experiences based on our previous experiences. This can result in some issues being viewed as problems while other issues are not. In other words, the lenses through which we view problems are also 'editing mechanisms' (Lawson, 1984, p. 52). What is more, much of the problem setting occurs at a tacit or non-conscious level. When it comes to naming problems, Lawson contends that the names that we use to describe a problem 'betray' our values. For example, the use of the word 'prehabilitation' hints at our values around injury etiology and the role of exercise, and intimates that we have a pretty good idea of what causes injury and can therefore prevent injury. Lawson contends that once a problem has been named, it provides a basis for action, and its name provides legitimacy for particular actions to occur. Terms such as overtraining, recovery and prehabilitation indicate a particular problematising orientation in the S&C domain and are biased towards a particular plan of action around the steps to be taken to mitigate risk.

What are the stimuli for Mau to undertake problem setting?

As we have discussed, social and technological change, along with anxiety about 'deprofessionalisation' can provide the impetus for problem setting (Lawson, 1984). In Mau's case, the latter two appear to be the primary stimuli for engaging with novel technologies. With the availability of widespread access to social media and technology, the athletes under Mau's care can readily source S&C information and may seek guidance from alternate non-professional sources. Importantly, S&C is a profession that tends to idealise innovation, and often new methods and technologies are accelerated to market with little testing rigour or scientific evaluation. There is a sense of self-imposed pressure for many S&C professionals to be early adopters of new methods and technologies, often before clients can source alternate information from non-professional sources. Consequently, an S&C professional may be using a technology or conditioning technique primarily because it is available, is seen to be cutting-edge, and promises to solve problems. Coutts (2014) points out that there is a tendency in sport sciences to yield to the temptation to over-utilise the available technologies and their data, before proof of concept and validity and reliability trials have been completed. Early uptake can help position the SCC as a ground-breaking leader rather than a follower. Subsequently, many SCCs use new technologies to measure or monitor athletes, without an in-depth understanding, let alone being certain of *what* they are measuring, *how* they are measuring 'it' and understanding *what problem* has been 'set' for the measurement to potentially solve.

Mau does not appear to have considered or understood the metrics and nuances of his newly adopted measurement and monitoring methods. Aside from attempting to identify how valid, reliable, specific and sensitive a test or screen might be, he could have also conceptualised the smallest worthwhile change (SWC) of the parameter of interest, and whether that SWC is in fact detectable with the methods employed. For example, he could ascertain from the literature how effective screening for injury in sport has been, and in particular how accurate (valid) movement screens have proved. Mau could have 'done his homework' – his due diligence – on the test-retest reliability of the screening method. He could also have attempted to ascertain the smallest improvements that could be reliably detected with the screening tool. That information would then inform some of his choices and whether screening was reliable and potentially meaningful. Mau's research would likely have revealed that although movement screens are promoted based on their ability to identify injury risk, support for screens by no means is unanimous or offers confidence (McCunn et al., 2016). For example, Rowan et al. (2015) screened athletes entering the National Hockey League using the Functional Movement Screen (FMS). Those researchers noted that identified asymmetries and 'infractions' demonstrated significant correlations that were seemingly slight, coincidental or even counterintuitive when linked with medical, physical and physiological fitness data. Bushman et al. (2016) reported similar misgivings when using FMS with military personnel, finding that although the FMS score was associated with a higher risk of injuries, sensitivity was poor with low predictive value and a tendency to misclassify injury risk (Monaco & Schoenfeld, 2019).

Mau appears to have not closely considered the stimuli for problem setting, and he also may not have been cognisant of the process of framing a problem. Key influencers as to how Mau goes about framing a problem are his socialisation as a former athlete, as a university S&C graduate, as a member of the football club and as part of the wider and local communities. These influences have undeniably, and tacitly, informed and edited what he views as problems as he attempts to 'transform the unfamiliar into the familiar' (Lawson, 1984, p. 52). Graduating from university with a specialisation in S&C would likely have a significant influence on the process Mau follows in order to name a given problem. According to Schön (2001), there is an emphasis on technical rationality in universities and particularly in professional schools. By this he inferred that students assume that cause-and-effect relationships exist and that these can be manipulated through rationally reasoned actions. This mindset can in turn encourage aspiring professionals to collect a greater repertoire of techniques such as movement screening, and to readily adopt new technologies like GPS. While professionals certainly need to master techniques in order to practice, there is a danger that 'knowing that' and 'knowing how' (Quinn et al., 1996) are assumed to be the most important attributes of a competent professional. Mau named his problems as preventable injury and preventable fatigue (overreaching/overtraining), which reflects a focus on technical efficiency. If he had named, and categorised, his problems in a way that had a moral focus, other questions could have been asked. For example, Quinn et al. (1996) argued that 'knowing why' and 'caring why' are just as important as 'knowing that' and 'knowing how', with all four elements being vital elements of professional competency.

By naming and framing his problem in a way that reflected a moral orientation, Mau could view the problem differently. For example, he might choose to first examine the team and squad statistics from previous seasons to explore trends in injury prevalence and perhaps distinguish preventable from non-preventable injury. He may also have wanted to clarify why he is gathering heart rate and GPS data. Is he concerned that athletes are doing too much, too little, or is it for prescriptive purposes to enable optimisation of individual training loads? If he is concerned about overloading, he may want to first explore the likely influence of fatigue by looking at match data, and talking to athletes and coaches about their experiences in previous seasons. These preliminary analyses may confirm if the problems he perceived are indeed true problems necessitating attention. For example, his enquiries may show that the club has experienced a lot of non-contact hamstring strains and groin/adductor strains. He may also find that during a winning season, fatigue did not seem to be the issue it appeared to be during their two recent losing seasons. Further analysis may indicate that the likely 'sticking spot' appeared to be the end of the regular season play and beginning of the playoffs, where more athletes and coaches reported fatigue. Closer monitoring may help detect whether these feelings of fatigue are perceived or demonstrated with objective measures.

Summary

In this chapter we introduced the quandary of an enthusiastic SCC contending with two issues that he has identified within his sport setting: injury and training fatigue. Through the SCC's eyes we are able to appreciate the temptation for him to seek to simplify these issues into manageable monitoring issues and settle on novel and convenient technological solutions. This chapter, however, accentuates the importance of taking the time to carefully name and frame these work challenges (problem setting, Chapter 3) to provide clarity about what is being done and why. While there are various external influences on an individual's willingness to problem set, we contend that a competent professional should be proactively using this approach with their work. As a supplement to problem setting, this chapter also emphasises the need for professionals to be able to 'peer under the hood' of new (and established) technologies and techniques, so as to fully understand and trust the metrics and nuances of monitoring methods. Finally, this chapter reinforces the need, when professionals problem set, to clearly strategise and plan for how information will be interpreted and used to contribute to, and improve, practice. The SCC in our pedagogical case is fortunate to have a group of critical friends who have helped him articulate and theorise about the issues that he has encountered, and to critically think about his learning and strategies for future practice.

End of chapter tasks

1   Use some of the questions and concerns raised in this chapter to develop an interview guide. Perhaps ask questions such as:

    •   What's the reliability and validity of 'such and such' technology or testing device?
    •   Where was this research published?
    •   Were there any financial conflicts of interest in this research?
    •   What were the participants' subjective experiences wearing 'such and such' technology?
    •   How much does this technology cost, and what are the human resources needed to implement it?

    Next, reach out to a sport scientist or SCC to interview them using your interview guide.
2   Drawing on the ideas of Lawson (see Chapters 3 and 4, e.g. problem setting or naming, socialisation, deprofessionalisation) critique a problem in S&C. Consider what values are involved in this problem, if it's highly essential, if it's reoccurring, and how it affects performance. Have others framed, and solved or tried to solve, this problem? Is it absolutely vital to solve this problem? What are some other problems capturing your attention, or failing to, and why not investigate those?

3 Watch investigative reporter and author David Epstein's TED talk on sport science and athletic performance: www.ted.com/talks/david_epstein_are_athletes_really_getting_faster_better_stronger?language=en

Consider the role of anthropometrics, technology and equipment, technique and rule changes, and other factors on athletic performance. Now consider your role as an SCC and how much you may, or may not, affect performance. What are some implications of your reasoning?

4 Investigate the origin of an S&C method, tool, piece of equipment, system of training, etc. Who invented it? Why? What were the social conditions at the time that helped produce this? What sorts of claims were made about the training or device? Was it developed through years of research and development, or a sudden epiphany? After you've had a chance to do this historical work, consider how your research has affected your understanding, and possible use or lack of use, of said object.

References

Bolino, M., Long, D., & Turnley, W. (2016). Impression management in organizations: Critical questions, answers, and areas for future research, *Annual Review of Organizational: Psychology and Organisational Behaviour*, 3: 377–406.

Bushman, T., Grier, T., Canham-Chervak, M., Anderson, M., North, W., & Jones, B. (2016). The functional movement screen and injury risk: Association and predictive value in active men, *American Journal of Sport Medicine*, 44(2): 297–304.

Coutts, A. (2014). In the age of technology, Occam's razor still applies, *International Journal of Sports Physiology and Performance*, 9(5): 741.

Irby, D.M. (2017). Constructs of professionalism. In R. Byyny, D. Paauw, M. Papadakis, et al. (eds.), *Medical Professionalism Best Practices: Professionalism in the Modern Era*, Aurora, CO: Alpha Honor Medical Society, pp. 9–14.

Jones, L., & Denison, J. (2018). A sociocultural perspective surrounding the application of global positioning system technology: Suggestions for the strength and conditioning coach, *Strength and Conditioning Journal*, 40(6): 3–8.

Lawson, H.A. (1984). Problem-setting for physical education and sport, *Quest*, 36: 48–60.

McCunn, R., aus der Funten, K., Fullagar, H., McKeown, I., & Meyer, T. (2016). Reliability and association with injury of movement screens: A critical review, *Sports Medicine*, 46(6): 763–781.

Monaco, J.T., & Schoenfeld, B. (2019). A review of the current literature on the utility of the functional movement screen as a screening tool to identify athletes' risk of injury, *Strength and Conditioning Journal*, 41(5): 17–23.

Quinn, J.B., Anderson, P., & Finkelstein, S. (1996). Managing professional intellect: Making the most of the best, *Harvard Business Review*, Mar.–Apr.: 71–80.

Rowan, C.P., Kuropkat, C., Gumieniak, R.J., Gledhill, N., & Jamnik, V.K. (2015). Integration of the functional movement screen into the National Hockey League combine, *Journal of Strength & Conditioning Research*, 29(5): 1163–1171.

Schön, D.A. (2001). The crisis of professional knowledge and the pursuit of an epistemology of practice. In J. Raven & J. Stephenson (eds.), *Competence in the Learning Society*, New York: Peter Lang, pp. 183–207.

5 Training volume – fear of missing out (FOMO)

Introduction
Part 1: pedagogical case
Part 2: commentary
Is deliberate weight gain advised?
    Training for weight gain
Periodisation rationale
Fatigue and workload monitoring
Professional competence
Summary
End of chapter tasks
References

Introduction

Training for sport has effectively become a year-round pursuit for many athletes. Driven by a quest to be fitter, bigger, stronger or tougher, and goaded by a fear of 'falling behind', athletes continually test the limits of how much training they can 'get away with'. The resulting dilemma for the strength and conditioning coach (SCC) is how to make a high training volume fit into an already tight schedule, whilst monitoring athlete workload. In the context of 'knowing why' and 'caring why', this chapter interrogates the logic and necessity of these practices (Quinn et al., 1996; see Chapter 2).

Part 1: pedagogical case

Recently I became involved in a local, informal group of SCCs who work in various sport settings, and I've been getting a lot of value from participating in that group. Perhaps it's the group dynamics, the topics that we've been discussing and debating, or it's just a bit of serendipity for me and the stage where I am in my career. Our group consists of seven members; six of whom regularly attend and contribute to the discussions. A few, like me, are new to the strength and conditioning (S&C) profession; two are 15-year-plus veterans, and the rest have a range of experience. Four of us have come straight into S&C from college courses, one has come to S&C through her sporting career and another has a background as physical training instructor in the military. The seventh member trained as a physical therapist and picked up S&C as an adjunct to her sports medicine practice. Everyone in the group works with a different sport, so that opens us up to a wide range of thoughts and issues.

The last two meetings have been really interesting. We've been discussing the concept of 'more, more, more' (more training, more intensity), with the debate getting a little heated at times. That topic was added to our agenda by Wade. He works with a high-level ice hockey club. Two sessions ago, Wade presented the background to his topic and gave us his preliminary thoughts on the issue. It turns out that Wade was contacted by Connor, a 28-year-old wing, who had played for the team that Wade currently works with. This season Connor had transferred to another club, and he had contacted Wade to discuss the struggles he was having with the SCC at his new club. The coaches of his new team want him to play a slightly different role (more physicality and finishing checks) and require him to add another 5 kg to his existing 90 kg body before the new season starts. Connor reported that he is finding the training volume too much. By all accounts, Connor has been a hard worker with a great training ethic and well-established training habits. According to Wade, Connor's issue is that the SCCs are trying to get him bigger and stronger at the same time. He simply doesn't feel that he has 'enough gas in the tank' to meet the demands of the hypertrophy and strength schedules, and on-ice trainings that they are expecting him to follow. Also, he does not feel like he is making any progress with either of the elements of his programme. Most of his weights are down from last season, he's feeling sluggish and he thinks that's slowing up in his skill sessions, where he feels like he's 'lost a step' on the ice. Connor is competing with six other right wingers in camp and feels like he's not demonstrating his best abilities with the team. He is experiencing a couple of lower body 'niggles', but he's unsure that those are not just some delayed muscle soreness combined with his low level of confidence.

Given his vulnerable situation, Connor is reluctant to discuss his concerns with the team coaches. The last thing he wants to do is to look like a quitter or malcontent with his new club. Nonetheless, he has talked with Bart, the team SCC, and explained that he is struggling physically with the training. Part of the reason for his this could be that his twin 18-month-old daughters have not settled well since the move to a new home; Connor and his wife are experiencing limited quality sleep, which is increasing the stress at home. Connor explained to Bart that when he came into the league as a 19-year-old he weighed 79 kg. Over time he gradually bulked up and physically matured, and three seasons ago successfully added about 5 kg to get to his current 90 kg. Knowing his body the way he does, Connor does not believe that further healthy weight gain is a possibility. According to Connor, while Bart did appear to listen to him, Connor found Bart relatively unsympathetic and was reluctant to move away from his established programme structure. Bart explained to Connor that he would just have to be patient because when faced with constraints, it is common practice to concurrently work on hypertrophy and strength. As hypertrophy is a precursor of strength, Bart assured Connor that once the weight is gained, they will drop the hypertrophy loading whilst maintaining the increased levels of strength.

Not only was Connor unconvinced that Bart was open to accommodate his situation, he was unsure, despite Bart's reassurances, that the skill coaches were aware of his high off-ice training volume. The skill coaches seemed to make no accommodations during Connor's skill sessions and scrimmages, and they had never mentioned anything that would indicate their awareness of his training situation. In an effort to placate Connor's concerns, Bart had agreed to re-examine his recovery programme, and in the meantime he wanted Connor to discuss his diet and hydration schedule with a club-affiliated dietitian and explore any supplements that might help with training recovery. Bart also wanted Connor to pay more attention to recovery and make use of the club's new cold water immersion system after training, as he believed this would help reduce soreness and speed up Connor's recovery time. Connor explained to Wade that he was not overly happy with these suggestions. He is not a fan of supplements and while he has no experience with cold baths, he has heard some negative things around their effect on muscle and strength adaptations, and on scar tissue. Connor is feeling anxious about his situation and fears that he is on a pathway to missing 'the cut' for the squad. He enjoyed and trusted Wade as an SCC and is now seeking some advice on how he might turn this situation around.

Wade told our group what he knows of Bart, and explains that he is a fairly inexperienced SCC who is new to the club and this level of competition. He knows that Bart has had a few years of experience as an assistant at a lower-level club and that he interned with one of the toughest S&C coaches in ice hockey, someone who had a reputation for being part of successful teams but also had a name for 'breaking' young players. He suspects that as an inexperienced S&C, Bart will be closely following the direction of his coaches and will not be 'sticking his neck out' by standing up for his athletes' individual needs. As an experienced professional, Wade explained that he wants to respect Bart professionally, so he won't intervene or question Bart's conditioning processes. However, he has provided Connor with suggestions on how he might help monitor and manage his own workload and fatigue.

As the group discussed Connor's situation, Wade shared with them one of Connor's comments that struck him as being the catalyst for rethinking commonplace practices. He said,

> the training seems so ridiculous and illogical. It's not about my hockey. They want me to train harder and recover faster so that I can go back in the gym and smash myself all over again – just to add more weight – I'm struggling to eat enough to hang on to the 90 kg I do have! To me it's like I'm siphoning my gas tank so I can get more in the next time I fill up! I thought part of conditioning was supposed to be to help prevent injuries; I really think that this programme is more likely to cause me injuries!

Having previously worked with Connor, Wade believes that he is an athlete who knows his training and body responses pretty well. To further stimulate our group's discussion around Connor's situation, Wade bought along a couple of papers on concurrent hypertrophy and strength gains, as well as a paper questioning the general adaptation syndrome and the potential for ongoing adaptation. The latter paper (Buckner et al., 2017) challenged a lot of the commonly taught principles. One of our group members raised a question about a hypothetical threshold for strength and fitness. What he meant was that with the modern obsession in sports like ice hockey for bigger, stronger and faster athletes, whether being any faster or stronger will actually make you a better player. He wondered, once you've reached a fitness threshold, whether you are really training to improve your game or just to improve your 'numbers'. I can see what he means and I've offered to find out what research there is on that topic and bring it back to the group. Someone also questioned whether gym-based strength has actually been shown to enhance athletic performance, particularly in 'open loop' team sports. Wanda, the ex-military SCC, thinks that Connor just needs to buckle down and demonstrate his physical and mental toughness. She thinks the coaches might be using this training not only to condition the athletes but also to test their resilience under duress. A couple of coaches in our group agree with her. We've discussed injury risk and fatigue, and we've also had some interesting discussions about communication and athlete-centred S&C. We've even explored ethics and some of the S&C ideologies that appear to be prevalent in our profession. I, along with the other novice SCCs in the group, hadn't expected that something like this could prove to be such a complex professional issue. My college course taught me how to write programmes, instruct exercise technique and put together a periodised training schedule, but it failed to prepare me for situations like this.

Part 2: commentary

In Chapter 3 we discussed how professionals can often get carried along on a wave of enthusiasm with the aim of finding and solving problems, problems that have in fact been poorly defined (Lawson, 1984; Schön, 2001). This appears to be what Connor is experiencing with Bart, his new SCC. Historically SCCs have been socialised, or explicitly educated in formal settings such as universities, into thinking that they need to conduct a thorough needs analysis as an initial step towards developing a training programme for an athlete. This would normally consist of analysing and understanding the position-specific needs of the sport, but also of understanding the circumstances and needs of the individual athlete. Taking initial direction from the sport coaching staff, who create the team's general sport plan and ancillary activities like S&C, an SCC would normally develop a generic and periodised training plan for the team and then provide more detailed individualised training programmes based on an individual needs analysis. Lawson (1984) suggests that our socialisation plays a significant role in how we frame problems because we interpret new experiences based on our previous experiences. This can result in some issues being viewed as problems while other apparent issues may not be. In other words, frames are 'editing mechanisms' (Lawson, 1984, p. 52), and this framing occurs at a tacit or non-conscious level. Not only are problems framed, but they also have to be named. As discussed in Chapter 3, the names that we use to describe a problem reflect our values, provide a basis for action and legitimatise the particular actions that are chosen or proposed (Lawson, 1984).

Is deliberate weight gain advised?

While the effects of unintended and undesirable weight gain on performance and health have been well described in the academic literature, strategic weight gain for sport has received scant attention. Some sport coaches often hold strong views on the suggested performance benefits associated with increased (and decreased) body size, perceptions that remain unchecked by critical challenges or research refutation. In general, if a prospective athlete is attracting the attention of selectors and scouts, they have likely performed well or demonstrated some potential. In collision sports, a prevalent coaching belief is that if a good athlete can become bigger, faster and stronger, they will also become more physically effective. There are also anecdotal assumptions (e.g. Gabbett et al., 2012) that increased body mass offers more protection from injury in combative sports such as rugby or ice hockey. While these suppositions are contestable (e.g. Fuller et al., 2013), rightly or wrongly, a coach's perceptions become a powerful form of pressure (Reel & Galli, 2006) that will directly affect athletes and S&C staff. The physicality argument may be difficult to critically evaluate, but research indicates that increased body mass and muscularity does not appear to offer any appreciable respite from injury (Gabbett et al., 2012). It would seem to be self-evident that larger bodies colliding at greater speeds are likely to cause more damage, more often. In terms of functional power and strength, increased body mass may offer no net benefit to an individual, as any activity that involves extensive bodyweight control is likely to penalise additional body mass. For example, Horn et al. (2018) demonstrated that higher body mass in football players was negatively correlated with reactive strength index – a proxy measure of the ability to move one's body rapidly – as measured during depth jumps. Increasing body weight, without a proportional increase in force-producing capacity, can affect the ability to jump, accelerate, decelerate and rapidly change direction. The subsequent impaired ability to land, decelerate and control movement can increase the risk of injury, particularly in older athletes (Young et al., 2019). Within the constraints of the sport, ice hockey involves many physical abilities. Although ice skating is arguably less influenced by body mass than running, the demands of starting and stopping still require an individual's body mass to be controlled, manoeuvred, accelerated and decelerated. Anecdotally, many players pressured to add weight for their sport have reported that their performance (finer motor skills and mobility) was perceived to deteriorate while their injury vulnerability increased.

A competent S&C professional should be constantly considering the health and wellbeing of athletes – values and ethical competence from Chapter 2. The pressure to gain weight can lead to behaviours such as compulsive exercise, disordered eating, and indulging in possibly indulging in hazardous and illegal muscle-building practices (Galli et al., 2011). Despite the best of intentions, lean body mass gains will, for some athletes, include fat accumulation (e.g. Kim et al., 2018). Pressured weight gain will often result in athletes having to eat when they are not hungry, making unhealthy choices and consuming food past satiety – habits that may be difficult to change post-sport. American footballers who had deliberately gained weight during their careers were found to have an increased risk of later-life health afflictions and disease (Churchill et al., 2018). Coaching preferences aside, a cognitively competent S&C professional would be advised to carefully consider the evidence base when evaluating the benefit-to-risk ratio associated with deliberate weight gain. At some point these larger athletes will retire from competitive sport and will likely want, or need, to return to a 'healthier' weight. Sporting organisations and SCCs need to consider how they can help these athletes transition, inclusive of biopsychosocial concerns, from a possibly 'at-risk' weight to healthier or non-athletic body composition.

Training for weight gain

Increasing body mass would normally be a major focus during the off-season and early preseason, but in Connor's case he feels pressured to continue weight gain 'deep' into his preseason training. It would seem that there are multiple pathways to hypertrophy, and Bart could explore less fatiguing options for Connor. Historically, methods of developing muscle mass have borrowed heavily from body building regimes, a sport which clearly seeks different outcomes from those of collision sports. Hypertrophy training regimes normally emphasise high-resistance training volumes, exercising to fatigue and generating prolonged metabolic stress (Howe et al., 2017). Aside from the fatiguing nature of the training, these methods may not be compatible with the strength and power objectives of an ice hockey player. For example, Dankel et al. (2017) suggest that hypertrophy is possible with more frequent and lower-volume training – a training method that may align better with Connor's strength and power expectations. Nobrega et al. (2018) demonstrated that training to a point of velocity decline rather than failure may be more optimal for hypertrophy, and Schoenfeld et al. (2015) have shown that hypertrophy is possible with both high and low loading routines. In summary, Bart could explore using different resistance training permutations with Connor to try to achieve his training goals in ways that are less fatiguing and more compatible with his other training objectives.

Periodisation rationale

As Kiely (2018) elegantly points out, SCCs have been educated – and, we would contend, socialised – to implicitly rely on and trust in periodisation and its vaguely rationalised ability to deliver highly predictable adaptations to applied training loads. Periodisation likely encourages a reckless confidence that often ignores the first principles of training and assumes that with careful planning, more and better training outcomes can be attained within a limited time frame (Kiely, 2018). Leaning heavily on Selye's (1936) general adaptation syndrome (GAS; Selye, 1936), periodisation is viewed as a systematic attempt to gain control of multiple adaptive training responses. Some have challenged these interpretations of the GAS, highlighting that Selye's original work was never conducted on humans, did not involve exercise and seemed to suggest that adaptation was not without limits (Buckner et al., 2017). Furthermore, Selye's original work inferred that adapting to one stressor may limit the ability to adapt to other stressors. The insight provided by Buckner et al.'s (2017) critique should perhaps encourage a bit more caution around training volume, yet the tendency is to continue to programme with the expectation that more training will be tolerated and will invariably lead to more improvements. In this respect, many sports or SCCs, and athletes, appear to knowingly err on the side of risk – it seems that athletes and SCCs fear not training enough far more than they fear training too much! In effect, SCCs continue to overfill athletes' training, mistakenly confident that this is all part of a scientifically based, periodised plan that will all work out.

The intentional programming of periods of substantial training volume increases, i.e. functional overreaching, is an increasingly common S&C strategy (e.g. DeWeese et al., 2015). Provided the overreaching is not too extensive, the athlete is expected to soon return to normal, in fact beyond normal with a little 'supercompensation' boost (Buckner et al., 2017). Be that as it may, there are likely to be widely varying individual differences in the ability to tolerate training volumes and the magnitude of any supercompensation benefits (e.g. Kiely, 2012). Some athletes will not bounce back from that training volume (non-functional overreaching). Non-functional overreaching not only has the potential to affect the capacity to train and perform, but it may have longer-term health sequelae (Delimaris, 2014). A competent SCC should possess more 'tools' and the cognitive competence to attempt to achieve the desired training adaptations without exposing athletes to undue risk. With respect to training volume, the risk is that SCCs become convinced that they can 'master' fatigue and failing adaptation. Given that Bart is unlikely to have that level of control, Bart might approach this situation asking how he could better organise Connor's training schedule to accommodate the athlete's needs and achieve acceptable outcomes without risking the fatigue that Connor is reportedly experiencing. Bart could also seek to reframe the context that he is working in and consider the social forces that have shaped SCCs to think that 'more is better', such as neoliberal production, work ethic and athlete over conformity, all that undoubtedly contribute to the 'do more', 'do faster' and 'outwork your opponents' mentality.

Fatigue and workload monitoring

Psychobiological models of fatigue generally acknowledge that an individual's perception of effort will interact with motivational factors to determine the exercise that the individual is willing and able to tolerate (Staiano et al., 2018). Connor has described lifestyle factors and sporting pressures that could be affecting his energy, but it is also likely that Connor is experiencing some of the physical effects of fatigue and possibly low-frequency fatigue. Low-frequency fatigue (LFF) is described as fatigue resulting from multiple cumulative stressors such as with high-intensity, moderate-to-high force and repetitive eccentric or stretch-shortening cycle (SSC) activities (Fowles, 2006). In addition, hypertrophic loading has been associated with significant peripheral fatigue (Walker et al., 2012) that impairs the ability to generate maximum force, something that Connor may be noticing on the ice.

Connor also reports that his training weights are down, but Cairns et al. (2005) argue that power measures may be better suited to detect dynamic exercise performance decrements, movements that are a large component of ice hockey.

Low-frequency fatigue can also manifest as fatigue-related effects on joint proprioception and dynamic neuromuscular control. Fatigue therefore has an influence on proprioception, and impairment of that ability increases one's susceptibility to injury as well as interferes with overall movement efficiency (Ribeiro et al., 2008). While Bart may be experimenting with functional overreaching with his ice-hockey squad, that particular strategy is causing anxiety for Connor. Even with multiple methods available for monitoring training load (Greenham et al., 2018), it remains difficult to determine when fatigue is verging on being excessive. The difficulty in identifying a threshold for excessive fatigue and the large intra- and inter-individual variability in typical measures of fatigue means that workload monitoring remains a relatively blunt instrument for the SCC.

Professional competence

In Chapter 2 we presented a professional competence framework adapted from the work of Cheetham and Chivers (1996); and attempted to map S&C professional competence in professional associations and certifications. In this chapter's pedagogical case, it is clear that Bart, the SCC, has good discipline-specific knowledge and is functionally competent to be able to deliver a quality programme to a team of athletes. The training responses and concerns of Connor have challenged Bart's cognitive competence as he contemplates his conditioning ideologies and how he might adapt training strategies and programmes to accommodate the needs and training responses of one of his athletes. To add complexity to his work, Bart faces the ethical dilemmas of acceding to coaching pressures, and in turn to pressure a reluctant athlete into gaining weight, knowing that it can negatively affect this individual's sporting future and long-term health. Consistent with the 'signature pedagogies' of the S&C field (see Chapter 2), Bart is less able to demonstrate his personal, behavioural, ethical and cultural competence when working with Connor. As a consequence of being less comfortable in those areas of competence, Bart struggled to identify ways to ensure that his practices could more readily accommodate Connor's situation, without interfering with team cohesion and development of a positive training culture. Moreover, his lack of comfort in these areas also meant that he found it difficult to advocate for his athletes and to explain his reasoning and conditioning strategies to the wider coaching staff.

For example, it appears that Bart has not fully appreciated that Connor has a nine-year training history and has successfully added 11 kg during his time in the sport. He could have enquired about Connor's training practices, his attitude and physical responses to strength and conditioning, his preferences and, most importantly, his life demands away from the sport. While reversible fatigue may be an objective and a desired outcome from an S&C programme, it can gain ascendancy and negatively affect training outcomes, performance and general health and wellbeing. As a relative novice, Bart may not be mindful that an athlete's workload consists of the combination of training-related as well as non-sport-related volume. While Bart may oversee the two hours each day that Connor is in the team gym, he has no real influence (or understanding) of the volume that Connor faces for those other 22 hours. Connor's sleep patterns and adapting to a new team environment and training regimen are important considerations for overall volume. With more information on Connor's life, training and injury history, Bart should be well placed to make better informed decisions about an optimal training plan for Connor.

Summary

In this chapter we continue the theme of naming and framing (Chapters 3 and 4). In particular, we draw attention to the need for SCCs to take every opportunity to progress their thinking from the superficial and routine, and to think more critically when exploring ways of challenging status quo positions within S&C, using research as well as personal and professional introspection. In this chapter we approach a stated S&C goal of deliberate weight gain from multiple and diverse perspectives that we believe encourage critical thinking and more rigorous consideration of the individual's health and wellbeing, their exposure to injury and the possibility of performance decrements. To do this, we argue, requires setting aside previously held beliefs that may be firmly embedded in personal ideologies and within the sporting habitus (culture), and adopting an athlete-centred approach to that individual's S&C needs. We suggest this requires a needs analysis that fully acknowledges the individual's sporting and training history as well as their personal and social circumstances (cultural competence). This process may inevitably require challenging commonly held assumptions and will also draw appropriately on an SCC's personal and behavioural competence, as well as values and ethical competence.

End of chapter tasks

1 Athletes, coaches and others are constantly trying to enhance performance – really trying to be their best and to beat their opponent. As such, there is a constant and dynamic tinkering of training practices. Yet, periodisation and the common use of statistics to inform S&C is based on predictability. Reflect on how these, and related practices, make working within sport challenging.
2 For many years, sociocultural scholars have shown how 'doing more' or 'training harder *ad nauseum*' can limit or hurt performance. What messages are commonly sent in S&C that facilitate the idea that more, or harder, is better? Reflect on how you might become aware of the messages that you and others convey in S&C settings.
3 Try to locate a current or retired athlete who attributed some of their failure or lack of progress in sport to S&C; perhaps the athlete injured him- or herself in an S&C session or gained/lost too much weight (either muscle mass or fat). Interview this athlete to understand their experience, and then consider what they say in regard to sport science and how this all may influence your coaching practice.
4 To enhance your critical thinking skills, search on the internet (e.g. YouTube, Vimeo) for videos of coaches or athletes engaged in training or talking about training. Pay close attention and note the logic of their argument. What evidence or reasons do they provide to justify their training? Do they provide any scientific support? Are you familiar with that science, or do you need to research it further? How confident are they in their conclusions, and how confident are you in their conclusions?

References

Buckner, S.L., Mouser, J.G., Dankel, S.J., et al. (2017). The general adaptation syndrome: Potential misapplications to resistance exercise, *Journal of Science and Medicine in Sport*, 20: 1015–1017.
Cairns, S.P., Knicker, A.J., Thompson, M.W., et al. (2005). Evaluation of models used to study neuromuscular fatigue, *Exercise Sport Science Review*, 33(1): 9–16.
Cheetham, G., & Chivers, G. (1996). Towards a holistic model of professional competence, *Journal of European Industrial Training*, 20(5): 20–30.

Churchill, T.W., Krishnan, S., Weisskopf, M., et al. (2018). Weight gain and health affliction among former National Football League players, *The American Journal of Medicine*, 131: 1491–1498.

Dankel, S.J., Mattocks, K.T., Jessee, M.B., et al. (2017). Frequency: The overlooked resistance training variable for inducing muscle hypertrophy? *Sports Medicine*, 47: 799–805.

Delimaris, I. (2014). Potential adverse biological effects of excessive exercise and overtraining among healthy individuals, *Acta Medica Martiniana*, 14(3): 5–12.

DeWeese, B.H., Hornsby, G., Stone, M., et al. (2015). The training process: Planning for strength – power training in track and field. Part 2: Practical and applied aspects, *Journal of Sport and Health Science*, 4: 318–324.

Fowles, J.R. (2006). Technical issues in quantifying low-frequency fatigue in athletes, *International Journal of Sports Physiology and Performance*, 2: 97–99.

Fuller, C., Taylor, A., Brooks, J., & Kemp, S. (2013). Changes in the stature, body mass and age of English professional rugby players: A 10-year review, *Journal of Sports Sciences*, 31(7): 795–802.

Gabbett, T.J., Ullah, S., & Finch, C.F. (2012). Identifying risk factors for contact injury in professional rugby league players – application of a frailty model for recurrent injury, *Journal of Science and Medicine in Sport*, 15: 496–504.

Galli, N., Reel, J.J., Petrie, T., et al. (2011). Preliminary development of the weight pressures in sport scale for male athletes, *Journal of Sport Behavior*, 34(1): 47–68.

Greenham, G., Buckley, J.D., Garrett, J., et al. (2018). Biomarkers of physiological responses to periods of intensified, non-resistance-based exercise training in well-trained male athletes: A systematic review and meta-analysis, *Sports Medicine*. Published online. https://doi.org/10.1007/s40279-018-0969-2

Horn, C., Klahr, D., Mokha, M., et al. (2018). Relationship of reactive strength and body composition in elite American football players, *ISBS Proceedings Archive*, 36(1): article 147.

Howe, L.P., Read, P., & Waldron, M. (2017). Muscle hypertrophy: A narrative review on training principles for increasing muscle mass, *Strength & Conditioning Journal*, 39(5): 72–81.

Kiely, J. (2012). Periodization paradigms in the 21st century: Evidence-led or tradition-driven? *International Journal of Sports Physiology and Performance*, 7: 242–250.

Kiely, J. (2018). Periodization theory: Confronting an inconvenient truth, *Sports Medicine*, 48: 753–764.

Kim, J., Delisle-Houde, P., Reid, R., et al. (2018). Longitudinal changes in body composition throughout successive seasonal phases among Canadian university football players, *Journal of Strength & Conditioning Research*, 32(8): 2284–2293.

Lawson, H.A. (1984). Problem-setting for physical education and sport, *Quest*, 36: 48–60.

Nobrega, S.R., Ugrinowitsch, C., Pintanel, L., et al. (2018). Effect of resistance training to muscle failure vs. volitional interruption at high- and low-intensities on muscle mass and strength, *Journal of Strength & Conditioning Research*, 32(1): 162–169.

Quinn, J.B., Anderson, P., & Finkelstein, S. (1996). Managing professional intellect: Making the most of the best, *Harvard Business Review*, Mar.–Apr.: 71–80.

Reel, J.J., & Galli, N.A. (2006). Should coaches serve as the 'weight police' for athletes? *Journal of Physical Education, Recreation & Dance*, 77(3): 6–55.

Ribeiro, F., Santos, F., Gonçalves, P., et al. (2008). Effects of volleyball match-induced fatigue on knee joint position sense, *European Journal of Sport Science*, 8(6): 397–402.

Schoenfeld, B.J., Peterson, M.D., Ogborn, D., et al. (2015). Effects of low- vs. high-load resistance training on muscle strength and hypertrophy in well-trained men, *Journal of Strength & Conditioning Research*, 29(10): 2954–2963.

Schön, D.A. (2001). The crisis of professional knowledge and the pursuit of an epistemology of practice. In J. Raven & J. Stephenson (eds.), *Competence in the Learning Society*, New York: Peter Lang, pp. 183–207.

Selye, H. (1936). A syndrome produced by diverse nocuous agents, *Nature* (London), 138(32): 33.

Staiano, A.E., Beyl, R., Hsia, D., Katzmarzyk, P., & Newton Jr., R. (2018). A 12-week randomized controlled pilot study of dance exergaming in a group: Influence on psychosocial factors in adolescent girls, *Cyberpsychology: Journal of Psychosocial Research on Cyberspace*, 12(2): article 3.

Walker, S., Davis, L., Avela, J., & Häkkinen, K. (2012). Neuromuscular fatigue during dynamic maximal strength and hypertrophic resistance loadings, *Journal of Electromyography and Kinesiology*, 22(3): 356–362.

Young, W., Talpey, S., Bartlett, R., et al. (2019). Development of muscle mass: How much is optimum for performance? *Strength and Conditioning Journal*, 41(3): 47–50.

6 'Helicopter' strength and conditioning

Questioning the role of monitoring

Introduction
Part 1: pedagogical case
Part 2: commentary
Questioning the value of monitoring

   The motives for monitoring
   What to monitor?
   How much monitoring is too much?
   Unintended consequences of monitoring

      The disciplined and docile athlete
      Implications for coaching staff

Summary
End of chapter tasks
References

Introduction

Some strength and conditioning professionals respond to the ambiguity of fitness and sport performance by seeking to control the apparently controllable. Contemporary sport performance models tacitly and explicitly promote the concept of micromanaging athletes' lives by planning, quantifying and prescribing elements such as fitness training, external recreational activities, nutrition, sleep and recovery strategies. One way micromanaging can occur in sport is via athlete monitoring. In this chapter we explain the differences between measurement and monitoring, and examine the merit and motivations to monitor athletes. The theme of appropriate problem setting is revisited in this chapter, as we explore and question the temptation for SCCs to scrutinise every aspect of an athlete's life and the effect that surveillance may have on athletes and others.

Part 1: pedagogical case

Coach Jones is entering his third year working at a large public university with a well-funded athletic budget. The strength and conditioning (S&C) facility is first-class, and the teams have access to all the latest equipment: custom dumbbells, weightlifting platforms, anti-gravity treadmills, a range of weighted pulley systems and hydraulic pressure-controlled machines. The S&C and medical staff also have access to an abundance of testing equipment and gadgets that include force plates, a metabolic cart, phlebotomy (blood draw), heart rate and GPS monitoring, body composition, brain and heart rhythms and vision training. The adjacent sports medicine room has several hot and cold tubs, an underwater treadmill and a resistance swim pool. The athlete performance team have, or can request to buy, virtually anything they desire. With such a vast inventory of equipment, Coach Jones feels an obligation to make good use of it all – after all, he had personally requested many of these things. Coach Jones is proudly able to declare that their training facility is outfitted for the 21st century. Appearances are very important in collegiate sports, and the coaches, facility, technology and equipment all contribute to making a good impression. In an unguarded moment, the coach will admit that part of his motivation to have these well-equipped facilities is to present an outstanding showcase for the university. When prospective athletes make recruiting visits, or new staff are being recruited by the Athletic Department, the S&C facilities are considered a strong selling point.

Coach Jones runs a 'tight ship' in the weight room. As the Director of S&C, he oversees all S&C for 17 different sports, involving hundreds of athletes, and he has responsibility for a staff of 11 S&C coaches. Whole teams, groups of athletes from the various teams, and individual athletes are tightly scheduled into the S&C's crowded workday; a day which operates from around 6 a.m. through until 6 p.m. Individual sessions are considered inefficient because they simply take up too much of an SCC's precious time and are therefore rarely accommodated. Groups keep 'the factory' moving along smoothly and efficiently. Scheduling is typically complicated by the athletes' classes and study hall, team meetings and video sessions, sport practices, community service responsibilities and specific athlete rehabilitation. Consequently, there's really no time for wandering or wondering. Football is the largest revenue-generating sport for the university, and Coach Jones has been the head S&C for that team for 10 years. In this role, Coach Jones directly coaches 85 scholarship athletes, and as the off-season training begins, he is anxious and eager to whip the team into shape.

This morning, a group of 25 football players are scheduled to lift weights and complete other aspects (agilities, running and testing) of their training. The athletes are expected to be ready to commence trainings promptly at 6:30 a.m., and they had better not be late or they risk facing some form of light physical punishment and a berating from the S&C and football coaches.

Individual management plans require some athletes to report to the sports medicine room earlier. Some will spend time in the cold or hot tubs, have the trainer apply balms to their aching bodies, or just chat with the SCCs. Michael arrived at 6:15 a.m. and immediately started foam rolling and putting on his right knee sleeve to hide the long scar from his ACL surgery two years ago. J.D. also arrived early and, after changing into his university-issued clothing, met with Matt, one of the assistant SCCs, to learn how he could use the latest mindfulness app on his smartphone. Matt had taken an elective course in sport psychology during his Master's studies in kinesiology and had informally talked with the players about mindfulness as a possible way to reduce player stress. Coach Jones thinks it's a little goofy, but J.D. has bought into the idea and the app is easy to use.

As the rest of the players drift in to be ready to go by 6:30 a.m., they take their regular urine tests to check hydration levels and for any weight loss. Players are also connected to the newly installed and expensive high-tech training device that records resting heart rates, heart rhythms and some propriety and confidential measures of brain functioning. While the SCCs haven't taken any formal courses in neuropsychology or neurobiology, the manufacturer's guarantee that the device can provide an objective report on athletic functioning, performance and injury risk are accepted as fact. Before 6:30 a.m. the players use tablets to complete a mandatory self-report questionnaire on their health status – a kind of readiness to train report. The tablets send data to a cloud-based server, accessible to all of the medical and athlete performance staff.

Promptly at 6:30 a.m., players head over to testing stations to record their vertical jump. Coach Jones watches carefully as his assistant coaches record the data. They murmur amongst themselves about the numbers. A couple of athletes look on curiously, but are ignored by the SCCs except when ordered to, 'Go and get lined up so we can get started. Hustle up!' Coach Jones reminds the group of 12 wide receivers and defensive backs that they'll need to come in before 6:30 a.m. on Friday to get their body composition testing completed before training. 'It's been six weeks and time to retest. Remember – fat don't fly!' he chuckles. 'There's a signup sheet outside the testing door. Y'all remember to sign up before you leave today. Only one guy every 10 minutes. Be here on time!' The players' faces say it all. They grimace and curse under their breath; just enough to express their displeasure at an even earlier wake-up call on a Friday of all days. But they're careful not to express their displeasure too loudly and risk facing the wrath of Coach Jones.

Coach Jones glances at his carefully and minutely detailed training session plan. The next 90 minutes have been planned based on the vast research on the science of S&C and is scripted into segments or blocks of training: dynamic warm-ups with light foam rolling or massage stick, plyometrics and agilities, short sprints for acceleration, resistance training and then recovery methods including partner stretching, more foam rolling and hot tub or cold tub. Every exercise, repetition, set, load, velocity, rest period, technique is explicitly informed by exercise and sport sciences – primarily exercise physiology and biomechanics and their corresponding tools to poke and prod the athletes for data. The coach's training prescriptions are carefully titrated, based on the mass of collected data, and are delivered to the electronic tablets provided at every lifting station. Velocity based training (VBT) devices are attached to each barbell and record every repetition and estimate power outputs. The athletes work through the exercises in groups of three; just enough to hold each other accountable whilst providing an appropriate rest period to keep the session moving. Athletes are also grouped by height and current performance, which makes changing weights and adjusting the equipment quicker. A massive clock on the wall keeps track of the time, with the coaches' booming voices and whistles keeping the bodies on task. Each repetition is measured by the VBT devices and the athletes' data are constantly being updated and projected on the large-screen video panels placed around the gym. When the screens were first installed, the players hovered over them hooting and hollering and cheering each other's efforts along. Now that that novelty has worn off, they barely take notice of their own data, let alone that of their teammates. The data analysis is left to Matt, the resident 'boffin' (i.e. a quirky science-y type coach) on the S&C staff. His job is to maintain the growing database and provide some analysis and updates for the various coaches. He feels like he's fighting a losing battle as the number of measured variables expands each season, and the sheer volume of data captured seems to grow exponentially. He's aware that most of the athletes and coaches don't bother logging in to their server, so with the limited time he has, he aims to provide a weekly summary of the variables that the S&C group have previously agreed are their key conditioning indicators.

The various devices let the coaches know when an athlete isn't working hard enough, and the GPS devices, put on before the warm-up, measure total distance covered in the session, changes in heart rate, and duration and distance of each acceleration. As the training session comes to an end, Coach Jones reminds the football players to complete their recovery routines, and then get to class or study hall, or to their assigned film sessions. He reminds the players of the importance of getting eight hours of sleep each night, and singles out Damien who had reported earlier that his sleep device had fallen off again; 'You're like the only one who's had a problem Damien – no one else's device ever falls off – well, what the hell were you doing at night for it to come off?' He also announces that the head football coach has added a motivational speaker to tonight's agenda. 'Make sure you get your nutrition shake on the way out and turn in those GPS and heart rate monitors – so help me if we've got to chase you down through the day to get those back! Good session fellas! Get yourselves ready for the same hardworking approach tomorrow.' Satisfied with the session, Coach Jones prepares for his next group, wondering whether the numbers will have picked up on anything that his coaching staff might have missed during the session.

Part 2: commentary

> [N]ot everything that can be counted counts, and not everything that counts can be counted.
> (Cameron, in Ekbia et al., 2015, p. 1531)

Questioning the value of monitoring

This pedagogical case reminds us of the need to continually interrogate our practices as it illuminates the motivations and perceptions of various interest groups; namely the perceptions of the coach and his coaching staff who initiate and control the monitoring, the perceptions of the athletes, and the interpretations of the many external observers of these practices. But the interest groups are not restricted to those assembled in the gym at 6:30 a.m. Others with vested interests include the sport coaches, the organisation (in this case, the university), the various donors, alumni and fans, and wider society who are drawn to the intrigue of competitive sport and constantly peer in on the reported practices and behaviours of sport coaches and athletes.

There is little doubt that technological advances have contributed significantly to the evolution of elite athletic performances. For example, the greater miniaturisation and improved sampling rates of devices like GPS trackers and heart rate monitors mean that these can be worn during all activities, and have enabled a better understanding of the physical and physiological sporting demands. This knowledge has in turn informed the tailoring of training to better match those sports activity profiles (Aughey, 2011). For SCCs, a goal of optimising training has often been frustrated by the apparent disconnect between the training loads prescribed and the training loads perceived by the athlete, with the athlete's fluctuating affective states suggested to strongly influence the physical training actually completed (Bailon et al., 2018; Fox et al., 2018). Monitoring technologies have helped bridge that gap by providing more objective measures of internal and external influencing factors (Bailon et al., 2018; Lambert & Borresen, 2010). This insight has brought SCCs closer to the concept of the 'auto regulated' athlete where ongoing decisions on optimally individualised training can be constantly informed by numerous monitored factors and variables (Nevin, 2019). While we might have access to the technology to monitor various variables, the pedagogical case should also raise questions about the accuracy, meaning and desirability of this expanding surveillance.

The motives for monitoring

From the pedagogical case we get a sense that Coach Jones and his staff have embraced the various gadgets and methods, possibly naively, with a high level of trust, and perhaps with only a vague idea of how the measures will actually contribute to athlete performances and the success of their programme. This situation is all too common in S&C programmes with many SCCs tacitly assuming that a better organised training programme will be more successful and outperform those that are not (Sands et al., 2017). This is similar to the view held in the wider sports coaching community which is that effective coaching involves having one's fingers on the pulse and leaving nothing to chance (Jones & Denison, 2018).

Seeking an edge over opponents has led SCCs to try to squeeze more training out of athletes by methodically increasing their training loads within compressed training periods. One consequence of those increased loading perturbations is that the training/regeneration balance can become increasingly fragile. Training stress has been recognised to originate from multiple sources (Campbell et al., 2017), and this insight has prompted many contemporary SCCs to have an increased interest in recovery, a curiosity that extends well beyond planned rest or down time. Monitoring of fatigue may now include things such as markers of injury risk, sleep quantity and quality, nutrition and hydration practices and a multitude of other lifestyle and 'wellness' factors (Sands et al., 2017); basically anything measurable, and modifiable, which is suspected to affect performance, may be tagged for tracking.

These escalating concerns mean that SCCs may no longer be content to control the one to two hours per day when athletes are undergoing physical loading under their supervision, but may also seek to know more about the other 22-odd hours of the day when athletes are not under their 'watchful eye'. The perceived need to measure recovery, and the lifestyle factors thought to contribute to fatigue and recovery, have prompted the proliferation and use of technical gadgets, as well as monitoring and tracking systems that ambitiously seek to quantify the unquantifiable.

What to monitor?

When SCCs can monitor so many things, a key question becomes, 'What is important?' The dilemma is captured beautifully in this unattributed quote:

> If you don't know what's important, then everything is important. When everything is important, then you have to do everything. When you have to do everything, you don't have time to think about what's really important.
>
> (Source unknown)

This quote, along with the quote at the beginning of this commentary, highlights the importance of knowing what to measure and monitor, and its dangers. Currently, there appears to be a tendency to measure and monitor all that we can, often without contemplating their relevance and relative importance. While it is recognised that the complexities of team sports make defining or evaluating an individual athlete's performance especially difficult (Robertson et al., 2017), proxy measures of performance (physiological markers), along with measures of other factors thought to impair performance (e.g. sleep, perceived stress), continue to be used to monitor an athlete's readiness to train and compete. Yet, despite performance being considered the gold-standard marker of physical readiness and overall wellbeing, questions are beginning to be asked as to the desirability and practicability of regularly evaluating an individual's maximal performances (Saw et al., 2016).

Many fatigue-inducing factors are relatively easy to measure within some exercise modes (e.g. loads in weight training or cycle ergometry), but these factors are less easy to quantify for game-specific training drills (e.g. blocking from the snap or making a series of tackles;

Campbell et al., 2017). Mills and Gearity (2018) call our attention to the conundrum provoked by the enormous complexity and elusiveness of precise and meaningful methods of measuring these things. They suggest that this results in relatively limited authentic scientific relevance for most applied S&C settings (Mills & Gearity, 2018).

The uncertainty over the authenticity of the measurement tools and gadgets provides a leverage point for questioning the many commercialised training devices and systems. Various commercial entities have recognised this increasing desire for answers and have sought to provide solutions, but this is a point where the alignment between neo-scientific promises of answers and scientific rigour and value begin to blur (Halson et al., 2016; Howard-Jones, 2014; Williams & Manley, 2016). The desire to be innovative can often lead SCCs to be early adopters of new methods and technologies (Buttfield & Polglaze, 2016) without due consideration of the veracity and value of the claims being made about the rigour or trustworthiness of the methods and technologies. Torres-Ronda and Schelling (2017) warn that many technologies often lack validity, a deficiency which may not be disclosed by companies, or may be disguised behind proprietary processing methods. For example, using heart rate variability (HRV) as a proxy measure of autonomic nervous system status, and thus fatigue, is commonly promoted. However, HRV is susceptible to random day-to-day variations (Pinna, 2007), and this method would need to be assessed in relation to the smallest detectable and meaningful change (Buchheit, 2014). Ultimately, as an end user, a competent S&C professional should be responsible for determining the magnitude of measurement error and seeking clarity around data veracity before placing too much trust in the numbers that are generated. It is particularly important for SCCs to do this if the numbers are going to be used as a basis for decision making. After all, the athletes, and not the technologies, should always be the focus (Torres-Ronda & Schelling, 2017).

How much monitoring is too much?

Data has practical value only if it is knowledgeably processed and interpreted. As discussed previously (see Chapter 3), framing the question is an important part of any process, and this is equally relevant when contemplating how much to measure. In our pedagogical case, we can see that Coach Jones and his S&C team appear to be unwittingly caught up in a data and technology quandary, and they are at risk of being trapped by the large variety and volume of data being captured. While the value of monitoring multiple variables is acknowledged, the various measurement and data collecting practices can be challenging and problematic. In the pedagogical case the S&C team are clearly enamoured with, value and want to use the gadgets and the data generated. But, they also appear to feel compelled to use particular tools, perhaps without really understanding how the information might be used to improve their practice.

The various streams of information that are collected on Coach Jones's programme in a sense become 'big data' for them. According to Ekbia et al. (2015), big data is that which demands additional analysis and that will necessitate more than a customary quick and simple evaluation. As illustrated in the pedagogical case, the volume and variety of data collected in this programme will need more than a cursory perusal if it is to yield meaningful information. On one hand, the coaches can readily access, respond to and appreciate the vertical jump data for its immediacy. On the other hand, much of the other data collected requires processing and analysis to provide any practical meaning.

Many measuring and subsequent monitoring methods will require expert staffing as well as an understanding of the individual and training context (Buchheit, 2014; Burgess, 2017;

Kerr, 2016). Dresp-Langley et al. (2019) suggest that only 10% of the data generated globally is likely to be stored or utilised. They explain the high amount of 'data wastage' as a consequence of end users of data being under pressure to cope with what these authors term as the '5-Vs' problem of data, namely the challenge of dealing with the amount of information generated (volume), the range of different measures that are captured (variety), the speed (velocity) at which it is generated, the trustworthiness of the data (veracity) and the ultimate usefulness (value) of the information gathered (Dresp-Langley et al., 2019).

In the pedagogical case, the S&C programme had a lot of data coming quickly, from a variety of sources, and tracking a large number of athletes. Yet it is unclear whether the S&C group had carefully considered the validity of the gathered data or how they would use it. The head sports coach and the S&C team do not appear to have asked themselves, 'Why are we measuring X or Y?' Once it is clear as to why, and 'what' to measure, the next question concerns how much to measure. The value of any data depends on the group's capacity to process that data and make professional sense of it. Rowley (2007) proposes a 'wisdom' hierarchy for data processing, where information is inferred from the raw data, which in turn has to be translated into knowledge or 'know how'. That knowledge then provides additional understanding that contributes to intelligent and wise decision making. An assumption within Coach Jones's programme is his overarching objective to use the information to help make better decisions that will result in more effective (wisdom) and more efficient (intelligence) S&C practices. A broad understanding of S&C is needed to understand data, and it would seem that that level of understanding also needs to be available at each stage of the data-to-wisdom process.

Spearheaded by business, sport scientists and S&C practitioners, most athlete monitoring systems have focused on methods for detecting the advent point at which training load crosses the adaptation/maladaptation threshold and begins to interfere with performance or wellbeing. Also, SCCs and medical staff have a vested interest in any apparent relationships between training overload and injury occurrence. Greenham et al.'s (2018) review of methods of monitoring training load responses have emphasised the need for a biomarker that can reliably detect the threshold for actual performance or health decrements. They observed that to date, no monitoring system has achieved that objective. Indeed, despite advances in objective measures of some things, subjective measures of fatigue still appear to be more responsive and useful than most objective measures (Saw et al., 2016).

Dresp-Langley et al. (2019) use the philosophical premise of Occam's razor to argue that the objective of monitoring should be to obtain the simplest possible explanation using the least number of measures possible. Occam's razor advocates parsimony, or the aim of seeking the most economical and effective interpretation of a phenomenon possible. To reduce the risk of bias and 'data fishing', Passfield and Hopker (2017) recommend having a priori hypotheses of relationships among variables before collecting data. Having a priori hypotheses can help guard against seemingly significant associations being interpreted, and detouring a programme down an ill-advised and perhaps spurious pathway. If Coach Jones and his staff were to conduct a stocktaking exercise, it could help to clarify areas of information strength and gaps and contribute to strategising a measurement and monitoring programme. That said, Coach Jones and his coaching staff would still have to invest time into evaluating and selecting from the various methods and systems available. They would also need to perform a pilot analysis of individual data to develop a system for identifying the smallest meaningful change in a monitored variable. That threshold will likely vary widely across individuals and therefore will require the capture of multiple data points over time in order to detect meaning individual data trends (Wiewelhove et al., 2015).

From this discussion it should be apparent that 'off-the-shelf' measurement products may not be the panacea for monitoring that they promise to be and will likely require significant investment of professional knowledge to add value. While monitoring systems will generate more information, a question to address is how much more useful information on individual athletes do they produce than would normally be available by working closely and conversing with, and listening to, athletes. More information may not equate to more useful information.

Unintended consequences of monitoring

The disciplined and docile athlete

Making use of various technologies may give the appearance of cutting-edge coaching, but Jones and Denison (2018) caution that excessive monitoring could also be interpreted as the anathema of the athlete-centred coaching that many aspire to achieve. Through a sociological lens, Jones and Denison (2018) posit that surveillance and monitoring may not always be a positive experience for an athlete (or a coach) and can be construed as attempting to exert undue control over athletes' lives. In an era where athlete autonomy and resiliency is both topical and advocated in sport coaching and the athlete development (Gonzalez et al., 2016), a high level of surveillance of athletes is counterintuitive. One perception is that constant surveillance and monitoring of athletes may relegate them to docile and dependent beings who are unable to think for and care for themselves in their sporting contexts. The risk is that athletes in these situations will in fact learn helplessness and begin to doubt their abilities to manage their own destinies within sport, becoming overly dependent on organisations and coaching staff. By way of example, Gearity, drawing on his experience as an SCC, discussed how his gym-based training session contributed to, amongst other things, the production of docile athletic bodies, underperformance and poor exercise technique (Gearity & Mills, 2012)

Kerr (2016) argues that athletes may react negatively to increased surveillance such as GPS tracking. Having their heart rates and movements constantly monitored could be construed as a coaching staff not trusting them to do the work or exert sufficient effort. In a similar vein, Williams and Manley (2016) suggested that surveillance in enclosed spaces, where 'no excuses' are tolerated, can start to erode the relationships within sport 'whereby the human aspect becomes increasingly redundant' (p. 848). This quote suggests that surveillance can reduce athletes to machines with measurable outputs. This approach risks not only affecting athletes' enjoyment of the sport, but the constant surveillance can also influence the health and wellbeing of the athletes. Yet, it is not only the explicit surveillance of athletes via GPS, and the like, that can have an impact on athlete wellbeing. Over a decade ago Denison (2007) ruminated on the possible unintended consequences that his coaching practices had on athletes. While his reflections were of his practices as a track and field (athletics) coach, we believe the questions he asked himself, and the process it illustrates, are also pertinent to SCCs. Denison raised questions around how the spaces in which athletes trained could function as a 'means of surveillance' and how they could become 'sites for the production of docile bodies; [by the athletes becoming] . . . well-disciplined, economically efficient and obedient' (p. 375). While this may sound ideal for many coaches, when training spaces are highly constrained by coaches, the spaces may provide few opportunities for athlete autonomy or joy, or the development of their decision-making skills. The constraining nature of spaces is linked to the way in which coaches use time. When Denison reflected on how his timetabled training sessions could contribute to the athlete feeling surveyed, he asked himself the following questions:

> by controlling the temporal nature of Brian's [athlete] running, was I also influencing how running was felt and experienced by him? Did my precision as a coach, that prevented any idle or useless movements, in effect remove Brian from the process or act of 'being a runner'?
>
> (p. 376)

Denison also questioned the process he used when talking with the athlete about race tactics. He wondered, if by talking about tactics as if they were rules, was he removing the opportunity for the athlete to design their own tactics and be free, to some extent, of the surveillance of the coach?

Implications for coaching staff

Coaches engaging in continuous athlete monitoring can also be vulnerable in various ways. At an elemental level, many of the features of athlete surveillance are contrary to the commonly espoused coaching values of many governing organisations. Bombarded with information from multiple data sources, coaches may be unwittingly drawn into overly technocratic coaching styles, which results in their becoming primarily purveyors of objective 'bits' of information. For example, with open access to athlete data, coaches could fall into viewing athlete bodies as machines, reacting to physical outputs but overlooking the psychosocial characteristics of individual athletes (Jones & Toner, 2016). Further, utilising 'big data' can effectively homogenise athletes and normalise workloads and efforts (Jones & Toner, 2016). Engaging with, and privileging this type of data may result in the coaching styles of coaches, which include SCCs, becoming more autocratic and controlling than they might otherwise aspire and/or desire to be.

Technological monitoring and testing also introduces additional 'noise' to an S&C programme. The gadgets and systems can be distracting for players and will generally require a higher level of engagement and learning for coaching staff. Large programmes may require the introduction of new staff, and their accompanying costs (e.g. financial, interpersonal, organisational), many of whom will work in emerging professional roles that will need to be carefully integrated into the athlete care interdisciplinary team. In our pedagogical case, these factors could all present as significant challenges for Coach Jones, who is already coordinating a large staff, catering to a wide range of athletes, with an already constrained timetable.

While the S&C staff in this pedagogical case may be doing all of the monitoring, the generated data also provides opportunities for the S&C programme and staff to be surveyed. While the data is primarily for internal programme accountability, there is no reason why it could not also be used by organisations as a form of external accountability of an S&C campaign. So an intriguing consideration here is that while S&C staff might be measuring the athletes, they may, at the same time, be unwittingly collecting data on their own performances. For example, a post-season review of team GPS-based workload data may not consider the real-time nuances that influence training loads and responses. This 'being monitored' realisation may be the catalyst for some SCCs to see the benefits of supplementing the generated data with contextual information and explanations to offer valid accounts of the status of the athletes (and potentially that of their programme). Coaching and training could be realised with less monitoring, less control; a stronger focus on training by 'feel' or other emotions; providing greater athlete autonomy/freedom; and promoting more creative and exploratory training environments. We have pointed out several caveats regarding monitoring, particularly that the data collected may provide an imperfect description of the physical conditioning and readiness to perform of the athletes. Monitoring can be a relatively blunt instrument that produces docile athletes. Rather than just monitoring variables because they can, coaches need to acknowledge the sociocultural considerations of power. How knowledge from monitoring data is constructed and used, and why; the values that are on display and how these values might be open to multiple interpretations; and the critical thinking and professional judgement of coaches, all need to consider the athletes in more holistic ways. Adding contextual information provides a broader understanding of what is actually happening to athletes and staff. So, when engaging in athlete monitoring, we argue that there is some value in SCCs adopting a critical sensibility and asking questions about the implications and possible misappropriation of surveillance technologies.

Summary

This chapter addresses two primary themes around monitoring; the challenges presented by the technology and pragmatics of athlete monitoring, and the psychosocial aspects of surveillance in S&C settings. The motivation for, and value of, accumulating objective and subjective training data on athletes is discussed from the perspective of how this contributes to the goal of 'auto-regulation' athlete S&C. We point out that the range, availability and ease of use of technologies now means that large amounts of data are being gathered on athletes, often without a reasoned context. We question the facility and ability of S&C programmes to effectively process that data and generate meaningful information expediently to contribute to S&C wisdom and efficiencies of practice. The need for clarity of monitoring purpose and process is discussed and reinforced as an a priori priority. This chapter also introduces the potential for psychological and sociological concerns associated with the constancy of athlete surveillance, with some discussion of the risk that monitoring can contribute to docile and unthinking athletes. We also consider whether the monitors can become the monitored, with the possibility that acquired data could be used to judge an SCC's practices. Overall, this chapter highlights the need for critical professional thinking when adopting or embracing the concept of athlete monitoring.

End of chapter tasks

1 Reflect and/or discuss with peers your own use of technology and monitoring devices as an athlete or coach. What were the goals of said technology? Did you achieve those goals, and how did that technology help or hinder goal attainment?
2 Out of the 168 hours in a week, athletes spend approximately 2% to 5% of the total weeks' time with coaches. How could SCCs organise the very limited time they do have with athletes in a way that would enable the athletes to continue developing when they're 'on their own'?
3 Sociologists of sports coaching argue that too much discipline or 'disciplinary practices' during athletes' training, through the control of time, space, flow, tempo, surveillance, judging, monitoring, etc., can result in negative effects. Describe how bioscience and technological knowledge have supported these practices and consider what psychosocial and pedagogical informed practices could disrupt these disciplinary practices. What fears, or barriers, exist that prohibit more creative and experimental practices in S&C?

4   Some SCCs have jumped on the positive psychology and mindfulness bandwagon. Read one or more of the articles in the following list and then consider how positive psychology or mindfulness may lead us to focus on inward, psychological problems and fixes rather than social issues such as neoliberalism and addressing social determinants of health and performance. Can you think of other examples where we 'treat the symptom, not the disease' in S&C?

- Binkley, S. (2011). Happiness, positive psychology and the program of neoliberal governmentality. *Subjectivity*, 4: 371–394. doi:10.1057/sub.2011.16
- www.theguardian.com/lifeandstyle/2019/apr/16/how-capitalism-captured-the-mindfulness-industry
- www.theguardian.com/lifeandstyle/2019/jun/14/the-mindfulness-conspiracy-capitalist-spirituality

References

Aughey, R.J. (2011). Applications of GPS technologies to field sports, *International Journal of Sports Physiology and Performance*, 6: 295–310.

Bailon, C., Damas, M., Pomares, H., et al. (2018). Intelligent monitoring of affective factors underlying sport performance by means of wearable and mobile technology, *Proceedings*, 2(19): 1202. DOI:10.3390/proceedings2191202.

Buchheit, M. (2014). Monitoring training status with HR measures: Do all roads lead to Rome? *Frontiers in Physiology*, 5(73): 1–17.

Burgess, D.J. (2017). The research doesn't always apply: Practical solutions to evidence-based training-load monitoring in elite team sports, *International Journal of Sports Physiology and Performance*, 12: S2-136–S2-141.

Buttfield, A., & Polglaze, T. (2016). People, not technology, should drive innovation in elite sport, *Sensoria: A Journal of Mind, Brain & Culture*, 12(2): 10–12.

Campbell, B.I., Bove, D., Ward, P., et al. (2017). Quantification of training load and training response for improving athletic performance, *Strength & Conditioning Journal*, 39(5): 3–13.

Denison, J. (2007). Social theory for coaches: A Foucauldian reading of one athlete's poor performance, *International Journal of Sports Science & Coaching*, 2: 369–383.

Dresp-Langley, B., Ekseth, O.K., & Fesl, J. (2019). Occam's razor for big data? On detecting quality in large unstructured datasets, *Applied Sciences*, 9: 3065.

Ekbia, H., Mattioli, M., Kouper, I., et al. (2015). Big data, bigger dilemmas: A critical review, *Journal of the Association for Information Science and Technology*, 66: 1523–1545.

Fox, J.L., Stanton, R., Sargent, C., et al. (2018). The association between training load and performance in team sports: A systematic review, *Sports Medicine*, 48: 2743–2774.

Gearity, B., & Mills, J.P. (2012). Discipline and punish in the weight room, *Sports Coaching Review*, 1: 124–134.

Gonzalez, S.P., Detling, N., & Galli, N.A. (2016). Case studies of developing resilience in elite sport: Applying theory to guide interventions, *Journal of Sport Psychology in Action*, 7(3): 158–169.

Greenham, G., Buckley, J.D., Garrett, J., et al. (2018). Biomarkers of physiological responses to periods of intensified, non-resistance-based exercise training in well-trained male athletes: A systematic review and meta-analysis, *Sports Medicine*. Published online. https://doi.org/10.1007/s40279-018-0969-2.

Halson, S.L., Peake, J.M., & Sullivan, J.P. (2016). Wearable technology for athletes: Information overload and pseudoscience? *International Journal of Sports Physiology and Performance*, 11(6): 705–706.

Howard-Jones, P.A. (2014). Neuroscience and education: Myths and messages, *Nature Reviews Neuroscience*, 15(12): 817–824.

Jones, L., & Denison, J. (2018). A socio-cultural perspective surrounding the application of GPS technology: Some suggestions for the strength and conditioning coach, *Strength and Conditioning Journal*, 40(6): 3–8.

Jones, L., & Toner, J. (2016). Surveillance technologies as instruments of discipline in the elite sports coaching context: A cautionary post-structural commentary, *Sensoria: A Journal of Mind, Brain & Culture*, 12(2): 13–21.

Kerr, R. (2016). *Sport and Technology: An Actor-Network Theory Perspective*, Manchester: Manchester University Press.

Lambert, M.I., & Borresen, J. (2010). Measuring training load in sports, *International Journal of Sports Physiology and Performance*, 5: 406–411.

Mills, J.P., & Gearity, B.T. (2018). Guest editorial: Special topic issue, sport sociology, *Strength and Conditioning Journal*, 40(6): 1–2.

Nevin, J. (2019). Auto-regulated resistance training: Does velocity-based training represent the future? *Strength and Conditioning Journal*, 41(4): 34–39.

Passfield, L., & Hopker, J.G. (2017). A mine of information: Can sports analytics provide wisdom from your data? *International Journal of Sports Physiology and Performance*, 12(7): 851–855.

Pinna, G.D., Maestri, R., Torunski, R., et al. (2007). Heart rate variability measures: A fresh look at reliability, *Clinical Science*, 113(3): 131–140.

Robertson, S., Bartlett, J.D., & Gastin, P.B. (2017). Red, amber, or green? Athlete monitoring in team sport: The need for decision-support systems, *International Journal of Sports Physiology and Performance*, 12: S2-73–S2-79.

Rowley, J. (2007). The wisdom hierarchy: Representations of the DIKW hierarchy, *Journal of Information Science*, 33: 163–180.

Sands, W.A., Kavanaugh, A.A., Murray, S.R., et al. (2017). Modern techniques and technologies applied to training and performance monitoring, *International Journal of Sports Physiology and Performance*, 12: S2-63–S2-72.

Saw, A.E., Main, L.C., & Gastin, P.B. (2016). Monitoring the athlete training response: Subjective self-reported measures trump commonly used objective measures: A systematic review, *British Journal of Sports Medicine*, 50: 281–291.

Torres-Ronda, L., & Schelling, X. (2017). Critical process for the implementation of technology in sport organizations, *Strength and Conditioning Journal*, 39(6): 54–59.

Wiewelhove, T., Raeder, C., Meyer, T., et al. (2015). Markers for routine assessment of fatigue and recovery in male and female team sport athletes during high-intensity interval training, *PLoS One*, 10(10): e0139801.

Williams, S., & Manley, A. (2016). Elite coaching and the technocratic engineer: Thanking the boys at Microsoft, *Sport, Education and Society*, 21(6): 828–850.

Part 3
Developing as a strength and conditioning professional

7 Developing as a competent strength and conditioning professional

Introduction
Part 1: pedagogical case
Part 2: commentary
How does socialisation influence the development of a competent S&C professional?
Broadening the scope of what constitutes competence in strength and conditioning
Summary
End of chapter tasks
References

Introduction

This chapter begins by asking, 'What do SCCs know and do?' We examine the everyday sociological life of an SCC, their common practices and interactions, and consider typical duties, tasks and expectations. In the chapter we discuss the importance and typical pathways of professional socialisation, a process that reinforces the need to integrate diverse forms of knowledge and to understand the influence of social forces, when making professional decisions. Following on from this theme, we discuss the need to broaden the scope of what we consider as professional competence. We argue that a better understanding of pedagogically informed reflective practice will in turn contribute to professional development and encourage SCCs to strive for professional excellence.

Part 1: pedagogical case

Over the past 30 years, the numbers of S&C coaching staff in Major League Baseball (MLB) have been steadily growing. Whereas teams used to have just one SCC for their major league team and one for all of their minor league squads, it's now commonplace for teams to have a full-time SCC at each minor league affiliate team, often one to three minor league coordinators and Latin American coordinators, and one to two SCCs for the major league team. As staff numbers increase, so does the importance of coach education, development, and human resource management. One MLB team, the Denver Pios (fictitious), has a staff of eleven coaches – let's take a peek at the profiles and experiences of some of these coaches, and the implications they might have for coaching competence and development.

The newest SCC for the Pios is Lorelei, a 21-year-old female who is completing an approved internship with the team. She is a senior in the final year of her undergraduate degree in exercise science at a nearby university. Lorelei is excited for the opportunity to intern with the team; she is the team's first-ever female SCC. Lorelei has completed two years of coursework in liberal education, but she took electives in biology to help with understanding the body's systems and structures. In her exercise science coursework, she has completed rigorous scientific courses on exercise physiology, biomechanics, nutrition, chronic disease and ageing, S&C essentials and programme design, research methods and statistics. Lorelei learned the fundamentals of using force plates, blood draws and exercise technique through the laboratory courses that she completed. Her four years as a starter on her school's volleyball team provided her with extensive resistance training experience as a participant, nicely complementing her theory courses.

Lorelei is eager to make a good impression and show the male coaches that she too can coach. She secretly worries that she will not be respected and wonders if the professional baseball players will listen to her and do as she tells them. After the first week of being with the team, she was surprised by the explicit language being used around the clubhouse and baseball field – cussing and yelling – these were not styles of communication that she had experienced in her degree programme or with her volleyball team! Lorelei was also surprised at the lack of mentoring type conversations she was receiving from the more experienced SCCs. When she asked one coach why they weren't doing any Olympic lifts, as she had learned that they're the best lifts for improving power, he had brusquely replied, 'Not now. Talk later. Go coach.' Having received such a curt response, she is now not sure who to approach with her questions regarding why the prescribed exercise intensity is around 60% for 8–10 reps, which she has been led to believe is a bit too easy for strength and power development. Her volleyball squad would never have lifted so light!

In the absence of quality conversations, and in the presence of prevalent, albeit questionable, communication styles, Lorelei decides that she will also be tough and demand respect, but she won't resort to the cussing and yelling she often hears. One of the positive things that occurred on the communication front was that Lorelei was assigned to work through the training sessions with four of the rookies from the Dominican Republic. Fortunately, Lorelei had taken a couple of years of Spanish in high school and remembered some of those words, as well as learning new ones by conversing with players during workouts. She has gained some satisfaction from the challenge of coaching in Spanish which she believes has tested and improved her instruction and communication abilities.

John is another SCC for the Pios and completed his internship with the team two years ago. He's now entering his third full season with the team and has just picked up a health and benefits package, which is a huge win for him. He no longer has to worry about health insurance, but he still barely gets by with his routine expenses like housing, food and student loan repayments. For the first two years he was a seasonal employee, which meant he coached during spring training and worked with the lowest-level rookie team for about eight months out of the year. In the off-season John would work at a local performance centre training athletes and a range of other clients. John's degree was in kinesiology and he started off as an athletic training major before switching to S&C, so he ended up enrolling in a care and prevention of athletic injuries course. He thinks most SCCs don't really understand mechanisms of injury and how to prevent them. John and Asher (the minor league coordinator) disagree on the efficacy of overhead lifting for baseball players and how best to design programmes for rotator cuff strengthening. Instead of stepping on Asher's toes, John has taken up an interest in speed and agility training. This past off-season he took a one-day course on sprinting and enrolled in an online agility course that also offered continuing education, credits that he requires to maintain his certification in S&C. When John was the SCC for the rookie teams, he primarily worked with late adolescents aged 18–21. For a lot of the players, it was their first time away from home for an extended time. John thought they all lacked discipline and most of them wouldn't get promoted because of it. Too often they would stay up late playing video games, chasing women, drinking alcohol or some combination of all three. When asked by the rookie team's head baseball coach why the player's looked so tired, John did not hesitate in placing the blame squarely back on the players and their lifestyles.

Asher, a 33-year-old male, is entering his sixth year with the Pios, which is the third team he has worked with. Since taking over the minor league system, Asher has totally revamped the S&C programme. He completed his college internship with a popular personal trainer who worked with a lot of professional baseball players during the off-season. When Asher started coaching with the Pios, he was allowed to do his own programming and coaching, so he mimicked what the personal trainer did. There were some things Asher really liked that the trainer did, but he also found that coaching one-on-one or in small groups, and during the off-season, was much different from coaching with a team and during pre- and in season. As such, Asher took a much more contextual and development approach to working with the minor league athletes.

Asher would love to experiment a bit more with conditioning methods but is fearful of losing his job by trying out new ideas, regardless of their evidence and his own critical evaluation of training, technology and the latest research. He's found that the organisation doesn't encourage innovation, and he has become a bit risk-averse, keeping many of his ideas to himself. A few years ago, in an attempt to satisfy his desire to keep learning, Asher committed to learning to speak Spanish, and he has also taken an interest in sport psychology. He likes that he can study effective coaching behaviours, communicate with players better in their native language, and he's become a strong proponent for mindfulness. While he enjoys mentoring the new interns and junior coaches and sharing some of his new learning, Asher is amused by, and dismissive of, Lorelei's talks about kettlebell training and her use of them in her own workouts. He never learned much about those things when he was at the university and wonders how they came back into style. Asher worries about how things like these come and go in the field, and how social media is used to promote 'the latest methods', making all sorts of grandiose claims about what works and why. He wonders why his colleagues don't share his scepticism of what he calls 'self-promoters looking to grow their brand and sphere of influence'.

Scott has been the head SCC for the Pios for 27 years. The team has had only one head SCC prior to Scott, but he lasted only a year before the organisation fired him. According to the rumours, he was fired because 'his people skills sucked'. Scott started out as a physical education teacher and a football, baseball and golf coach. As the field of S&C rapidly grew, he took at a job at a local university coaching baseball and serving as the head SCC. Scott can rapidly correct any athlete's exercise technique, write periodised S&C programmes in his sleep and has the credibility and institutional history of a living legend in the field. Scott finds most S&C boring nowadays. He's seen kettlebells come, go and come back again. He's heard all the best coaches and the charlatans and phonies, and has seen the use of technology and data grow exponentially. But injuries continue to occur and athletes still periodically underperform, and he has come to the realisation there are no guarantees for complex athletes and systems.

At 54 years old, Scott is thinking about retiring from the field and trying other things. One of the things holding him back is his concerns about a succession plan for the SCC programme. He does not have a lot of confidence in any of his assistants being able to assume leadership of the programme. They are all good practitioners, but he worries about their professionalism and their broader understanding of S&C in the Pios environment. They all seem fixated on what to do and how to do it. He expects Lorelei, along with every intern before her, to want to ask a million questions about programme design and the latest gadget to purportedly enhance performance, but like the veteran ball players, he knows only too well that if something were really that effective, they'd have already done it by now.

As a veteran SCC, Scott knows all too well the importance of energy systems and muscle activation. For years he's been preaching about other aspects such as relationships, addressing athletes one-on-one, not jumping to conclusions about what works, when, how and why, and the importance of valuing athletes as people. He wonders whether he could have been a better mentor to his staff and encouraged them to think more about the people and better decision making.

Part 2: commentary

This chapter is underpinned by an understanding that becoming a competent SCC professional is a process enmeshed with moral, ethical and societal concerns. Given this, what follows does not resemble a 'how to coach' list. In Chapter 3 we pointed out that one stimuli for problem setting is a desire to develop as a professional. We supported the suggestion made by Lawson (1984, 1993) that to understand the process of setting a problem, it is useful to reflect on how problems are named and framed. A significant influence on how we frame problems is our socialisation, because previous experiences will influence what we view to be, or not, a problem.

How does socialisation influence the development of a competent S&C professional?

Whereas S&C is a relatively new profession, discussions of socialisation in the contexts of education and physical education have occurred for decades (see Andrew et al., 2017; Lawson, 1983a, 1983b; Lawson & Stroot, 1993; Lortie, 1975; Zeichner & Tabachnick, 1981). Despite the origin and age of much of this literature, we believe there is some merit in members of the S&C community heeding some of the lessons from this literature, particularly if the profession wants to encourage reflection on the process of developing competent S&C professionals and understanding how SCCs learn the values, behaviours and expectations associated with the profession.

Lawson (1983a, 1983b) named three phases of socialisation: acculturation, professional socialisation and organisational socialisation. Drawing on examples from education, Lortie (1975) explained that acculturation, or 'apprentice-of-observation', has significant influences on the development of becoming a teacher because future teachers, as pupils in schools, have over the years spent thousands of hours watching what teachers do and say. As a consequence, potential teachers develop assumptions about what it is that a teacher does, which may indeed be flawed because of the limited insight into what teachers do behind the scenes. While the 'apprentice-of-observation' for a budding SCC is not as lengthy as those of future teachers, we contend that athletes will have witnessed SCCs in action and have developed some assumptions about, and understanding of, what is required to be an SCC. An individual's belief that they can meet the requirements of being, for example, an SCC has been described by Lortie (1975) as a person's 'subjective warrant'. From our pedagogical case we get a sense that Lorelei has been inspired to pursue S&C based on her collegiate sport experiences. She has a concept of what an SCC should look like, how they should behave and practice. We also have the example of Asher replicating the methods and persona of a high-profile SCC.

The second phase of socialisation is 'professional socialisation', which can also be referred to as 'pre-service training' (Lawson, 1983a, 1983b) and in the case of education occurs in teacher training programmes most often connected to tertiary training institutions. In these programmes the future teacher is introduced to current knowledge, skills and evidence-based initiatives. While S&C associations have accreditation processes that focus primarily on functional competence (see Chapter 2), increasingly more SCCs are gaining tertiary qualifications in programmes that take a research-informed and evidence-based view of S&C. While there appears to be no S&C literature that has explored the effectiveness of the 'pre-service training' of SCCs, the evidence in the education and physical education context suggests that pre-service training for future teachers has a limited effect and does little to change the belief systems they developed in their 'apprentice-of-observation' (Cassidy & Tinning, 2004). John, in our pedagogical case has a well-developed theoretical knowledge base of athletic injury and injury etiology. Without any direct experience in the realities of sport and conditioning for injury prevention, John has ideological concerns about the practices of Asher, a more experienced SCC. Although John is entering his third season with the Pios organisation, he has not had the opportunity to test his knowledge and understanding, and we get a sense that he is holding on to his evidence-based ideologies on injury prevention.

The third phase of socialisation is 'organisational socialisation', also known as induction, and is keenly felt by new teachers in the first three years of employment (Stroot & Ko, 2006). It is during this time that new teachers regularly interact with pupils, other teachers, senior managers (e.g. principals), administrators, parents and sports coaches within and outside of the school respectively. All these 'stakeholders' play a role in what the new teacher says and how they do it (Cassidy & Tinning, 2004). In the context of S&C, while the organisational socialisation literature does not currently exist, the anecdotal evidence does suggest that those new SCCs, who have been encouraged to question the status quo in their pre-service training, face an environment that does little to support them to ask 'why' questions. The 'stakeholders' in many S&C environments are content to continue to focus on the 'what' and the 'how', and new SCCs are encouraged to do so as well. This apparent reluctance of existing SCCs to nurture the new SCCs' curiosity and willingness to experiment with new ideas illustrates what Schempp et al. (1993) identified, albeit in the context of physical education teacher education programmes, that often many new teachers (or in this case, SCCs) abandon what they learnt in their pre-service teacher programmes because of the reality shock of the school environment. The cussing and yelling and training methods were at odds with Lorelei's assumptions regarding S&C. The practice of abandoning what they had previously learnt is what Zeichner and Tabachnick (1981) called the 'washout effect'. This effect can be lessened if the new professional enters an environment which is supportive and rewards curiosity.

For example, Lorelei has unresolved questions about her resistance training assumptions, so her opportunities for timely learning is limited within the current organisational structure. Within the Pios organisation there are undoubtedly sound rationales to support why they resistance train a certain way, or how best to protect players' shoulders, but these are not being readily communicated across the staff. Lorelei will coach as she is told, but there will be some inevitable 'washout' of her theoretical understandings. This can have a flow on effect in that SCCs who are not 'in the know' will fear being exposed for not knowing, will avoid a particular area in order to save face or, to avoid conflict, may seek an alternate niche within S&C. Sharing information and reasoning provides opportunities for the whole S&C staff to reflect, discuss critically and contribute to mutual professional development.

A significant challenge faced by all professions, especially those that experience a 'washout effect' (Zeichner & Tabachnick, 1981), is to be able to relate to an increasingly diverse world. An example of that diversity is reflected in the 2013 New Zealand (NZ) census, which identified NZ as being home to more than 200 ethnic groups with 160 languages spoken (New Zealand Internal Affairs, 2019). A 2011 England and Wales census found that 80% of the total population identified as White British, yet only 45% of the population living in London identified as such (Institute of Race Relations, 2019). In an education context in the United States, Flory (2017) noted that earlier research documented that in the 2012–2013 academic year 'nearly 49 percent of K-12 students in the U.S. identified as Black, Hispanic, Asian/Pacific Islander, American/Alaska Native or multi-racial' (p. 162). Yet, this diversity was not reflected in those teaching in US public schools, where 83% of the teachers identify as White Americans. Even if prospective teachers in pre-service training learn initiatives, such as culturally relevant pedagogies which aim to engage with diverse student populations (see Azzarito & Simon, 2017; Flory & McCaughtry, 2011), it is possible that the new teachers, especially those who go to work in urban (and more diverse) communities, and who are not supported, will experience a 'washout effect' and will struggle to engage with students who are culturally, ethnically and socioeconomically very different from them. A consequence of this 'cultural clash' can be disengagement and burnout (Flory, 2017).

Education programmes taken by aspiring SCCs typically assume that such professionals will be interacting with a largely homogenous and compliant client base that will respond in consistent and predictable ways to interventions. A supportive environment that encourages critical enquiry will go some way to minimising the possible 'washout effect' and potential disillusionment with the chosen professional pathway. In our pedagogical case, Scott hints of supporting this personally but perhaps not sharing that support collectively.

If we look at the make-up of the attendees of S&C conferences, review the S&C literature and map the S&C field (see Chapter 2), it does not appear that understanding diversity is prioritised. Yet, if SCCs are working in urban populations, at least in the USA, the UK and New Zealand, they will be working with diverse populations. So, if SCCs genuinely desire to engage with *all* their athletes, then the SCCs face a real challenge to become more culturally competent (see Chapter 3). Lorelei and Asher have both taken steps to be able to communicate better with the organisation's Latin American players, and those conversations will likely teach them more about these players than simply knowing Spanish words and phrases.

Broadening the scope of what constitutes competence in strength and conditioning

In Chapter 2 we highlighted the challenges that have arisen over an increasing focus on competence, one of which was focusing on professionals having the 'ability to do things' (functional competence). According to Frelin (2013) the ability to do one thing is never enough in highly dynamic professional situations where 'educational judgement' or 'professionality' is required (p. 6). In this chapter we still engage with ideas of competence in a way that we consider supports and gives recognition to those professionals who do use their 'educational judgement' or 'professionality'. We consider it important for SCCs to be not only competent but also able to display 'educational judgement' because, as Biesta (2016) pointed out, albeit in an education setting, 'a teacher who possesses all the competences . . . but who is unable to judge which competence needs to be deployed when, is a useless teacher' (p. 130).

Many proposed models of professional competence (e.g. Quinn et al., 1996) come from business applications. Yet Collins (2006) has challenged the view that the 'primary path to greatness in the social sectors [which we argue include many contexts in which SCCs work] is to become "more like a business"' (p. 1). He argued that '[w]e need to reject the naïve imposition of the "language of business" on the social sector, and instead jointly embrace a *language of greatness*' (p. 2). One way to do this to recalibrate what success looks like without using business metrics. According to Collins, a 'great' business or social sector organisation 'is one that *delivers superior performance* and *makes a distinctive impact* over *a long period of time*' (p. 5, *emphasis added*). While there will never be one perfect indicator to illustrate greatness, Collins contends it is important to settle 'upon a *consistent and intelligent* method of assessing your output results and the tracking your trajectory with rigor' (p. 8, *emphasis in original*).

Another challenge with subjecting professional disciplines to business models is the common strategy of attempting to standardise and routinise the work of the professional (Ponnert & Svensson, 2016). These authors characterise this as a shift from occupational to organisational professionalism, with a resulting fragmentation of duties and a loss of discretion and decision making (Ponnert & Svensson, 2016). We get a sense in our pedagogical case that delineation of roles and duties is restrictive for someone like Asher, who is described as unwilling to move beyond his assigned roles and duties. Fragmentation of the Pios S&C work environment may be seen as being efficient organisationally but may not be particularly conducive to personal and shared professional development.

One of the outputs that SCC organisations could track is the diversity of their workforce and client base. Once that baseline data has been determined, either locally, nationally or globally, then SCC organisations can make plans to become great and work in ways that value diversity and inclusion. Consistent with Collins's view of what makes a great business, Kirk Hope (2019), the CEO of BusinessNZ, observed that some leaders are recognising diversity and inclusion as being 'important for our social and economic future', noting that a diverse society enables a range of perspectives, ideas and skills to come to the fore but also requires leaders to increase their cultural competence.

Another way SCC organisations could encourage ideas and practices to flourish and challenge the dominance of the orthodox business models is by focusing on developing excellence. There are many ways of conceptualising and discussing excellence, two of which are via ethics and organisations. In discussions on virtue-based ethics in the sporting context, McNamee (2011) suggested there is some merit in pursuing the development of 'good people living good lives' (p. 33). He went on to say that the pursuit of *eudaimonia* (human wellbeing or flourishing) is worthwhile because we prefer people keep to the rules, not because they fear they will be punished if they get caught, but because they want a contest that is 'fair and an equal test of relevant abilities and powers' (p. 33). A perceived difficulty with such a position, especially when living in this diverse world, is there is no universal understanding of what constitutes a 'good life'. Yet McNamee (2011) contended that we can view a 'good life' as

> one that is lived in accordance with virtue against a given background. . . . . *Arete* (excellence) is that which enables persons to achieve their telos (proper end) of flourishing, yet *arete* is also an ingredient of the attainment of that goal at the same time.
>
> (p. 33)

An important point here is that what constitutes a 'good life' or 'excellence' is not universal; rather it is judged against a 'given background'. Consequently, a focus on developing excellence could be one way to engage more broadly with the ideas of competence, recognising that judging excellence and competence is influenced by the context in which it occurs and therefore the judgement requires flexibility and 'professionality'. In our pedagogical case,

John is unimpressed with the 'professional sport ethic' of the rookie players that he is working with, mainly because of the impact on training outcomes. He could reframe his approach with these young athletes and find ways to subtly educate players about how to live and behave as a flourishing and excellent collective.

When discussing excellence in the contexts of organisations, which operate in an increasingly diverse world, Burke (2011) drew on psychological literature to argue that performers, and those working with them, have to adapt to working in rapidly, and continually, restructured landscapes. To be successful in such an environment, she made a case that people in organisations can 'no longer be parochial in their thinking. They must take account of changes in the wider environment likely to impact upon their work' (p. 100). For example,

> [t]he top-down 'rational' approach to organizational structure is not adequate in this new context. . . . Management no longer represents the exclusive control of resources and information. Individuals have choices about where they focus their attention, how they behave and with whom they want to work. Increasingly, important decisions are arrived at through informal means via loosely configured networks of individuals, focused around common aims, coalitions or activities as the decision-making capability is dispersed more evenly throughout the organization.
>
> (Burke, 2011, p. 100)

Socialising less experienced SCCs into the profession and an organisation is an important part of developing an effective staff. Schwab and Starbuck (2016) use two useful analogies to describe ways to support professional development and collegiality. They suggest that '[i]t is helpful to have companions when you walk an untrodden path' (p. 169), and argue that '[s]ometimes individuals have unique insights that astound others; sometimes collaborators challenge each other or counteract missteps; sometimes teamwork is the only way to make progress' (p. 169). In our pedagogical case, Lorelei's questions and Asher's ideas, if shared across the SCC staff, could stimulate more critical thinking and discussion to the benefit of individuals and the organisation. An other analogy, used by schwab & Starbuck (2016, p. 171) is that '[m]ultiple expeditionary patrols are better than an army for opening up a large and diverse territory' which encourages staff to explore new and well-reasoned methods, and to lead the S&C programme in new directions. While such actions may be perceived as a threat to the integrity of a programme, our pedagogical case demonstrates that a static and siloed programme can provoke different and often destructive responses in individual staff.

Summary

Entering the S&C profession is not as simple as obtaining a formal qualification; one of the professional developmental challenges is being aware of the need for, and the value of, appropriate socialisation. Constructive socialisation can assist a novice professional to identify and self-audit against the key professional competences in S&C. A subsequent challenge is to securing work environments, experiences and mentoring that will provide for effective socialisation into the profession. In this chapter we have suggested that many neophyte SCCs enter into S&C having passed through the first phase of socialisation – being acculturated – having personally experienced S&C and formulated an understanding of what they believe S&C involves and requires. The second phase, professional socialisation, is commonly accessed through study, often directed by the signature pedagogies of the profession, and typically involves accumulating untested knowledge, theories and skills. The third and final phase, organisational socialisation, introduces SCCs to the realities, vagaries and nuances of professional practice. Within this chapter we encourage SCCs to embrace the broadening scope of practice, resist attempts to fragment and routinise their professional roles and constantly seek ways to flourish within a professional culture of excellence.

End of chapter tasks

1. Create some sort of visual (e.g. concept or mind map, coloured sticky notes, chronology) that charts key experiences, such as schooling, courses, experiential learning, (in) effective mentors, that show how you learned to coach. After you've created this visual, enhance your understanding by: reflecting on your trajectory, come back to it after a week or two and see what stands out or what you now realise was omitted, or ask others to comment and engage them in dialogue.
2. Use Flory and McCaughtry's (2011) three-step approach explained in the chapter to inform how you can implement a culturally relevant pedagogy within your S&C setting, or a hypothetical setting where you would like to work.
3. In the coaching science research, scholars often cite the example of former University of California, Los Angeles (UCLA) head men's basketball coach John Wooden, a 10-time NCAA Division I champion, as an exemplar on reflective practice and continuous learning. At the end of every season, Wooden would identify one aspect of coaching to improve upon and rigorously study it throughout the next year. Identify one highly essential aspect of your coaching to improve upon over the next year that will improve your coaching. You might also create a list for the next 5, 10, 15+ years where you forecast one thing to learn deeply every year. Over the years you could also revisit this list to see if it has changed and ponder why this might be the case.
4. Part of developing a profession is identifying what, and to what extent, knowledge, skills, and attitudes should be required. Alone, with a peer, or perhaps a class of students or group of coaches, identify, categorise, and rank what you think all SCCs should know and be able to do.
5. Identify one or more of the following: popular S&C textbooks, websites of leading S&C organisations, the social media accounts of S&C organisations or 'celebrity' coaches or scientists in S&C, or clinic and conference proceedings and materials. Next, review the material(s) with the aim of pointing out any patterns: What knowledges or practices are dominant? What are some things they do not talk about? Speculate as to why these knowledges and practices became popular or hidden or obscured.

References

Andrew, K., Richards, R., & Lux Gaudreault, K. (2017). *Teacher Socialization in Physical Education: New Perspectives*, London: Routledge.
Azzarito, L., & Simon, M. (2017). Interrogating Whiteness in physical education teacher education: Preparing prospective PE teachers to become educators of culturally relevant pedagogy and social justice. In K. Andrew, R. Richards, & K. Lux Gaudreault (eds.), *Teacher Socialization in Physical Education: New Perspectives*, London: Routledge, pp. 176–193.
Biesta, G. (2016). *The Beautiful Risk of Education*, London: Routledge.
Burke, V. (2011). Organizing for excellence. In D. Collins, A. Abbott, & H. Richards (eds.), *Performance Psychology: A Practitioners Guide*, Edinburgh: Elsevier, pp. 99–120.
Cassidy, T., & Tinning, R. (2004). 'Slippage' is not a dirty word: Considering the usefulness of Giddens' notion of knowledgeability in understanding the possibilities for teacher education, *Journal of Teaching Education*, 15(2): 175–188.

Collins, J. (2006). *Good to Great and the Social Sectors: Why Business Thinking in Not the Answer*, London: Random House Business.

Flory, S.B. (2017). Culturally responsive pedagogy and teacher socialization. In K. Andrew, R. Richards, & K. Lux Gaudreault (eds.), *Teacher Socialization in Physical Education: New Perspectives*, London: Routledge, pp. 162–175.

Flory, S.B., & McCaughtry, N. (2011). Culturally relevant physical education in urban schools: Reflecting cultural knowledge, *Research Quarterly for Exercise and Sport*, 82(1): 49–60.

Frelin, A. (2013). *Exploring Relational Professionalism in Schools*, Rotterdam: Sense Publishers.

Hope, K. Diversity and inclusion is important for our social and economic future. www.stuff.co.nz/%20business/budget-2015/111619561/diversity-and-inclusion-is-important-for-our-social-and-economic-future (accessed 3 Dec. 2019).

Institute of Race Relations. Ethnicity and religion statistics. www.irr.org.uk/research/statistics/ethnicity-and-religion/ (accessed 3 Dec. 2019).

Lawson, H. (1983a). Toward a model of teacher socialization in physical education: The subjective warrant, recruitment, and teacher education, *Journal of Teaching in Physical Education*, 2(3): 3–17.

Lawson, H. (1983b). Toward a model of teacher socialization in physical education: Entry into schools, teachers' role orientations, and longevity in teaching (part 2), *Journal of Teaching in Physical Education*, 3(1): 3–16.

Lawson, H. (1984). Problem-setting for physical education and sport, *Quest*, 36(1): 48–60.

Lawson, H. (1993). Dominant discourses, problem setting, and teacher education pedagogies: A critique, *Journal of Teaching in Physical Education*, 12(4): 149–160.

Lawson, H., & Stroot, S. (1993). Footprints and signposts: Perspective on socialization research, *Journal of Teaching in Physical Education*, 12(4): 437–447.

Lortie, D. (1975). *Schoolteacher: A Sociological Study*, Chicago, IL: University of Chicago Press.

McNamee, M. (2011). Celebrating trust: Virtues and rules in the ethical conduct of sports coaches. In A. Hardman & C. Jones (eds.), *The Ethics of Sports Coaching*, London: Routledge, pp. 23–42.

New Zealand Internal Affairs. Briefing to the incoming minister for ethnic communities. www.beehive.govt.nz/sites/default/files/2017-12/Ethnic%20Communities.PDF (accessed 3 Dec. 2019).

Ponnert, L., & Svensson, K. (2016). Standardisation – the end of professional discretion? *European Journal of Social Work*, 19(3–4): 586–599.

Quinn, J., Anderson, P., & Finkelstein, S. (1996). Managing the professional intellect: Making the most of the best, *Harvard Business Review*, Mar.–Apr.: 71–80.

Schempp, P., Sparkes, A., & Templin, T. (1993). The micro-politics of teacher induction, *American Educational Research Journal*, 30(3): 447–472.

Schwab, A., & Starbuck, W.H. (2016). Collegial 'nests' can foster critical thinking, innovative ideas, and scientific progress, *Strategic Organization*, 14(2): 167–177.

Stroot, S., & Ko, B. (2006). Induction of beginning physical education teachers into the school setting. In D. Kirk, D. Macdonald, & M. O'Sullivan (eds.), *The Handbook of Physical Education*, London: Sage Publications, pp. 425–448.

Zeichner, K., & Tabachnick, R. (1981). Are the effects of university teach education 'washed out' by school experience? *Journal of Teacher Education*, 32(3): 7–11.

8 Women and strength and conditioning coaching

Introduction
Part 1: pedagogical case
Part 2: commentary
Who is a strength and conditioning coach?
Gendered stereotypes and norms in strength and conditioning
Education, diversity and developing strength and conditioning coaches' competence
Summary
End of chapter tasks
References

Introduction

Despite the participation in, and popularity of, women's sport dramatically increasing over the past 50 years (Acosta & Carpenter, 2014) female participation in sports coaching, administration and S&C has not followed suit. Although slightly more women graduate with kinesiology and exercise science degrees (DataUSA, 2014) very few become S&C professionals, a situation that saw Gearity et al. (2016) suggest that S&C has become (or continues to be) a hyper-masculine space. In this chapter we look at who are SCCs, and who athletes prefer to work with. We explore the systemic discrimination faced by female SCCs and some of the gendered stereotypes and norms that remain prevalent in S&C. In the pedagogical case that follows, we present Rosa's experience in this area.

Part 1: pedagogical case

It was the subject heading that caught my eye: 'Hi, can I pick your brain?' The sender of the email was Annie, a professor of exercise science, whose class I had enrolled in 10 years earlier. Wow! Annie wants to 'pick' my brain. Now that was a first! She didn't explain why she wanted to meet, and I was a bit afraid to ask, but we arranged to meet up at a local café.

When we met at the café, Annie was keen to tell me about her experience of attending the annual conference of the UKSCA (the leading professional strength and conditioning organisation in the UK). She showed me a photo she took of the conference attendees and asked me for my impression. I had been to these conferences before, so I laughed because the photo was of hundreds of men wearing polos or T-shirts, shorts and runners. I suspected this is what had surprised Annie and why she had taken the photo. Annie said that prior to attending the conference, she was aware that the demographics of the attendees would not represent the demographics of the athletes with whom they were working, but she was unprepared for seeing such a discrepancy in person. During the conference, she became aware that a mere 7% of the UKSCA members were female, and it was very clear that not all of them had attended the conference. Not only were there few women in the audience, but approximately 95% of the audience was White and only a handful of people were over the age of 50. After a bit of chatting, Annie said; 'Rosa, what is your experience of being a strength and conditioning coach [SCC]?' So, this is what Annie wants to pick my brains about!

I often get asked what it's like working in a masculine and male-dominated environment. What I am always keen to highlight is that while I face challenges on a regular basis, I am not a victim. By saying this, I am aware some people may think I am gender blind or naïve. I don't think I am either. Instead, I like to think it is because I grew up in a family where my siblings were brothers (two younger and one older). We were all interested in and played a lot of different sports. Whenever any of us wanted to play 'pick up', 2v2 games in the back yard, our sex was not one of the selection criteria. It was the same at school. I went to co-educational primary (elementary) and secondary (high) schools and I played a lot of 'pick up' sport during lunch breaks and after school. I was quite skilful at basketball, football (soccer) and cricket, so when it came to choosing teams, I was never picked last – a good indication that I wasn't considered a liability. In fact, once we had a new kid move to the school, and when he joined in the games, he didn't realise I was a girl until I had to change back into my school uniform. I had similar experiences throughout university, and because I enrolled in a sport science degree, there were males and females who were used to 'mucking in' together. These experiences influenced my values and perceptions when I entered the world of S&C. Now the case is that the majority of SCCs I work with on a daily basis are male, and I have found that we all instruct technique and design S&C programmes in very similar ways. What I have found to be the most obvious difference is that male SCCs are more likely to say degrading things to each other and to the athletes.

I have been in my current position for eight years, which is a permanent, half-time SCC for athletes on the national women's football and cricket teams. My employer is a national high-performance organisation that oversees the high-performance environment of all sports. Given that I am not employed full-time, if I wish to supplement my income, which I do, I freelance as an SCC with other sporting organisations. For the first three years as an SCC, I worked really hard to establish my credibility and grabbed every opportunity presented to me. This meant I was working with any athlete or team I could, and I worked very long hours. I didn't mind too much because I really enjoyed meeting lots of interesting people, and I learned a lot working with a range of athletes, in a variety of sports, who were participating at the community, developmental as well as elite levels. Even though I was working harder than ever, I felt as if I was living my dream. However, after three years, I was exhausted. I felt as if I was always at the beck and call of some sport coach or supervisory SCC. I hardly had a weekend to relax and I wasn't getting anywhere financially. Because the sporting sector never has enough money to pay for 'extras', or support staff like an SCC, a large part of my work was unpaid, with the idea that 'paying your dues' would lead to future reward. I remember feeling, at times, that I was being taken advantage of, but what can you do when you know they won't pay more, but you're convinced you can make a difference? I'm still working on the solution to following one's passion whilst perpetually trying to make ends meet. At the UKSCA annual conference that I attended that year, I met up with a women's-only group of SCCs; some of us went to university together, others I came to know through mutual colleagues and networking. Despite the similarities of our education and career trajectories, at the beginning of my fourth year as an SCC, I told these peers that I didn't think I could continue on in the field as it stood.

Another reason for feeling this way was that I wasn't getting promoted to a full-time permanent position. There was one position I applied for, and didn't get, which really annoyed me. Initially, I assumed I didn't have the same experience as the successful candidate. However, I later found out the successful applicant had graduated the same year as me, but he didn't have my breadth of experience. Apparently, he had played a couple of years with the national junior football team, but he had never made it to the senior national team. When I learned this, my annoyance grew because. I had grown up believing that if you work hard, pay your dues and learn everything you can, you'll be rewarded.[1] Months later, my frustration multiplied because I heard that the guy who had got the job wasn't even that good at coaching exercise technique, yet he had gone to the same secondary school as two members on the selection committee. Apparently, networks, and looking the part, matters more than being a quality coach!

After these experiences, and heading into my fourth year as an SCC, I decided to work the hours the organisation paid me, and use my time strategically to complete the most recent certification on rehabilitation techniques and became more familiar with the latest research in the field. One consequence of adopting this new strategy was that I made the decision to attend an international S&C conference, where I hoped to network and seek out new opportunities. As I was only employed on a 0.5 contract, I wasn't eligible to receive any funds for professional development from my employer, and I was even required to take leave (vacation days) to attend the conference. This surprised me, but it did open my eyes to how institutional practices were contributing to what I was beginning to see as injustices.

When I arrived at the conference, I was excited, nervous and a little intimidated because everyone seemed to know each other. I felt like I was the only one hanging around on my own. As luck would have it, I spotted two other SCCs who were also flying solo, so we gravitated to each other. One was a young man who told me he identified as British-Asian, and the other was a White British woman somewhere in her 50s. They both lived locally, so while on the first day, we could hang out during the breaks between sessions, they were not attending the conference dinner, nor were they attending the conference on the second day because it was too expensive. The woman had been in the field for about 30 years and worked mostly as a personal trainer. She had tried for years to affiliate with a high-performance sports team but could never gain entry, so she refocused her aspirations to the personal training and business side of the field. The young man had recently graduated from a small university with a degree in Exercise Science and was coaching part-time at a local secondary school and doing some personal training on the side.

I too had considered not attending the conference dinner because attending any formal dinner on your own is tough, and I guessed that I would have to randomly join an existing table of people who already knew each other. Despite those reservations, I decided to be brave and attend. As predicted, when I sat at an available seat, I was the only woman at the table and aside from their polite offers to buy me a drink, the group at the table didn't seem too interested in talking to me about actual S&C coaching. After the dinner, I followed the crowd to the pub for a pint, and there I finally introduced myself to a couple of well-respected head SCCs and asked for their business cards. They were also polite and told me that I was welcome to contact them in the future should I need any advice about SCC. On the second day of the conference, I went to the graduate student research poster sessions, and another session specifically for first-time attendees. In talking with the graduate students, it turned out most of them weren't funded to attend the conference. Yet, many of them said they reduced their expenses by either sharing a room with another graduate student or with their supervisor. That's great for them, but while I am good friends with my male colleagues, they would never entertain the idea, let alone offer, to share a room with me. Sharing a room with a woman would just not be seen as 'proper'.

At this point, Annie interrupted me to ask for any 'take home messages' about my experiences of being a female SCC that she could use in class. Pausing for a while, I finally said: don't attend conferences with the expectation that 'experts' will provide you with the 'holy grail' of how to be an S&C (because they won't); don't accept the view that women are only token hires or variables to control for, or are a problematic and homogenous group (because we aren't); make an effort with networking, as it's important for professional development, and finally, you need to be resilient, self-reliant and resourceful.

Part 2: commentary

In this section of the chapter, we discuss Rosa's experiences and related literature on identities (or demographics, as is it often called in research), focusing on gender and coaching in S&C, whilst connecting to large social and historical discourses. We analyse Rosa's case to better understand how women SCCs typically, but not always, come into the field, how they develop, and their gendered experiences of coaching. But first, an essential caveat – we believe people are complex, and although we share similarities and differences, in this chapter we are mindful about categorising all women, or coaches, as a homogenous group. Such labelling takes us away from the view that people are complex and that homogenising an entire group, for example through stereotyping, can lead to negative effects such as marginalisation or stigmatisation. We're also cautious writing about women from a deficit position or using a blame-the-women narratives. LaVoi (2016) argues that such narratives can 'serve to construct, reinforce and sustain marginalization . . . while simultaneously deterring women from entering the profession' (p. 20). Yet another way that women coaches are commonly discussed is through a difference narrative. That is, women bring different (which in the eyes of some means lesser) inherent gendered skills to coaching compared to men, such as being caring, emotional, or nurturing. This sort of 'essentialising' of women can lead to unintended consequences that does little to promote women as coaches, diversity amongst coaches, and a more accurate depiction of human behaviour. For example, in order to motivate athletes to lift a heavier load, if a male SCC yelled, jumped up and down and slapped athletes on the back, then this might be seen not as a man being overly emotional, but as just good coaching (Fielding-Lloyd & Meân, 2008). Whereas if a woman did this or something similar, they might be viewed as being yet another overly emotional woman; a difference narrative that serves 'to perpetuate femininity and gender stereotypes' (LaVoi, 2016, p. 26). Such a difference narrative assumes, and positions, 'all women and all men into separate (read unequal) categories, and erases similarities between men and women, while simultaneously erasing difference among men and among women' (LaVoi, 2016, p. 27). Indeed, coaching has been, and will continue to be, a gendered, contested terrain, which warrants our critical analysis and subsequent preparation of students and coaches for this reality (Messner, 1988; Mullin & Bergan, 2018).

Who is a strength and conditioning coach?

In the S&C literature, no evidence exists on any work-related performance differences based on gender, or any other identity. Schull (2016) observed in her review of research, which focused on gender preferences in sport, that there was some support for the claim that female athletes had a preference for male sport coaches, or that masculine qualities and behaviours were preferred and were strongly identified with leadership. However, Schull showed how these masculine ideological preferences have developed as a result of power and hegemony, not some inherent development or truth. Interestingly, and in contrast to sport coaching research, recent studies specific to S&C suggest athletes possess minimal gender preferences, next to no conflicts or problems exist around the sex of the SCC, and if a clear problem existed, it's likely a male one in the sense that some male athletes hold sexist views, mirroring many societies' general sexist attitudes (O'Malley & Greenwood, 2018).

In one of the few studies on athletes' preferences of SCC, it was found that collegiate football players reported being less comfortable with a female strength coach than collegiate women athletes from soccer and volleyball (Magnusen & Rhea, 2009). In a similar study, researchers found that male and female collegiate athletes' perceptions of positive SCC behaviours (e.g. constructive feedback, in control of emotions) positively correlated with perceptions of SCC-athlete compatibility, whereas negative behaviour did not predict compatibility (Lee et al., 2013). They also found that female athletes, but not male, rated compatibility higher when SCC behaviours were perceived as positive. In a qualitative interview study with 10 NCAA Division I juniors (third year) and seniors (fourth year), the athletes reported hardly any gender preferences for an SCC but did report desiring positive coaching behaviours such as leadership ability, professionalism, trust, respect, support, dependability, a positive relationship and personality (Shuman & Appleby, 2016).

Based on the available evidence, it seems that athletes prefer and report greater compatibility for positive coach behaviour, which can be offered by a person of any sex or gender, and is consistent with years of research and scholarly reports on athletes' preferred coach behaviour (Chelladurai & Miller, 2017) and effective coaching (Côte & Gilbert, 2009). So rather than gender preferences, or gendered ideologies, informing decisions about coaching, what warrants our attention is the preparation of competent coaches who can deliver positive, supportive and desirable behaviours to enhance performance and other psychosocial outcomes. When we pause to consider how women SCCs have endured, and thrived, in a male-dominated, hyper-masculine setting, it would now seem obvious that they would develop a range of skills. Indeed, having a history of being challenged in, and out of, S&C settings via interpersonal and social gender norms and harmful stereotypes, and obtaining extensive qualifications, women SCCs appear to be quite competent and resilient. Perhaps this demonstrates how quality coaching and gender trailblazers in S&C can foster, and have fostered, positive social change.

However, we must not use the development of resilience as a reason to ignore issues of injustice such as systemic discrimination. That is, logic like 'See, these coaches are better today because of the challenges they've experienced and thus all is well' is a problematic narrative. Cassidy et al. (2014) provide an overview of some of the questions that have been asked, and debates that have occurred, about the value of resilience:

> Can resilience be distilled into a few global aggregates? (Rutter in Howard et al., 1999) Others have pointed out that we can be more, or less, resilient at various points in our lives depending on the accumulation of resources, experiences, and the interactions we have with individuals and the environment (Masten et al., 1990). More recently, MacKinnon and Derickson (2012, p. 2) argue that the concept of resilience is neoliberal because it 'privileges established social structures, which are often shaped by unequal power relations and injustice' and the onus is placed on individuals 'to become more resilient and adaptable to a range of external threats'.
>
> (pp. 126–127)

Whilst the development of resilience is a useful psychological skill, it cannot be advocated in lieu of fairness and opportunity. Furthermore, LaVoi (2016) offers many reasons why we should support women's paths into coaching, including: women coaches are role models and can encourage girls to become sport leaders and reduce boys' sexist attitudes; women coaches add diversity and differences to thinking, practice and enhance outcomes; and women coaches are less likely to sexually abuse athletes.

Finally, although this chapter focused on women in S&C, additional considerations need to be paid to overlapping identities such as race, socioeconomic status and others. Attendance at conferences, professional development, certification courses and universities more broadly are becoming, or already are, expensive. As shown in Rosa's story, and in the field of S&C more generally, those working in universities, or high-performing organisations with hearty financial resources (e.g. endowments, grants, generous state or federal funding), will likely disproportionately reap the rewards. Thus, the adage 'the rich get richer and the poor get poorer' rings true in S&C. Although not yet studied in S&C, this same phenomenon was identified 50+ years ago by the sociologist Merton (1968), who labelled it the 'Matthew Effect'. What Merton showed was how the organisation of, and rewards provided in, higher education favours institutions and their professors who already possess great wealth, fame and resources. These issues are played out within S&C organisations who provide grants and awards to well-known and accomplished researchers, many of whom go on to leadership positions in the same organisations, thus reproducing this system. As women, and people of colour, tend to also have less wealth and receive less compensation for their work, they are doubly penalised, and breaking into the system is more of an outlier than the norm (Pfeffer & Killewald, 2018).

Further related to diversity, a recent report, jointly written by an Australian Human Rights Commission and Deloitte, found a diverse workplace creates happier workers who believe that the workplace is more successful. The report noted that, 'the more included an employee feels, the more likely they are to be at work . . . to receive a higher performance rating. . . . [and] innovation levels increased when employees felt they were in a more inclusive and diverse workplace' (Sawyer, 2013, p. 1). Other identified benefits of a diverse workplace include: having a competitive edge, increased ability to attract talent, enhanced decision making, ability to tap into new opportunities, improved business image as well as increased productivity and engagement (Cunningham, 2011; also see https://diversityworksnz.org.nz)

Gendered stereotypes and norms in strength and conditioning

Historically, White men have dominated higher education and science, and engaging in weight training activities was seen as a White masculine domain to build character and proper hygiene (Shurley, Todd et al., 2019; Shurley, Felkar et al., ahead of print). So Professor Annie in our pedagogical case is a rarity because historically, and in contemporary times, most exercise physiologists have been, and are, men. Women are not well represented as conference keynote speakers in this domain, as Rosa witnessed when she attended the international S&C conference. What she witnessed is not isolated to the UK.

Several studies have shown that most SCCs tend to be White men (Martinez, 2004; Todd et al., 1991). Acosta and Carpenter (2014) found that in the USA, while 41.4% of Division I universities employ at least one female SCC, the percentage drops to 22.9% at the Division III level, and 10.8% at the Division II level. Division II universities have the lowest percent of female coaches across all sports (36.4% compared to 43.4% for Division I and 47.3% for Division III) and thus, as we will explain, more likely to reproduce the status quo that favors male coaches. Division II has the least number of women's teams by division, and some believe more women SCCs would be hired if there were more female athletes to coach (Laskowski & Ebben, 2016; Massey & Vincent, 2013). In comparison, Division I universities have large budgets to hire more coaches, and they also face enormous public pressure and media attention, and therefore might be more inclined to hire women SCCs in an effort to appear more equitable. Although Division III universities have a relatively large number of women's sports, they are more likely to employ only one full-time SCC, which is biased towards men. Across the three levels combined, the percentage of colleges or universities that employ a female SCC is 28.6%.

While progress has been made in terms of equitable representation of female SCCs and leaders in the field of S&C, we can see that SCCs like Rosa are more outliers than the norm. To better understand how to address these inequities, we now turn to addressing what we know about women's experiences in the field. Rosa's experiences capture what it's like for many women SCCs. When she was a newcomer to the field, Rosa was full of enthusiasm and highly satisfied in her role. As an SCC, she felt the work was meaningful and her coaching helped athletes achieve enhanced performance. Women SCCs, similarly to men, usually find great satisfaction in their work due to these reasons, along with the opportunity to build relationships with athletes and seeing them mature, developing character and hard work habits, and to identify with the larger mission of the athletic department or university (Laskowski & Ebben, 2016; Massey & Vincent, 2013; Sartore-Baldwin, 2013; Shuman & Appleby, 2016). However, women SCCs face unique challenges related to gendered stereotypes that can affect their, and their peers', thoughts, emotions and behaviours. For example, whether it be in the weight training facilities or coaching conferences, many women SCCs report concern about their impression management. They think about what clothing to wear and how it could be construed as too revealing; or the opposite, such as too frumpy and unathletic. They worry about losing their credibility or professionalism by being seen intoxicated, acting silly or in poor physical fitness (Shuman & Appleby, 2016). Women SCCs report feeling as though they are constantly being surveyed and judged by others, which can be internalised and cause anxiety (Gearity & Mills, 2014; Laskowski & Ebben, 2016; Mullin & Bergan, 2018; O'Malley & Greenwood, 2018).

Women SCCs often report tensions and contradictions relating to gender norms. For example, if they yell and curse at an athlete, they could be seen as bitchy, mean or trying too hard to fit in and be 'one of the guys'; whereas when men adopt such practices, it is considered normal, if not desirable and effective, coach behaviour. Again, relating back to stereotypes, in this example, the same behaviour might be considered a positive stereotype for men but a negative stereotype for women. Of course, people can critique and change stereotypes and problematic practices. In multiple studies, women SCCs have problematised the norm of yelling obscenities and degrading athletes (Gearity & Mills, 2014; Laskowski & Ebben, 2016). Yet, other women SCCs will attempt to live up to the hegemonic masculine norm in S&C by being (extra) tough and stern and by standing up to athletes or sport coaches who challenge their authority. These complexities, of going along with, or disrupting, stereotypes, is also found in research on sport coaches' experiences of gender relations (Norman, 2012, 2016; Norman & Rankin-Wright, 2018; Rankin-Wright et al., 2019).

Throughout Rosa's career, she had coached a variety of sport teams and athletes. Absent from Rosa's pedagogical case was any descriptions of meaningful conflict or 'problem' with athletes. Some women SCCs report being 'tested' interpersonally in the workplace (Gearity & Mills, 2014; Laskowski & Ebben, 2016). Can they spot a heavy load? Can they coach complex exercises such as Olympic lifts – or even perform them? If an athlete physically or verbally assaults them, will they be able to defend themselves? Will anybody take them seriously? There is a paucity of research on these topics, and yet these issues seem to be identifiable in the S&C community – it's as if they've been made real without evidence, perhaps to marginalise and diminish women SCCs. In contrast, male SCCs generally do not get asked the type of questions just identified. Supervisors of SCCs need to become aware of gendered biases that work to position women SCCs as being less able than their male counterparts. Specifically, consideration needs to be given to how institutional arrangements, and well as individual behaviours, in the S&C training site continue to produce harmful stereotypes.

Specific to S&C, and taking heed from Denison's (2019) similar work in sport, Kuklick and Gearity (2019) have argued that a core competency for SCCs should be to know how to problematise often taken-for-granted practices. Examples of such practices include the clothing one wears, (degrading) communication with an athlete and the lack of women in leadership positions (for more, see LaVoi & Calhoun, 2016). Armed with such knowledge, SCCs could be more inclusive and embrace differences and diversity, which empirically has been linked to a host of psychologically positive outcomes (Cunningham, 2011; Sawyer, 2013); a point we elaborate upon in the next section.

Underlying S&C is an assumption of heteronormativity, or the idea that heterosexuality is normal and the only proper way to express one's sexual behaviours (Sartore-Baldwin, 2013). Most of the early social and behavioural research in the field did not ask participants a host of demographic or identity questions such as their sexual orientation. Perhaps because of its conservative, religious and hegemonic masculine foundations, there was an assumption that all the men must be straight, or as put in one paper on the topic, 'athleticism = masculinity = heterosexuality' (O'Malley & Greenwood, 2018, p. 41). Researchers have shown that women SCCs often find the hypersexualised-objectifying-misogynistic music common in weight rooms to be a problem; however, the insidious nature of these microaggressions have been normalised and thus often go unnoticed (Gearity & Mills, 2014; Gearity & Henderson Metzger, 2017; Massey & Vincent, 2013). One popular, and mostly biophysical, S&C textbook considers music only from the perspective of how it affects ratings of perceived exertion or effort, or that high-volume music could impede an SCC's ability to give instruction and safety warnings (Haff & Triplett, 2016). Nonetheless, another leading, more recent, mostly biophysical S&C textbook does state, 'Do not play music or television programs in the weight room that are offensive or sexist' (Evetovich & Eckerson, 2019, p. 578). While this example is focused on music, we reiterate the larger social point and connection to show how the dominant biophysical knowledge in S&C textbooks, and typical professional development opportunities, omit acknowledging or addressing these issues.

Education, diversity and developing strength and conditioning coaches' competence

To our knowledge, there is no research exploring the sexual orientation, practices, of male SCCs from their own, or others', perceptions. This would seem to indicate the dominance of heteronormativity for men in S&C and the view that their sexuality is unproblematic or a legitimate area of study. This is not the case for woman SCCs. In the same vein as woman sport coaches, the subject of sexuality for women SCCs has been reported in the literature (Gearity & Mills, 2014; Massey & Vincent, 2013). Aptly captured by Mullin and Bergan (2018) marking women as lesbian, and thus breaking with heteronormativity, seeks to discredit and impede their progression and causes anxiety and distress, that men or heteronormative conforming coaches (i.e. the female SCC who goes out of her way to demonstrate her male partner or husband) do not experience. In the case of Rosa, we don't know anything of her sexual orientation or partnership status. Amongst some of the reasons why women SCC conceal their sexual orientation is to protect themselves from stigma, or because it's deemed irrelevant to their coaching (i.e. it should be a non-issue despite it being one). Rosa also indicated, as male coaches also have, that she works long hours and that given the focus she's put on her career, she may not have prioritised finding a significant other (Gearity & Mills, 2014; Laskowski & Ebben, 2016; Massey & Vincent, 2013). It is worth reiterating here that we bring up these points not to offer definite interpretations or conclusions, and we are mindful of the way in which our own biases inform our stance. However, as stated as a purpose of this book, we seek to expose the intersection of these biopsychosocial issues in order to name this social milieu and remove discriminatory practices. As women SCCs have experienced these gendered norms, they naturally affect how women prepare to coach, so the following section explores this, as well as issues for the field related to diversity, inclusivity and competence.

Consistent with research on women sport coaches (Norman, 2010), women SCCs state a need to have unparalleled qualifications; such as having been a high-performing athlete, multiple certifications and a Master's degree, and several experiential learning milestones such as coaching at multiple sites with numerous athletes and teams (Gearity & Mills, 2014; Laskowski & Ebben, 2016; Sartore-Baldwin, 2013). The research suggests that women, and many men, ultimately leave the S&C field because of issues such as long hours, low compensation and lack of appreciation for their role. Yet, for those who have endured in the field, women SCCs in particular obtain extensive formal education, experiential or on-the-job experiences and additional professional development, including certifications and conference attendance (Laskowski & Ebben, 2016; Massey & Vincent, 2013; Sartore-Baldwin, 2013). For example, women SCCs usually possess a Master's degree, have been collegiate, professional or Olympic level athletes, work 55–60 hours per week and have obtained certifications with the NSCA (e.g. Certified S&C Specialist) and other weightlifting, speed or S&C organisations (e.g. USA Weightlifting, Collegiate S&C Coaches' Association) (Laskowski & Ebben, 2016; Massey & Vincent, 2013).

Rosa's career trajectory demonstrates her growing awareness of the perceived need to commit to ongoing professional development, obtain additional certifications and develop networks. As was shown in the pedagogical case, developing networks were easier said than done. Also apparent in the pedagogical case was the way in which men, when in positions of power, tend to hire people that look like them (also called homologous reproduction; see Stangl & Kane, 1991) and are not actively recruiting diverse representation in their coaching staff. Consequently, the status quo endures, and women and members of other groups who do not fit the dominant group are marginalised, often receiving only fractional SCC appointments and having to secure alternative employment in related fields, as evident from the employment trajectories of the colleagues Rosa met at the conference. Yet, despite possessing these qualifications, believing they are effective coaches (i.e. enhance athletic performance, good role models) and desiring to stay in the field, some women SCCs intend to leave, or do leave, because of these circumstances (Gearity & Mills, 2014; Massey & Vincent, 2013). Awareness of these issues can lead SCCs and other sport leaders and policy makers to take actions to support the inclusion of skilled women SCCs. Indeed, an important area for future research is 'allyship' and the allies who are 'people with privilege taking action to end the oppression that gave them their privilege' (Bishop, 2015, p. 102). With respect to S&C, this might entail understanding why some male SCCs recognise their male privilege and work towards uplifting women's opportunities in the field (Rook & Gearity, 2019).

Summary

In this chapter, we focused on describing and analysing the lived experiences of women SCCs and referenced related research on gender, identity and diversity in S&C. Through the pedagogical case, we described how an SCC was socialised into S&C, and problematised ethical dilemmas and behaviours that she felt did not fit with her essence as a coach and person. We also noted individual, organisational and social implications and recommendations that could enhance diversity and inclusivity, and ultimately a host of desirable outcomes. Nearly 30 years ago, a former NSCA President recommended that the NSCA's Women's Advisory Committee should 'assume an advocacy role for the female members of the organization' (Todd et al., 1991, p. 38). Nowadays, a more progressive view acknowledges that these issues in fact concern us all. We all share in producing and lessening or removing barriers like sexism and systems of oppression, and like good allies, all SCCs should advocate for women SCCs, and others from traditionally underrepresented or marginalised groups.

End of chapter tasks

1. If you were the head SCC, or in charge of developing a staff of SCC, how would your awareness of gender affect the coaches in your charge? After considering gender, bring in other identities (e.g. race, religion, sexuality) to consider how multiple identities might affect their experiences and your leadership.
2. What are some ways your own biases have affected your view of coaching? What was the catalyst for you to begin becoming aware of your own biases? If these questions are challenging, why might that be? Some people find it easier to point out others' biases. Consider that claim, and see if you can point out biases you recognise in other people or, better, coaches.
3. Watch sport movies or documentaries, and/or the next time you're at the gym, observe what men and women are doing, how are they being portrayed, what structures and institutional arrangements exist to support particular portrayals.

Note

1 This point relates to the idea of the myth of meritocracy (Coakley, 2014).

References

Acosta, R.V., & Carpenter, L.J. (2014). *Women in Intercollegiate Sport: A Longitudinal, National Study, Thirty-seven Year Update*, West Brookfield, MA: Authors. www.acostacarpenter.org/2014%20Status%20of%20Women%20in%20Intercollegiate%20Sport%20-37%20Year%20Update%20-%201977-2014%20.pdf.

Bishop, A. (2015). *Become an Ally: Breaking the Cycle of Oppression in People* (3rd ed.), Winnipeg: Fernwood Publishing.

Cassidy, T., Jackson, A-M., Miyahara, M., & Shemmell, J. (2014). Greta: Weaving strands to allow Greta to flourish as Greta. In K. Armour (ed.), *Pedagogical Cases in Sport, Exercise and Physical Activity. Volume 1: Physical Education and Youth Sport*, London: Routledge, pp. 117–129.

Chelladurai, P., & Miller, J.J. (2017). Leadership in sport management. In R. Hoye & M.M. Parent (eds.), *The Sage Handbook of Sport Management*, Thousand Oaks, CA: Sage Publications, pp. 85–102.

Coakley, J. (2014). *Sports in Society: Issues and Controversies* (11th ed.), New York: McGraw Hill.

Côte, J., & Gilbert, W. (2009). An integrative definition of coaching effectiveness and expertise, *International Journal of Sports Science & Coaching*, 4: 307–323.

Cunningham, G. (2011). The LGBT advantage: Examining the relationship among sexual orientation diversity, diversity strategy, and performance, *Sport Management Review*, 14: 543–461.

DataUSA. (2014). https://datausa.io/profile/cip/kinesiology-exercise-science#demographics (accessed 5 Dec. 2019).

Denison, J. (2019). What it really means to 'think outside the box': Why Foucault matters for coach development, *International Sport Coaching Journal*, 6: 354–358.

Evetovich, T.K., & Eckerson, J.M. (2019). Age and gender training considerations. In T.J. Chandler & L.E. Brown (eds.), *Conditioning for Strength and Human Performance* (3rd ed.), New York: Routledge, pp. 573–600.

Fielding-Lloyd, B., & Meân, L.J. (2008). Standards and separatism: The discursive construction of gender in English soccer coach education, *Sex Roles*, 58: 24–39.

Gearity, B.T., & Henderson Metzger, L. (2017). Intersectionality, microaggressions, and microaffirmations: Towards a cultural praxis of sport coaching, *Sociology of Sport Journal*, 34: 160–175.

Gearity, B.T., & Mills, J.P. (2014). Identity development and coaching practices of collegiate, women strength and conditioning coaches. Paper presented at the North American Society for the Sociology of Sport, Quebec, Canada.

Gearity, B.T., Mills, J.P., & Callary, B. (2016). Theoretical underpinnings among qualitative research. In N. LaVoi (ed.), *Women in Sports Coaching*, London: Routledge, pp. 234–252.

Haff, G.G., & Triplett, N.T. (2016). *Essentials of Strength Training and Conditioning* (4th ed.), Champaign, IL: Human Kinetics.

Howard, S., Dryden, J., & Johnson, B. (1999). Childhood resilience: Review and critique of literature, *Oxford Review of Education*, 25(3): 307–323.

Kuklick, C., & Gearity, B.T. (2019). New movement practices: A Foucauldian learning community to disrupt technologies of discipline, *Sociology of Sport Journal*, 36(4): 289–299.

Laskowski, K.D., & Ebben, W.P. (2016). Profile of women collegiate strength and conditioning coaches, *The Journal of Strength and Conditioning Research*, 30(12): 3481–3493.

LaVoi, N.M. (2016). Age and gender training considerations. In N.M. LaVoi (ed.), *Women in Sport Coaching*, New York: Routledge, pp. 1–9.

LaVoi, N.M., & Calhoun, A.S. (2016). Women in sport media: Where are the women coaches? In N.M. LaVoi (ed.), *Women in Sport Coaching*, New York: Routledge, pp. 163–176.

Lee, H., Magnusen, M.J., & Cho, S. (2013). Strength coach-athlete compatibility: Roles of coaching behaviors and athlete gender, *International Journal of Applied Sports Sciences*, 25(1): 55–67.

Magnusen, M.J., & Rhea, D. (2009). Division I athletes' attitudes toward and preferences for male and female strength and conditioning coaches, *The Journal of Strength and Conditioning Research*, 23(4): 1084–1090.

Martinez, D. (2004). Study of the key determining factors for the NCAA division 1 head strength and conditioning coach, *Journal of Strength & Conditioning Research*, 18(1): 5–18.

Massey, C.D., & Vincent, J. (2013). A job analysis of major college female strength and conditioning coaches. *The Journal of Strength and Conditioning Research*, 27(7): 2000–2012.

Merton, R.K. (1968). The Matthew effects in science: The reward and communication systems of science are considered, *Science*, 159: 56–63.

Messner, M.A. (1988). Sports and male domination: The female athlete as contested ideological terrain, *Sociology of Sport Journal*, 5: 197–211.

Mullin, E.M., & Bergan, M.E. (2018). Cultural and occupational barriers facing women professionals in the field of strength and conditioning, *Strength and Conditioning Journal*, 40(6): 15–20.

Norman, L. (2010). Bearing the burden of doubt: Female coaches' experiences of gender relations, *Research Quarterly for Exercise and Sport*, 81(4): 506–517.

Norman, L. (2012). Gendered homophobia in sport and coaching: Understanding the everyday experiences of lesbian coaches, *International Review for the Sociology of Sport*, 47(6): 705–723.

Norman, L. (2016). Is there a need for coaches to be more gender responsive? A review of the evidence, *International Sport Coaching Journal*, 3(2): 192–196.

Norman, L., & Rankin-Wright, A.J. (2018). Surviving rather than thriving: Understanding the experiences of women coaches using a theory of gendered social well-being *International Review for the Sociology of Sport*, 53(4): 424–450.

O'Malley, L.M., & Greenwood, S. (2018). Female coaches in strength and conditioning – why so few? *Strength and Conditioning Journal*, 40(6): 40–48.

Pfeffer, F.T., & Killewald, A. (2018). Generations of advantage: Multigenerational correlations in family wealth, *Social Forces*, 96(4): 1411–1442.

Rankin-Wright, A.J., Hylton, K., & Norman, L. (2019). Negotiating the coaching landscape: Experiences of Black men and women coaches in the United Kingdom, *International Review for the Sociology of Sport*, 54(5): 603–621.

Rook, M., & Gearity, B.T. (2019). More women in the weight room: Exploring gender-allyship in strength and conditioning coaching. Presentation at the 2019 ISSA World Congress of Sociology of Sport, 25 Apr.

Sartore-Baldwin, M.L. (2013). The professional experiences and work-related outcomes of male and female strength and conditioning coaches, *The Journal of Strength and Conditioning Research*, 27(3): 831–838.

Sawyer, R. (2013). Workers happier in more diverse workplaces, Jan. www.dynamicbusiness.com.au/hr-and-staff/report-on-diversity-in-the-workplace-reveals-happy-workers-17012013.html.

Schull, V.D. (2016). Female athletes' conceptions of leadership: Coaching and gender implications. In N.M. LaVoi (ed.), *Women in Sport Coaching*, New York: Routledge, pp. 126–138.

Shuman, K.M., & Appleby, K.M. (2016). Gender preferences? National collegiate athletic association division 1 student-athletes and strength and conditioning coaches. *The Journal of Strength and Conditioning Research*, 30(10): 2924–2933.

Shurley, J.P., Felkar, V., Greviskes, L., & Todd, T. (ahead of print). Historical and social considerations of strength training for female athletes. *Strength and Conditioning Journal*.

Shurley, J.P., Todd, J., & Todd, T. (2019). *Strength Coaching in America: A History of the Innovation That Transformed Sports*, Austin, TX: University of Texas Press.

Stangl, J.M., & Kane, M.J. (1991). Structural variables that offer explanatory power for the under-representation of women coaches since title IX: The case of homologous reproduction, *Sociology of Sport Journal*, 8: 47–60.

Todd, J., Lovett, D., & Todd, T. (1991). The status of women in the strength and conditioning Profession, *Strength and Conditioning Journal*, 13(6): 35–38.

9 Finding a professional voice and collaborating

Introduction
Part 1: pedagogical case
Part 2: commentary

    Naming and framing the problem

Boundary work
Boundary crossing
Summary
End of chapter tasks
References

Introduction

Despite strength and conditioning coaches (SCCs) spending many hours engaging with athletes, it can be a lonely profession with limited opportunities for collegiality. In this chapter we consider how the process of framing a problem can assist, or not, SCCs to develop their professional voice and enhance the opportunities for working collaboratively. In addition, we introduce the idea that working in an environment, in which there is a degree of tension, can actually be a productive and collaborative space. For this outcome to occur, we identify mechanisms and strategies that can help facilitate opportunities for working at, and crossing over, professional boundaries in productive ways.

Part 1: pedagogical case

Bronwyn is a third-year SCC for the Scorpions netball club, a competitive side in an elite netball league. While the players are effectively amateur, the club strives to model a professional management structure, so several part-time support staff are employed. In addition to a coaching staff of three, a manager and a logistics person, the team also employs a team doctor, a physical therapist, a sports dietitian, a sports psychologist and a videographer/analyst on part-time bases. In Bronwyn's full-time role she has responsibility for the strength and conditioning (S&C) of the Scorpions' premier and development squads. When the competitive elite league is in progress, responsibility for the delivery of S&C sessions for the development squad is handed to two volunteer interns.

    Having worked her way into the role through volunteering with club netball teams, Bronwyn now finds that in her third season at the elite level, she has a very good structure in place for the athletes. Her programming is consistent, the athletes are predominantly receptive to her system and, with the help of her interns, she has a good instructional and training environment within the shared S&C facility and the team's adjacent training facility. In those respects, Bronwyn's chosen career has followed the path she had expected. Her undergraduate education had prepared her for the seasonal planning and programming, her experiences have helped to develop her instructional style and by attending local S&C conferences and regularly reading journal articles, her ideas are up to date and her practice is innovative. However, nothing in her undergraduate programme had prepared her for some of the interprofessional issues that have arisen in the past two seasons. She is unsure whether this is because she simply didn't perceive the issues during that frantic first season when her focus was on survival, or whether it has something to do with the recent changing team dynamic. At the end of her first season with the Scorpions, the head coach was replaced and the incoming coach brought with her two new coaching assistants.

In her second year Bronwyn was faced with some initial challenges as a consequence of working with a completely new coaching staff, but by the end of the season she was feeling reasonably comfortable about her relationships with the coaches and her role within the organisation. Her only real concern was with the team physical therapist, Sandy, who Bronwyn found to be a 'stickler' for everyone respecting her physiotherapy knowledge and scope of practice. Interestingly, Sandy did not appear to reciprocate that professional respect. Sandy constantly reminded coaching staff, players, the team doctor and of course Bronwyn, not to encroach into her physical therapy domain. It had not always been so segregated. Initially, Sandy had sought Bronwyn's advice and collaborated with her when returning injured players to training and competition. However, over time, Sandy had increasingly excluded Bronwyn from those processes. The most obvious example of this was that Sandy had taken some of the return-to-play type exercises and drills that Bronwyn had developed and shared with her, and was now delivering these to athletes herself. Bronwyn wondered why this was the case. Was the new coaching structure causing Sandy to be concerned about her job security? Was she trying to demonstrate her worth to the organisation?

Bronwyn's values inform her athlete-centred practices and her willingness to collaborate with other professionals. While some think she is idealistic, Bronwyn believes that a shared care approach requires putting one's professional and personal egos aside for the benefit of the athletes and the team. So, while Bronwyn is flattered that Sandy is using the exercises she developed, she also feels aggrieved that Sandy is using the exercises and drills, which were developed using her knowledge, experience and innovation, without any attribution. This is compounded by Sandy overlooking the fact that Bronwyn would normally work closely with a rehabilitating athlete and would progress returning athletes methodically and carefully through drills before progressing to some of the exercises that Sandy has co-opted. Bronwyn feels that because Sandy has not worked closely with the athletes' strength and conditioning, she is not understanding or observing those progressions – Sandy just replicates the exercises without much wisdom. Added to Bronwyn's frustration, Sandy has also developed a habit of removing athletes from her regular conditioning sessions in order to provide treatment and oversee return-to-play conditioning drills. All of this is occurring without consulting Bronwyn or considering her overall conditioning plan. From Bronwyn's perspective, this is clearly encroaching on her scope of practice and is disruptive for the overall team communication and functioning. This approach is insidious and appears to be affecting other members of the management team, with both the sports dietitian and the sports psychologist also recently straying into providing conditioning and injury advice. Bronwyn is unsure what effect this is having on the athletes but suspects that, in the eyes of some athletes, her role has been subtly undermined.

Bronwyn is unsure about how to approach this issue in a way that resolves the effects it is having on her enjoyment of, and effectiveness in, the workplace. Bronwyn has tried talking to Sandy about her concerns but found Sandy to be quite dismissive of her role and professional knowledge; knowledge that she had once valued. With this avenue exhausted, and with there being no identified team leader of the sports medicine and science staff, she can really only take the issue to the head coach or the team manager. However, she fears that by doing so she would very likely come out of such a conversation looking trite, professionally jealous and possibly a team disruptor. With job security always at risk in professional sport, she does not want to be seen to be 'rocking the boat'. Bronwyn is also aware that she is in effect a mentor and role model for the two interns, so she has been particularly careful about how she reacts and what she says around the interns and athletes.

Bronwyn is quite distressed by the situation because she is noticing that she is now thinking twice before referring an athlete to Sandy for physical therapy. Previously, if she had noticed athletes experiencing training or movement difficulties, which could signal early signs or symptoms of an impending injury, she would suggest that they immediately consult with the team physical therapist. She tells herself that she would never knowingly put an athlete at risk. But now, with the expectation that Sandy is likely to unnecessarily withhold an athlete from training and prescribe her own S&C practices, she gives more thought to every situation before drawing Sandy's attention to any potential problems.

Bronwyn's distress is exacerbated by the feeling that she is being undermined as an S&C professional and that her discipline, training and education is being demeaned and devalued. Even though she tells herself that her role has never been about her own profile and ego, and that the interests of the athletes and team come first and foremost, she realises that professional recognition and respect is in fact important to her. More than anything Bronwyn is missing the collegiality that they all enjoyed in her first season with the team. She has no real support structure beyond the Scorpions team environment. While there are other local SSCs, they are all busy and tend to work independently and largely in isolation. So, there is not really an S&C colleague, or someone with similar interests, who she feels comfortable going to with her concerns. She has tried to research the problem but has found that the S&C world is primarily focused on the biophysical science of S&C and the practice of how to programme and coach. She has considered approaching a counsellor external to the organisation and sport for guidance, and she is coming to realise that her education and professional experiences have not really prepared her for this type of issue.

Part 2: commentary

Naming and framing the problem

Bronwyn has a problem, but what is less clear is whether or not she has clearly articulated, or set, the nature of the problem. In this pedagogical case it appears that Bronwyn views Sandy's behaviour to be problematic, but we contend that it is more complex than 'fixing' Sandy's behaviour. As mentioned in Chapter 3, if SCCs desire to be recognised as professionals, there is some benefit in understanding the process of problem setting, with its associated processes of naming and framing. Lawson (1984) claimed there are numerous stimuli for problem setting; but the two which resonate with Bronwyn's situation are: (a) a desire to become, or develop as, a professional and (b) the threat of deprofessionalisation. It is possible that if Bronwyn spent less emotional energy trying to 'fix' Sandy's behaviour, and more time on understanding how she names and frames the perceived problem, she may find more affirmation of her work and develop a deeper understanding as to why she is feeling undermined.

As mentioned in Chapter 3, the *names* given to problems generally fall into two categories, 'technical efficiency' and 'morality', with the former focusing on fixing problems and the latter concerned more with matters such as privileges, needs and rights (Lawson, 1984). In the pedagogical case, it appears that Bronwyn is implicitly naming the problem in a way that focuses on technical efficiency, whereas it may be more useful to understand what is going on if she named it as a moral problem, with its concerns with privileges, needs and rights. This way, if and when Bronwyn raises the issue with the team management and sports coaching staff, the focus of the discussion would be about needs and rights (not only her own, but those of other members of the coaching team) and her desire to act professionally. Naming the problem as such has the potential to shift the discussion away from technical efficiency and fixing the problem. Such a focus has the potential to become a discussion about 'them' and 'us' or she' and 'me', rather than discussions that look at the bigger picture by asking 'what' and 'why' type questions of the entire coaching team. Yet the names we use to describe a problem 'betray' our values. So, if Bronwyn does not value 'knowing why' or 'caring why', or does not view this as being integral to becoming a competent professional (Quinn et al., 1996), then she is not going to name the problem as having a moral focus and thus will potentially adopt the view of technical efficiency and continue to focus on trying to 'fix' the problem, i.e. Sandy's behaviours.

Yet the naming of problems does not happen in isolation. Our socialisation, past and recent, plays a significant role in how we *frame* problems because we interpret new experiences based on our previous experiences (Lawson, 1984). We can see this is the case with Bronwyn. While she is not consciously framing the problem, she is nonetheless interpreting the current situation, i.e. working with new coaching staff and a shift in Sandy's behaviour, based on what she experienced in her first year working with the team. For many of us, we have become socialised into viewing interprofessional competition as an inevitable fact of life (Abbott, 1988). In their review of terms being used to describe the ways in which professionals work collaboratively, Nancarrow et al. (2013) identified interprofessional to be one such term. While they found many related terms were used interchangeably to describe such work, one noteworthy point for the discussion in this chapter where we use the term interprofessional, is that:

> [t]he terms inter/multi-professional are generally narrower than the terms inter/multi-disciplinary [13–16] and refer to teams consisting exclusively of professionals from different professions or disciplines, or at least to the relationships between professionals in teams that may also include other non-professional staff.
>
> (pp. 2–3)

Interprofessional competition can occur because professionals feel that they have to protect their autonomy, exclusivity and dominance through professional accreditations and ethical codes (Abbott, 1988). Arguably, interprofessional competition may also be linked to one's professional identity. As Reid et al. (2004) wryly observe, a common trait of experts is a high level of confidence in their own opinions, and therefore they may fear being perceived as not knowing, or not being sufficiently competent (Phelan & Griffiths, 2019). Whatever is the driver for the interprofessional competition, one of the outcomes of being competitive is that professionals can be reluctant to co-operate and share ideas (Wright et al., 2007). When this is the case, it is very likely that professionals will engage in boundary protection, rather than being open to working in ways that encourages interprofessional or boundary crossing work. We discuss boundary crossing in more detail in a later section.

In the pedagogical case we can see how Bronwyn has been socialised into being concerned about the relevant knowledge base and skills her colleague has to deal with, in this case, an exercise rehabilitation or return-to-play situation. Bronwyn's own academic training reinforced the professional responsibility of understanding one's scope of practice and respecting the prescribed professional boundaries. An actual example of this type of prescription is evident in the National Strength and Conditioning Association's (NSCA) *NSCA Strength and Conditioning Professional Standards and Guidelines* (Triplett & Chandler, 2017), where accredited strength professionals are instructed not to misrepresent their knowledge and skills, provide services that they are not qualified or permitted by law to provide, and to refer to more qualified individuals as appropriate. Sandy, as the team's physical therapist, was bound by a very similar code of ethics and professional conduct. For example, New Zealand Sports Physiotherapists work under an ethical code that states that individuals working in the profession must:

- be 'aware of the limits of their clinical competence and sports-specific knowledge at varying levels of competition and refer to, or seek advice from an appropriately skilled professional as required';
- 'work within their scope of practice, and ensure that they maintain their knowledge and skills through regular continuing professional development';
- 'not undermine relationships between another sports health care provider and their patient' (Physiotherapy New Zealand, 2019).

Such approaches adopted by professional associations could be viewed as isolationist (i.e. deliberately setting themselves apart), and have implications for those professionals, like SCCs, who are required to collaborate, work, and function with colleagues in multi- or interprofessional teams.

Providing opportunities for individual professionals to work within a team is not the same as having them work as a team (Wilhelmsson et al., 2012). Interestingly, Reid et al. (2004) speculated that professional teams may often be just a by-product of assembling a wide range of professional services, and that multi/interprofessional teams may have often not been adequately conceptualised or embraced. Wilhelmsson et al. (2012) suggested that some form of organisational infrastructure may need to be (re)negotiated and agreed upon for the sake of all parties; in particular for the benefit of the athletes. If, for example, a sport organisation failed to adequately conceptualise or embrace its professional team(s), then athletes can be unintentionally placed in situations where they feel pressured to 'choose' who to trust, and at times that choice may not be endorsed by the coach or professional support staff (Reid et al., 2004). In the pedagogical case, this might explain why Bronwyn perceives Sandy's practices to be undermining, and to undermine her role as the SCC, in the eyes of some of the athletes.

Further, failure of organisations to adequately conceptualise or embrace the professional team(s) can provide opportunities for the actions of individual professionals to influence collaborative working approaches. Bos-de Vos et al. (2019) suggest that these micro-practices by professionals can be constructive or destructive. In relation to the latter, they state that professionals who seek to cast other professionals in a negative light often do so with the aim of strengthening their own claims as a logical professional choice. Professions may also elect to (re)frame emergent areas using their professional reputation, thereby extending their traditional services or occupying a particular domain of work. This can be seen in the pedagogical case where return-to-play is a relatively new and emergent area that is not specifically covered in the scopes of practice of medical, physical therapy or S&C professionals. From Bronwyn's perspective, Sandy is staking a personal and professional claim for this area of work. When a profession reframes their activities, there are possibilities for role ambiguities. Eys et al. (2006) point out that roles can be organised around performing core responsibilities relative to the group's objectives, or they can be socio-emotional in orientation, promoting harmony and integration within the group. While role ambiguity is often viewed negatively in terms of productivity and social cohesion, Fletcher and Wagstaff (2009) suggest that role ambiguity and conflict can provide the impetus for reconsidering policies and structures, as well as inter- and intra-group relationships. Similarly, others have viewed 'friction' (Asad & Le Dantec, 2019) or 'interruptions' (Biesta, 2006) as productive (see Byrne & Cassidy, 2017). This supports the claim that collaborative working approaches, despite the potential for tension, can provide an impetus for the beneficial reimagining of professional roles within a teamwork setting (Bos-de Vos et al., 2019; Reay et al., 2017).

Viewing the tension as productive might also encourage individuals to reconsider the role they play, for example, when the creation of an athlete-centred coaching environment becomes mandated. Bronwyn is frustrated by what she sees as Sandy, the dietitian and the sports psychologist, straying into providing conditioning and injury advice, and therefore occupying what Bronwyn would consider to be her domain of work. If the expected practices are not compatible with current practices, then this can create boundary conflicts or confusion (Fletcher & Wagstaff, 2009). While boundary conflicts and tension may provoke professional insecurities, some are still optimistic that working across boundaries has the potential to yield more positives than maintaining the status quo. For example, Bos-de Vos et al. (2019) suggest that the micro-practices of professionals working in collaborative ways with other professionals may mean that they have made a conscious choice to 'pioneer role boundaries' by offering to provide new services, or by negotiating new opportunities for collaboration. This work can be considered as 'boundary work'. To understand the following discussion on boundary work, it is worth noting that our understanding of boundaries has been informed by Akkerman and Bakker (2011) who define them as 'sociocultural differences between practices leading to discontinuities in actions and interactions' (p. 133). The benefits of undertaking boundary work are not just that it potentially builds collaborations. Rather, for some learning theorists (e.g. Engestrom, 2001; Roth & Lee, 2007; Wenger, 1998), boundaries 'are potential resources for learning, as they can trigger efforts – of individuals, groups, or large systems – to cross boundaries' (Akkerman & Bruining, 2016, p. 245).

Boundary work

The way in which people can work and learn in groups was discussed in Chapter 3, where we provided a brief outline of community of practice (CoP) (Lave & Wenger, 1991; Wenger, 1998; Wenger et al., 2002). From the pedagogical case, it can be seen that despite Bronwyn and Sandy working in the same environment, i.e. the Scorpions netball club, they do not genuinely work in a CoP because they are not exhibiting the three dimensions that Wenger (1998) lists as a requirement of a CoP, namely being *mutually engaged* in a *joint enterprise* in which they have a *shared repertoire* of practices, e.g. tools, routines and regimes. In the literature, it is clear that, over the years, as the concept of CoP has become more sophisticated, the links between CoPs, boundary work and learning have become more apparent

(Lave & Wenger, 1991; Wenger, 1998, 2010; Wenger-Trayner & Wenger-Trayner, 2015; Wenger et al., 2002). This is illustrated in the following quote.

> The term boundary often has negative connotations because it conveys limitation and lack of access. But the very notion of community of practice implies the existence of boundary. Unlike the boundaries of organizational units, which are usually well defined because affiliation is officially sanctioned, the boundaries of communities of practice are usually rather fluid. They arise from different enterprises; different ways of engaging with one another, different histories, repertoires, ways of communicating, and capabilities. That these boundaries are often unspoken does not make them less significant.
> (Wenger, 2010, p. 125)

Wenger (1998) discussed in detail the processes and practices associated with crossing boundaries, but later asked the question, 'Why focus on boundaries?' (Wenger, 2010), to which he replied that boundaries 'connect communities' as well as provide 'learning opportunities'. These learning opportunities occur in a very *Goldilocks and Three Bears* sort of way, i.e. too hot, too cold and just right. He explained:

> [a]t the boundaries, competence and experience tend to diverge: a boundary interaction is usually an experience of being exposed to a foreign competence. . . . If competence and experience are too close, if they always match, not much learning is likely to take place. There are no challenges; the community is losing its dynamism and the practice is in danger of becoming stale. Conversely, if experience and competence are too disconnected, if the distance is too great, not much learning is likely to take place either . . . Learning at boundaries is likely to be maximized for individuals and communities when experience and competence are in close tension.
> (p. 126)

Like Wenger, Beck (2000) was also interested in the opportunities that can arise around points of tension. Beck explored what it means to live and work in the rapidly changing social world, which includes the changing nature of work. He examined the way in which, in the modern world, work practices have become 'unstable', and he highlighted how this instability can result in an environment where a person's skills can suddenly be devalued and positions obliterated. Beck noted that while these changing and destabilising practices can be extremely challenging, they also can provide opportunities for developing new ideas and ways of working. However, for these opportunities to occur, there has to be a commitment to provide an environment in which everyone can be included in the process of developing new ideas and ways of working. Many people working in the sports and coaching contexts are acutely aware of the instability of work environments. Often the win-loss record of a team, or athlete, can determine the futures of the sports coaches and support personnel. Nonetheless, exciting opportunities can occur when a group of related professionals genuinely work together for a common purpose, i.e. the betterment of the athlete(s).

It is apparent that in some SCC communities there is an appetite for new ways of working with groups of professionals for the betterment of the athlete. One example is the conceptual model outlined by Arvinen-Barrow and Clement (2015) for the multidisciplinary management of sports injury. While they advocate for the various disciplines to work together for the benefit of athletes, their model still reinforces traditional roles, with primary and secondary rehabilitation teams. They explain that in the initial stages of recovery and rehabilitation, the physiotherapist will, with other medical staff, lead the management of the athlete's injury. But, what could these initial stages of recovery look like if the SCC, with their knowledge of the sport as well as the physical and physiological demands and forces involved in the sports action, was involved in rehabilitation and the return-to-play assessment? Also, what if the fitness maintenance work, overseen by the SCC, was incorporated early in the injury tissue healing and repair stage, under the direction of the physiotherapist? The model proposed by Arvinen-Barrow and Clement (2015), and our subsequent questions, highlight how challenging it is to work outside of one's primary profession. While it is important to recognise that the demarcation of boundaries is often 'ideological', it is still worthwhile to explore the potential of, and possible strategies for, collaborating and undertaking boundary crossing work.

Boundary crossing

As alluded to in the previous section, the value of exploring the concept of boundary crossing is its potential for developing a greater sense of how, in this case, professionals learn (Akkerman & Bakker, 2011). We contend that understanding how SCCs learn (signature pedagogies) provides opportunities to support them to develop their professional voice and become willing, open and confident to collaborate with colleagues from professional domains other than their own. To successfully achieve this outcome, Akkerman and Bruining (2016, p. 245) suggested 'four learning mechanisms' need to occur in boundary crossing situations. These include:

1   'a process of mutual *identification*. . . . In this process, people are concerned with (re) defining the way in which the intersecting practices are different from one another and how they can legitimately coexist'.
2   'a process of *coordination* of the different practices that can take place. . . . [Here people attempt to] find a communicative connection between actors or translate between them, efforts to organise the activity as smoothly as possible, and attempts to create routines to rely on'.
3   'a *reflection* process . . . [which is about an] openness to take up others' perspectives to look at one's own practice'.
4   'a *transformation* process, in the sense that change becomes visible either in terms of changes in the existing practices or in terms of new in-between practices that are created'.

Let us consider for a moment what incorporating these four mechanisms might mean for the Scorpions netball club, which was the context for this chapter's pedagogical case. As an organisation that employs professionals from various domains, the club could explicitly incorporate these mechanisms into their strategic plans and employees' job descriptions. By doing so, all employees could be held accountable for how they are working collaboratively across professional boundaries. Furthermore, by requiring all employees to report on their progress on implementing these strategies, the Scorpions netball club establishes an expectation, and provides opportunities, for employees to find their professional voice.

Akkerman and Bruining (2016) made a further contribution to our understanding of boundary crossing by proposing, and illustrating, the ways in which it can occur at multiple levels, i.e. intrapersonal, interpersonal and institutional, either independently or simultaneously. Drawing on this work, and applying it to the S&C context, we can see that boundary crossing at the institutional level requires a commitment from 'multiple organisations or organizational units' (p. 247). For example, the NSCA or support staff in a sport organisation like Netball New Zealand would be required to begin searching for ways to align practices within the organisation, a process that would also include their reconsidering its organisational identity, such as what position it holds on weight training for children. At the interpersonal level, boundary crossing requires 'actions and interactions between specific groups of people from different practices' (p. 247). In the S&C context, this might mean that SCCs, physical therapists, mental skills trainers, head coaches and assistant coaches would agree to work on a particular issue together, and in doing so create a collaborative process that would necessitate their developing some sort of relationship with each other. Boundary crossing at the intrapersonal level requires people to become brokers (see Chapter 1 for what this looks like in an S&C context) and facilitate connections and collaborations. Being a broker is not easy because it can be isolating, and as a consequence it can take its toll of the psychological wellbeing of the broker. While boundary crossing can occur at multiple levels and either independently or simultaneously, it has been suggested that boundary crossing can occur at the intra- and interpersonal level without it necessarily occurring at the institutional level. Yet, boundary crossing can occur at the institutional level only when both inter- and intrapersonal boundary crossing has already occurred (Akkerman & Bruining, 2016; Gustavsson & Säfsten, 2017).

Summary

Finding a comfortable professional identity within any work environment can be challenging. We noted in this chapter that a professional work team is not merely a collection of like-minded individuals 'thrown' together; to work successfully together requires an organisational infrastructure that supports collegial endeavours, and there needs to be a collective will to collaborate and share ideas and practices. We suggest in this chapter that professional conflicts can arise when a professional inaccurately names and frames an issue. Specifically in our pedagogical case, the SCC appears to have framed the problem based on technical efficiency and using a 'who knows best' argument. We contend that it may be more productive to frame such an issue as a moral challenge that considers the rights and needs of professional colleagues. This chapter also discussed 'boundary work' which we situated as a potential opportunity and possibly the genesis of productive connections and interprofessional collaborations. The mechanisms for helping to realise boundary crossings are presented. We question in our discussion whether professional organisations may at times be counterproductive to boundary crossing collaboration, by organisationally attempting to secure and protect work boundaries for their membership.

End of chapter tasks

1   In your country, there are likely to be regulations governing numerous fields or professions such as medicine, physiotherapy, psychotherapy, teaching, real estate, electricians and plumbers, but perhaps not for S&C or sport coaching. See if any government regulations exist or if there are standards and guidelines provided by a professional organisation (e.g. NSCA, UKSCA, ASCA). Compare these regulations or standards with those of another, more formalised and regulated profession such as physiotherapy or psychology. What are some implications of these similarities and discrepancies for working on an interprofessional team?

2   Consider your own academic preparation to become an SCC. Analyse the curricula to see how much time, and to what extent, biopsychosocial-pedagogical aspects are developed. Discuss what you find in relation to working on interprofessional teams.
3   Use Akkerman and Bruining's (2016) 'four learning mechanisms' (i.e. identification, coordination, reflection, transformation) to analyse a case (i.e. your own, a peer's, an evaluation of a nearby staff) of boundary crossing in a sport setting that includes an SCC.
4   As you progress in your career and develop a vast knowledge base and a deep understanding of many things, how will you likewise develop an attitude of humility and appreciation of the contributions of others?

References

Abbott, A. (1988). *The System of Professions: Essay on the Division of Expert Labour*, Chicago, IL: Chicago University Press.
Akkerman, S.F., & Bakker, A. (2011). Boundary crossing and boundary objects, *Review of Educational Research*, 81: 132–169.
Akkerman, S.F., & Bruining, T. (2016). Multilevel boundary crossing in a professional development school partnership, *Journal of the Learning Sciences*, 25(2): 240–284.
Arvinen-Barrow, M., & Clement, D. (2015). A preliminary investigation into athletic trainers' views and experiences of a multidisciplinary team approach to sports injury, *Rehabilitation Athletic Training & Sports Health Care*, 7(3): 97–107.
Asad, M., & Le Dantec, C.A. (2019). 'This is shared work': Negotiating boundaries in a social service intermediary organization, *Media and Communication*, 7(3): 69–78.
Beck, U. (2000). *The Brave New World of Work*, Patrick Camiler (trans.), Cambridge: Polity Press.
Biesta, G.J.J. (2006). *Beyond Learning: Democratic Education for a Human Future*. Boulder, CO: Paradigm.
Bos-de Vos, M., Lieftink, B.M., & Lauche, K. (2019). How to claim what is mine: Negotiating professional roles in inter-organizational projects, *Journal of Professions and Organization*, 6: 128–155.
Byrne, G., & Cassidy, T. (2017). 'Pleased to be sacked': Coach Pat Lam's 'learnings' and the evolution of a professional rugby union organisation, *International Sport Coaching Journal*, 4(3): 326–334.
Engestrom, Y. (2001). Expansive learning at work: Toward an activity theoretical reconceptualization, *Journal of Education and Work*, 14(1): 133–156.
Eys, M.A., Beauchamp, M.R., & Bray, S.R. (2006). A review of team roles in sport. In S. Hanton & S.D. Mellalieu (eds.), *Literature Reviews in Sport Psychology*, Hauppauge, NY: Nova Science, pp. 227–255.
Fletcher, D., & Wagstaff, C. (2009). Organizational psychology in elite sport: Its emergence, application and future, *Psychology of Sport and Exercise*, 10: 427–434.
Gustavsson, M., & Säfsten, K. (2017). The learning potential of boundary crossing in the context of product introduction, *Vocations and Learning*, 10(2): 1–18.
Lave, J., & Wenger, E. (1991). *Situated Learning: Legitimate Peripheral Participation*, Cambridge: Cambridge University Press.
Lawson, H.A. (1984). Problem-setting for physical education and sport, *Quest*, 36: 48–60.
Nancarrow, S., Booth, A., Ariss, S., Smith, T., Enderby, P., & Roots, A. (2013). Ten principles of good interdisciplinary team work, *Human Resources for Health*, 11(19): 1–11.
Phelan, S., & Griffiths, M. (2019). Reconceptualising professional learning through knowing-in-practice: A case study of a coaches high performance centre, *Sports Coaching Review*, 8(2): 103–123.
Physiotherapy New Zealand. (2019). Sports physiotherapy code of conduct, physiotherapy New Zealand. https://sportsphysiotherapy.org.nz/sportsphysiotherapy.org.nz/documents/Sports-Physiotherapy-Code-of-Conduct_v-Dec-2013.pdf.
Quinn, J., Anderson, P., & Finkelstein, S. (1996). Managing the professional intellect: Making the most of the best, *Harvard Business Review*, Mar.–Apr.: 71–80.

Reay, T., Goodrick, E., Waldorff, S.B., et al. (2017). Getting leopards to change their spots: Co-creating a new professional role identity, *Academy of Management Journal*, 60(3): 1043–1070.

Reid, C., Stewart, E., & Thorne, G. (2004). Multidisciplinary sport science teams in elite sport: Comprehensive servicing or conflict and confusion? *The Sport Psychologist*, 18(2): 204–217.

Roth, W-M., & Lee, Y-J. (2007). 'Vygotsky's neglected legacy': Cultural-historical activity theory, *Review of Educational Research*, 77(2): 186–232.

Triplett, N.T., & Chandler, B. (2017). NSCA strength and conditioning professional standards and guidelines, *Strength & Conditioning Journal*, 39(6): 1–24.

Wenger, E. (1998). *Communities of Practice: Learning, Meaning, and Identity*, Cambridge: Cambridge University Press.

Wenger, E. (2010). Communities of practice and social learning systems: The career of a concept. In C. Blackmore (ed.), *Social Learning Systems and Communities of Practice*, London: Springer.

Wenger, E., McDermott, R., & Snyder, W. (2002). *Cultivating Communities of Practice: A Guide to Managing Knowledge*, Boston: Harvard University Press.

Wenger-Trayner, E., & Wenger-Trayner, B. (2015). Learning in a landscape of practice: A framework. In E. Wenger-Trayner, M. Fenton-O'Creevy, S. Hutchinson, C. Kubiak, & B. Wenger-Trayner (eds.), *Learning in Landscapes of Practice: Boundaries, Identity, and Knowledgeability in Practice-Based Learning*, London: Routledge.

Wilhelmsson, M., Pelling, S., Uhlin, L., et al. (2012). How to think about interprofessional competence: A metacognitive model, *Journal of Interprofessional Care*, 26: 85–91.

Wright, T., Trudel, P., & Culver, D. (2007). Learning how to coach: The different learning situations reported by youth ice hockey coaches, *Physical Education and Sport Pedagogy*, 12(2): 127–144.

Part 4
Conditioning across the lifespan

10 Healthy development of youth for sport

Introduction
Part 1: pedagogical case
Part 2: commentary

    Parenting

Deliberate practice
Early sampling and deliberate play
Fundamental movement skills
Summary
End of chapter tasks
References

Introduction

The pressure to succeed in sport, a desire to emulate elite athletes or the fear of being 'left behind' at an early age have resulted in many youth being introduced to purposeful fitness training and conditioning. While expert position statements might agree that S&C practices may not be physically harmful for youth (e.g. Faigenbaum et al., 2009), we argue that harm may present in other forms. Developing good physical activity habits, having fun and making sure 'the balance' is right are equally important considerations for youth. To help SCCs navigate these challenging issues, this chapter examines youth conditioning from sociocultural and pedagogical perspectives by raising questions regarding parental influences, and the need for, and wisdom of, early specialisation and deliberate practice.

Part 1: pedagogical case

Scene from a suburban home:

Reg: (throwing a bag of sports gear into the laundry) Sorry we're late. I got into a bit of a 'discussion' with Nick's coach after practice.
Bronny: OK, but let's not get into that now. Whitney and I have been waiting on you guys for dinner. I'll call her. You go and wash up for dinner Nick!

Later, after the family had left the dinner table.

Bronny: So, what was this drama at Nick's rugby training?
Reg: Oh, it was just the way that their coach runs the kids' trainings. This was the first time all season that I've had the chance to watch Nick's practice. Afterwards,

	I thought I'd offer the coach a few suggestions and observations, but he didn't take it well – got very defensive. Nick's been down there at rugby training for about an hour and a half all told, all for about seven minutes of rugby action! The coach has the girls and boys lined up for virtually the whole practice. They stand and wait in line to touch the ball or execute a skill drill. If they're not lined up, he's got them doing fitness drills over and over. I'm just not convinced that Nick or the other kids are really getting much from those 90 minutes.
Bronny:	So, what did you suggest? You were polite I hope?
Reg:	Of course – yeah, I thanked him for giving up his time and coaching the team. I suggested that he could maybe go with smaller groups and have a few more balls in play so that there was less waiting around time, and so the kids can have more time actually doing something meaningful and sport specific. That didn't go down well, and then when I questioned whether 11-year-old kids really need to be doing fitness drills during rugby practice time, he really lost the plot [lost his cool]. I mean the kids spent a good 35 minutes just on fitness training tonight. Come on! Active 11-year-olds don't need a lot of extra fitness to play this game. Nick is already getting a ton of fitness work with his wrestling trainings and most of his teammates are also involved with other sports. It just seems so 'old school'. He's got them running up and down the sand dunes, doing 'down and ups' and sit-ups until they were groaning and couldn't move. It seems kind of like punishment. That's not fun for a kid – I think he's missing the essence of kids' sport.
Bronny:	Sure – how did he take your criticism of his focus on fitness?
Reg:	Not well, really. He went on about all of the rugby coaching courses that he had been doing and how modern youth were lazy and how a lack of fitness was letting the team down in games. So, he really seemed pretty defensive and kind of set in his ways. I think he's seeing how senior rugby teams train and not thinking about the fact that he's actually dealing with 11-year-olds. We didn't part well. Of course, he played the old – 'if you think you can do better, you're welcome to take over' card.
Bronny:	Hmmm, well Nick still seems to enjoy his rugby. I've never really heard him complain about practices or the fitness work.
Reg:	Yeah, that's true, but I'm wondering how long that love affair with rugby can last. You know I was thinking on the drive back about my childhood memories of rugby. Growing up in a farming community, rugby was the only sport accessible to us. Hell, rugby was all we thought about in those days – the sport dominated. The players on my club team were spread far around that community – most of us lived at least a 30-minute drive from the club. So, the only time that we got together was for our Saturday morning games – no practices at all to interfere with our enjoyment. But man, we played rugby constantly. There was always an impromptu game of rugby going on at school during morning and afternoon intervals and at lunch time. As soon as we got home, my brother and I were out in a field kicking a ball around and taking shots at the goal posts that my dad had made for us. Most weekends we'd have a marathon game of rugby with friends, cousins, whoever we could find. And wow, in those small-sided games we were continuously running, catching, passing, kicking, inventing new moves. Fitness drills never entered our head, but we never 'ran out of steam' and we never stopped running. Fast forward now to Nick's era and his only time with a rugby ball is those 90-minute practices and games. He reckons they play pick-up games at school

occasionally, but he doesn't join in – he says the bigger kids tend to dominate. Nick's learning how to run and do push-ups, but I don't think he's learning much about playing and enjoying the sport. I don't know, maybe I'm living in the past too much!

Bronny: Well it's kind of hard for me to relate. Remember, my main sport was track. I didn't have a great interest in team sports and it was only when I moved up to middle school and blitzed the field in the 800 m that I kind of got shoulder tapped by an athletics club. And wow I really enjoyed that. We got a lot of coaching, but when I think about it, track was mainly about conditioning – although we didn't think of it that way. We did long runs, intervals, speed sessions, starts, and we kind of understood that this is what would help us run faster. We learned to push ourselves and I seem to remember it being six days per week, but we were all in it together. While it wasn't fun, fun, I really enjoyed the discipline and commitment and feeling fit. I don't think I ever missed a session. You know, maybe that wasn't such a good thing. The total focus on running did mean that I became obsessed with my weight and somehow became convinced that I needed to be lighter to go faster. No one told me that directly, but perhaps I picked up some subtle messages about weight. I'm pretty sure that starving myself didn't help my running or my long-term health and wellbeing. You know, I can't believe my parents didn't pick up on that food obsession and actually do something about it. I also played field hockey through high school. That was much more like your rugby experience, although my family lived in town and close to school, so we had a couple of practices each week. But practices were mainly games and scrimmages against the boys' team or small-sided games. I don't remember doing a lot of standing around or fitness drills. So, I do get what you are saying; hockey was fun! Fitness was always really just part of our warm-ups and really our own responsibility; the focus was on learning to play hockey as a team.

I think Whitney is getting a similar experience to mine. I've watched her ballet classes and her netball training. Her ballet is a bit more like my track experience. A lot of repetition, a lot of discipline but that combination is working on developing their strength, balance, and control. I think Whitney loves ballet, but needs netball as a bit of a social and fun outlet. Sure, there's some standing around and lining up for netball passing drills, but by and large, they are all engaged, and the coaches leave it up to the girls to work on their own fitness. Although recently they've introduced a 'Netballsmart' dynamic warm-up that kind of works on basic movement skills. It seemed to consume a lot of time and drain the fun. Of course, her ballet teacher would much rather that she gave up the other activities and concentrated on ballet. Whitney is not willing to do that, and good on her.

Did I tell you she has been asking about joining a gym lately? Quite a few of her friends and netball teammates have gym memberships. I get the sense that other parents are really pushing the fitness thing. I think Whitney already has enough going on in her busy life, and a part of me is a bit dubious about the gym environment and their emphasis on the 'body beautiful' [aesthetic appeal and looking good]. I would hate for Whitney to get caught up in the weight and body image thing the way that I did.

Reg: Yeah, I think you're right – Whitney has got good balance there. But you know, Whitney might find the gym thing is a real positive for her ballet and netball. After all, she's 15, she is probably ready for a bit of resistance and circuit training. Ballet is pretty hard on the body, and that hockey turf is pretty unforgiving. I think gym work might help with reducing the possibilities of injuries. But Nick, at 11 years old – I don't think he's old enough or ready for the fitness emphasis in sport. I'm not sure that fitness drills at his age are that healthy or helpful. I want him to love the game and get some of that enjoyment that you and I have had from sports. I think I'll quietly reach out to some of the other parents to get their thoughts on the fitness emphasis. Also, I might contact my buddy, Garth. We lived in a residential college together at Otago – he studied physical education and went on to become a strength and conditioning coach in rugby. I'm sure he would have the knowledge and experience to give us a steer on this.

Several days later, following a phone call to Garth, Reg received a lengthy email in response to his queries. It was clear from the email's detail that Garth had encountered Reg's concerns before and had given them careful consideration.

Dear Reg,

Thanks for your recent call – lovely to hear from you again. I'm really pleased that you reached out with those questions, as those are some of the issues that regularly trouble me. I routinely encounter parents seeking guidance to develop the fitness of their children. Although I realise that they are wanting the best for their offspring, I really find some of the trends in contemporary youth sport disturbing. For children, say under the age of 13, I see the primary role for an SCC to really be educating the parents about the pros and cons of early specialisation and fitness training. In that respect, I've been preparing for a talk that I'm about to give at the local high school – I even hoped that I might be able to turn it into an article eventually. What follows are my notes for that talk – I think you'll find that some of the research will resonate with Bronny and your experiences with your kids' sports.

Part 2: commentary

Parenting

It is regularly acknowledged in the coaching literature that parents and guardians have a clear and significant influence on the sporting pathways of children (e.g. Baxter-Jones & Maffuli, 2003; Gould et al., 2016; Positive Coaching Alliance, 2019) and therefore youth attitudes to, and engagement with, S&C. From tacitly, or intentionally, steering them towards certain sports and activities, to funding, transporting, supporting and organising, parents are inextricably involved in the sports that are selected and pursued by their children. Studies on sport coaching and participation have shown that parental influence can also derail and interfere with a child's sport development (e.g. Dorsch et al., 2018; Harwood & Knight, 2015). With changing circumstances, parental involvement can morph from positive and supporting to negative and controlling, particularly as pressure mounts with the child's progression through a sport (Gould et al., 2016). In recognising the key roles that parents play, Dorsch et al. (2018) urge that parents should not be viewed from a deficit perspective and instantly problematised. Rather, they should be considered as a coach's ally and asset. Working in a junior tennis setting, Gould et al. (2016) sought to create a coaching environment that was conducive to optimal parent involvement. This involved seeking to periodically inform and educate parents and to provide them with guidance on what parents could do (as well as should not do) to help support their child's tennis experiences and progression. This is not to suggest that parents should become de facto SCCs, but rather someone who assists with decision making and supports appropriate habits.

An example of this ethos is the Positive Coaching Alliance (PCA), an organisation that acknowledges the importance of educating the family of the young people who play in youth sports, as well as educates coaches and challenges the culture of 'win at all costs'. Jim Thompson, the PCA founder, talks about being a 'Double Goal Coach', which means the coach has two goals: first, winning on the scoreboard, and second, promoting good life lessons. He also describes a 'Second goal parent' as one who lets the coaches and athletes focus on the scoreboard, but who 'relentlessly' focuses on the second goal of promoting good life lessons. He provides the example of what that could look like at the end of a game when their child does not play as well as they had expected; 'the parent could begin the conversation with "you know, one of the things I like about you is that you're the kind of person who doesn't get discouraged easily. You're the kind of person who bounces back when things go wrong"' (PCA, 2019). To facilitate the education of family members associated with youth sport, the PCA offers a 'toolkit' that includes ideas for how to re-define a winner, fill the emotional tank, honour the game and debrief the game.

It may be that the most important contribution an SCC can make in the area of the development and wellbeing of young athletes is through educating parents and guardians – providing reality checks. Depending on their level of engagement, an SCC in collaboration with the sport coach can help parents to understand the overall plan for their child's sport development and provide guidance on the elements that typically facilitate or hinder that development. In terms of S&C, correcting disinformation and misinformation may be an important preemptive area for education and discussion. We believe that this has become even more important in contemporary contexts where contrary information and opinions, often wrapped up in commercial interests, are freely available. These are commonly highlighted and propagated through electronic and printed media. For example, numerous commercial facilities offer performance-based conditioning programmes for youth, targeting children as young as five. One would assume that a five-year-old is not making the decision to enrol in, and pay for, such programmes. Knight et al. (2016) identified that parental involvement varies widely and will often reflect the previous experiences and values of parents. In that respect, SCCs should be particularly mindful of individualising messages when communicating with parents. We suggest the following key education points for sports parents.

Deliberate practice

There continues to be considerable debate concerning the most suitable sporting pathway for children and youth. The two primary, and seemingly divergent, pathways are to encourage either early specialisation or early sport sampling (generalisation). The former has predominantly been encouraged by interpretations of the work by Ericsson et al. (1993) and their claim that deliberate practice, and lots of it, is critical to expert performance. While Ericsson and colleagues advocated for deliberate practice, they did acknowledge that deliberate practice could include activities that were not intrinsically motivating, that required high levels of effort and attention and that did not lead immediately to social or financial rewards. While their work focused on music and chess expertise, the emergent 10,000 hours or 10 years of deliberate practice concept, has been directly adopted for other endeavours such as sport performance (Malina, 2010). The 10,000 hours concept has also been popularised in non-fictional works (e.g. Gladwell, 2008). Despite widespread criticism of this concept (e.g. Malina, 2010), parents in particular have fixated on the 10,000 hours threshold and interpreted this as a basis for pursuing more sporting engagement for their children, often without consideration of the possible consequences (Nyland, 2014).

While parents may often be the ones pushing for more sport participation, Nyland (2014) points out that coaches are the most likely to encourage early sport specialisation. That may be a reflection of coaches' abilities to spot latent talent, or they may simply be attempting to build as large a pool of potential talent as possible within their coaching squads. There are certainly some sports (e.g. figure skating and gymnastics) where peak performance appears to occur at younger ages, and where earlier specialisation seems to be necessary to success (LaPrade et al., 2016). LaPrade et al. (2016) characterised early sport specialisation as prepubertal children participating in intensive training or competition for more than eight months of the year, and with a level of engagement that precludes playing other sports. For SCCs the concern may be that physical conditioning becomes just another proxy means of 'depositing' or accumulating more hours of sporting engagement. There are of course highly publicised examples of early sport specialisation that have resulted in outstanding success (e.g. Tiger Woods, Michelle Kwan). But, as Gilbert (2017) pointed out, early specialisers like Tiger Woods and Ronaldinho still developed creative skills through unstructured free play. As Malina (2010) emphasises, however, it is often the success stories from early specialisation that are publicised. We hear fewer stories from the many potentially great athletes who specialised at a young age only to fall by the wayside. While there are likely gains from intensive training and coaching, it is also important to consider what might be lost in the process. Nyland argues that violinists and chess moves are one thing, but these individuals are not enduring the high and repetitive loading of young joints and musculotendinous units that would be required of young sportspeople (Nyland, 2014). Sports specialisation consumes time; it also takes away opportunities for rest, recovery and the simple contemplation and enjoyment of just being a kid (Nyland, 2014). Hours committed to early sport specialisation can lead to social isolation of children and a concomitant fostering of dependence on others. These factors can compromise the development of important skills that would normally contribute to later life resilience (Malina, 2010). Given that the chances of reaching the elite level of a sport are low, Wiersma (2000) challenges early specialisation, asking whether it is ethical to be advocating this when around 98% of participants are unlikely to benefit. To date, there has been little research to support or refute early specialisation in many sports (Feeley et al., 2015), so the points raised next are important for SCCs to consider when advising on S&C for children.

Early sampling and deliberate play

In Côté's (1999) discussions of children's sport participation, he emphasised 'early sampling', which he later described as comprising two fundamental elements; 'involvement in various sports' and 'participation in deliberate play' (Côté et al., 2009, p. 7). Côté and his colleagues claimed that when children participate in various sports, they 'experience a number of different physical, cognitive, affective, and psycho-social environments', which in turn provides them with opportunities to develop the 'physical, personal, and mental skills required to specialize in one sport during adolescence' (p. 9). The second element of early sampling is deliberate play and is reflected in activities like backyard cricket and 'pick-up' 3v3 basketball. According to Côté et al. (2007) deliberate play is 'intrinsically motivating . . . provide[s] immediate gratification . . . [and is] specifically designed to maximise enjoyment' (pp. 185–186). What is more, the 'informality' of deliberate play provides children with an opportunity to 'engage in sports with minimal equipment, in any kind of space, with any number of players, and with players of different ages and sizes' (Côté et al., 2009, p. 9). Informal play is also likely to contribute to fitness and provide individuals with experiences in regulating their emotional and cognitive responses to competition (Côté et al., 2007). While deliberate play is unstructured and play-like, it should not be confused with play associated with infancy. Nor should deliberate play be thought of as a mechanism to increase the chances of 'falling behind'. DiFiori et al. (2017) maintain that deliberate play will instead provide children with a diverse and responsive foundation for later competitive sport development. Deliberate play enables children to experience enjoyment, as well as the freedom to experiment with movements and tactics without the constraints of structured sessions or being concerned about perfecting the execution of a technical movement (Santos et al., 2017). This license to informally hone new skill elements, which is unlikely to be encouraged or practiced in more organised settings, is a salient feature of deliberate play (Côté et al., 2007).

Many of the above benefits of deliberate play were highlighted when Coutinho et al. (2016) explored the practice experiences of Portuguese volleyball players. In their study, they found that the opportunity for children to spend time together enjoying spontaneously created games – games that were constantly being adapted to satisfy changing contexts (different locations and spaces, varying numbers and interacting with older peers) – provided the children with opportunities to be inventive in developing physical, technical and tactical abilities. Coutinho and colleagues argued that the nature of those practice activities had a greater impact on skill acquisition than the time spent in formalised practice. Such outcomes would arguably have been more difficult to acquire in adult structured sports. Although structured sports may be well intentioned, their primary focus on performance tends to overshadow the importance of enjoyment, participation and personal development to children's sporting experiences. However, early sampling and deliberate play does not suit participants in all sports, particularly those where peak performance usually occurs before full physical maturation. For example, in women's gymnastics and figure skating, as well as contemporary snow sports like the Big Air and Half Pipe, peak performance 'generally occurs in the middle and late teens, thus indicating the value of early specialization' (Côté et al., 2009, p. 11).

The Australasian College of Sport and Exercise Physicians (ACSEP) compiled a position statement on sport Specialisation in Young Athletes, identifying the potential harms associated with young athletes involved in sport specialisation. In particular they suggested that highly specialised young athletes were more susceptible to overuse injuries. Along with physical harms, the ACSEP position statement also drew on evidence of general harms associated with early sport specialisation, specifically a lower overall perception of health, earlier cessation of sport and possible burnout, less fun from sport participation and less psychological satisfaction with sport. Of particular interest to SCCs is that the ACSEP noted that resistance training has been shown to reduce injury risk (by up to 68%), contribute to sport performance and health, and accelerate physical literacy development. The ACSEP reminds practitioners that they have a 'duty of care' for young athletes and should discourage specialisation until after the age of 12, consider each individual's social, emotional and psychological maturity as well as age, and use simple guidelines to minimise the risk of issues relating to early specialisation, sport specialisation and training volume. It is not only the medical profession that has articulated their stance on early specialisation. The International Society for Sport Psychology (ISSP) also published a position paper on young athletes specialising at an early age in a single sport (Côté et al., 2009). In this position paper, the ISSP advocates for a 'comprehensive' approach to be taken when working with young athletes, one that recognises the complex interplay between the environment, the task and the person.

Recently, Gilbert (2017) discussed sampling and documented the growing trend of coaches and athletes recognising the value of adopting a sampling approach to sport participation in their early years of playing sport. He went on to point out that 'most college and Olympic athletes in the United States also played multiple sports up to high school, and college coaches typically prefer recruiting multisport athletes' (p. 114). The call being made for sampling is not just restricted to sports, but within sports as well. Some successful coaches and sports clubs are adopting a 'position-sampling approach to athlete development . . . e.g. Sevilla Football Club in Spain, one of the world premier football clubs does not designate athletes to a particular position until the ages of 16 or 17' (Gilbert, 2017). The International Olympic Committee identified sport sampling as a key recommendation on its consensus statement on athlete development (Bergon et al., 2015).

Fundamental movement skills

A criticism of early sport specialisation is that youth opting to intensively train for one sport are unlikely to be exposed to the range of movement experiences that would be expected with a range of different sports. Anecdotally, this deficit has been associated with an increased risk of injury and reduced activity options in later life (e.g. Jayanthi et al., 2015). The logic presented is that single-sport athletes tend to place greater emphasis on intensive training and sports-specific skill development, which leaves little time or opportunity for learning fundamental movement skills (FMS; LaBella & Myer, 2017). Often associated and confused with being physically educated and having physical literacy (Robinson & Randall, 2017), the concept of FMS is intriguing. For some, the logic is appealing, while for others it represents reductionist thinking that possibly misinterprets sport and movement skills. To suggest that there are movement skills that are fundamental to all physical activity, and that these fundamentals need to be taught, makes several assumptions. It assumes that the question of movement skills and sport performance has been adequately and clearly framed (Chapter 3). Otherwise, how could we know what to measure, and how to measure it? Barnett et al. (2016) define fundamental motor skills as basic learned movement patterns that do not occur naturally and are argued to be foundational for more complex physical and sporting activities. But this definition raises a number of questions, including how the movements have been identified as being fundamental to all activities. Given the global differences in the sports adopted and played, how do FMS acknowledge cultural appropriateness? (Barnett et al., 2018). Are FMS stable abilities? Are they transferable across activities? What role does perceived FMS competence play in sporting ability and engagement? Are FMS dependent on thresholds of physical and fitness capabilities? What is the relationship between FMS products (test element), processes (learning element) and performances (sporting ability)?

Many sports bodies have adopted quasi-FMS programmes as part of injury prevention strategies (e.g. FIFA 11+, Netballsmart). These programmes often focus on warm-up and preparatory activities, usually with an explicit injury prevention objective. In respect of the latter, encouraging reductions of lower limb injury have been reported following FMS styled conditioning (McKay et al., 2019). Based on our critique of FMS in the previous paragraph, some SCCs, drawing on their exercise sciences understanding, may baulk at some of the FMS claims. We might, for example, attempt to reconcile the fact that there have been generations of elite athletes with exceptionally high levels of movement competency, but who were never explicitly taught fundamental movement skills. Discussions regarding the value and necessity of remedial fundamental movement skills could benefit from critical thinking. For example, in the field of motor control and motor learning, the Dynamical Systems Theory (DST) postulates that all movements depend on the dynamic interaction between the (moving) individual, the movement task to be performed and the environment in which it takes place (Sigmundsson et al., 2017). Ostensibly, DST suggests movement demands are episodic and unpredictable. Arguably, there is no harm in performing the FMS, but there are many research questions to be answered before there can be agreement over whether this is the most valuable use of a child's time during play.

Summary

Youth development and the place of S&C present some authentic challenges to an SCC's professional competence. We argue in this chapter that youth sport has been enveloped by a kind of dysfunctional norm, where specialisation, high training loads and adult-like conditioning practices have become more normalised. We argue that these trends are likely persuaded by popular culture and pseudoscientific arguments but can result in detrimental parental influences and injured, tired and disaffected young athletes. SCCs can get caught up in this messy reality, often by trying to do the 'right' thing in a 'wrong' situation. An SCC could easily engage with youth strength and conditioning, utilising their extensive knowledge and functional competence and believing that they are doing the right thing. However, our message in this chapter is that while it may be safe to engage in delivering S&C to youth in these environments, the challenge is to decide what is sensible and ethically acceptable. A competent S&C professional should have the ability to think in context (cognitive competence), be able to evaluate the benefit-to-risk balance of each situation (values and ethical competence, cultural competence), and ultimately be able to communicate with and gently educate (personal and behavioural competence) all parties with a vested interest in youth S&C.

End of chapter tasks

1   Educating parents on the biopsychosocial aspects of S&C was identified as an essential task of an SCC. Drawing on the research, create something concise and effective (e.g. infographic, flyer, video or cartoon) to address the key biopsychosocial aspects of youth S&C.
2   Sport and S&C can be very disciplinary and prescriptive, which can lead to negative outcomes. What are some ways you could integrate play, games, fun, friends and developing friendships, exploration, creativity, autonomy, throughout S&C activities?
3   In an ideal world, what should our sport and S&C activities look like throughout our lifetime (e.g. infant, toddler, child, adolescent, adulthood, masters)?
4   We often mistakenly believe we must do specific practices, in a specific and structured way, at an exact time. What are some biopsychosocial reasons this occurs? Imagine your job is to prepare SCCs for practice. How would you facilitate their knowledge and practice to become masters of their craft who exercise dynamic professional judgement, and not merely robots or technocrats?

References

Australasian College of Sport and Exercise Physicians. Position statement: Sport specialisation in young athletes. www.acsep.org.au/content/Document/Early%20Specialisation%20Position%20Statement.pdf (accessed 4 Dec. 2019).
Barnett, L.M., Lubans, D.R., Timperio, A., et al. (2018). What is the contribution of actual motor skill, fitness, and physical activity to children's self-perception of motor competence? *Journal of Motor Learning and Development*, 6: S461–S473.

Barnett, L.M., Stodden, D., Cohen, K., Smith, J., Lubans, D., Lenoir, M., Iivonen, S., Miller, A., & Laukkanen, A. (2016). Fundamental movement skills: An important focus, *Journal of Teaching in Physical Education*, 35(3): 219–225.

Baxter-Jones, A., & Maffulli, N. (2003). Parental influence on sport participation in elite young athletes, *Journal of Sports Medicine and Physical Fitness*, 43(2): 250–255.

Bergon, M., Mountjoy, M., Armstrong, N., et al. (2015). International Olympic committee consensus statement on youth athletic development, *British Journal of Sports Medicine*, 49: 843–851.

Côté, J. (1999). The influence of the family in the development of talent in sport, *The Sport Psychologist*, 13(4): 395–417.

Côté, J., Baker, J., & Abernethy, B. (2007). Practice and play in the development of sport expertise. In R.C. Eklund & G. Tenenbaum (eds.), *Handbook of Sport Psychology* (3rd ed.), Hoboken, NJ: John Wiley & Sons, Inc., pp. 184–202.

Côté, J., Lidor, R., & Hackfort, D. (2009). ISSP position stand: To sample or to specialize? Seven postulates about youth sport activities that lead to continued participation and elite performance, *International Journal or Sport and Exercise Psychology*, 9: 7–17.

Coutinho, P., Mesquita, I., Davids, K., et al. (2016). How structured and unstructured sport activities aid the development of expertise in volleyball players, *Psychology of Sport and Exercise*, 25: 51–59.

DiFiori, J.P., Brenner, J.S., Comstock, D., et al. (2017). Debunking early single sport specialisation and reshaping the youth sport experience: An NBA perspective, *British Journal of Sports Medicine*, 51(3): 142–143.

Dorsch, T.E., King, M.Q., Tulane, S., et al. (2018). Parent education in youth sport: A community case study of parents, coaches, and administrators, *Journal of Applied Sport Psychology*, 31(4): 427–450.

Ericsson, K.A., Krampe, R.T., & Tesch-Romer, C. (1993). The role of deliberate practice in the acquisition of expert performance, *Psychological Review*, 100(3): 363–406.

Faigenbaum, A., Kraemer, W.J., Blimkie, C.J., et al. (2009). Youth resistance training: Updated position statement, *Journal of Strength and Conditioning Research*, 23: S60–S79.

Feeley, B.T., Agel, J., & LaPrade, R.F. (2015). When is it too early for single sport specialization? *The American Journal of Sports Medicine*, 44(1): 234–241.

Gilbert, W. (2017). *Coaching Better Every Season: A Year-Round System for Athlete Development and Program Success*, Champaign, IL: Human Kinetics.

Gladwell, M. (2008). *Outliers: The Story of Success*, New York: Little, Brown and Company.

Gould, D., Pierce, S., Lauer, L., et al. (2016). Examining expert coaches' views of parent roles in 10-and-under tennis, *Sport, Exercise, and Performance Psychology*, 5(2): 89–106.

Harwood, C.G., & Knight, C.J. (2015). Parenting in youth sport: A position paper on parenting expertise, *Psychology of Sport and Exercise*, 16(1): 24–35.

Jayanthi, N.A., LaBella, C.R., Fischer, D., et al. (2015). Sports-specialized intensive training and the risk of injury in young athletes: A clinical case-control study, *The American Journal of Sports Medicine*, 43(4): 794–801.

Knight, C.J., Dorsch, T.E., Osai, K.V., et al. (2016). Influences on parental involvement in youth sport, *Sport, Exercise, and Performance Psychology*, 5(2): 161–178.

LaBella, C.R., & Myer, G.D. (2017). Youth sports injury prevention: Keep calm and play on, *British Journal of Sports Medicine*, 51: 145–146.

LaPrade, R.F., Agel, J., Baker, J., et al. (2016). AOSSM early sport specialization consensus statement, *The Orthopaedic Journal of Sports Medicine*, 4(4): 1–8.

Malina, R.M. (2010). Early sport specialization: Roots, effectiveness, risks, *Current Sports Medicine Reports*, 9(6): 364–371.

McKay, C.D., Cumming, S.P., & Blake, T. (2019). Youth sport: Friend or foe? *Best Practice & Research Clinical Rheumatology*, 33(1): 141–157.

Nyland, J. (2014). Coming to terms with early sports specialization and athletic injuries, *Journal of Orthopaedic & Sports Physical Therapy*, 44(6): 389–390.

Positive Coaching Alliance (PCA). https://devzone.positivecoach.org/resource/video/youth-sports-development-zone-jim-thompson-tedxfargo (accessed 4 Dec. 2019).

Robinson, D.B., & Randall, L. (2017). Marking physical literacy or missing the mark on physical literacy? A conceptual critique of Canada's physical literacy assessment instruments, *Measurement in Physical Education and Exercise Science*, 21(1): 40–55.

Santos, S., Jiménez, S., Sampaio, J., & Leite, N. (2017). Effects of the Skills4Genius sports-based training program in creative behaviour, *PLOS ONE*, 12(2): e0172520. https://doi.org/10.1371/journal.pone.0172520

Sigmundsson, H., Trana, L., Polman, R., & Haga, M. (2017). What is trained develops! Theoretical perspective on skill learning, *Sports*, 5(2): pii:E38.

Wiersma, L.D. (2000). Risks and benefits of youth sport specialization: Perspectives and recommendations, *Pediatric Exercise Science*, 12: 13–22.

11 Talent identification and development and creating an environment for success

Introduction
Part 1: pedagogical case
Part 2: commentary
    Acknowledging the complex environment of talent identification and development
Talent identification
Talent development
Summary
End of chapter tasks
References

Introduction

This chapter deals with the emerging phenomena of early talent identification, sporting academies and the growing prevalence of single-sport athletes. While sport, parents and athletes generally view these as contributing to positive performance, such initiatives can present new challenges for SCCs. To assist SCCs to examine these challenges, this chapter discusses some of the complexities associated with player talent identification and development. We discuss the difference between giftedness and talent and debate the concept of talent identification. We review some of the common talent development models and examine the contributions that SCCs can make to talent identification and development.

Part 1: pedagogical case

Getting to the airport for an early flight was never easy, so Joan, Charlie and Ivan had agreed to car pool to make sure that they all caught the flight that would take them to the biennial Connecting Coaches conference. It was a quiet drive to the airport, not just because of the early hour but because the three did not really know each other well, and they were venturing into the unknown by attending a conference for sport coaches. While they were affiliated to the same sports club, they were SCCs working independently with different sports that shared social and training facilities. Joan focused on track and field, Charlie worked with rugby and Ivan was associated with the gymnastics club. Their respective clubs had amalgamated three years earlier to reduce costs, increase their chances of obtaining funding and make better use of their community's sports facility, which had previously been used exclusively by track and field. The club's governing board were pleased with the financial benefits of the combined sports club concept. There had been very few issues around sharing the facilities and resources, largely because of the different times and seasons when the sports were active. However, the board members were disappointed that there appeared to have been very little integration and sharing of 'best practices' across the three sporting codes. As a trial to encourage the sharing of ideas, the board had sponsored Joan, Charlie and Ivan to attend the Connecting Coaches conference. The stipulation was that the SCCs had to be willing to work with their colleagues across the sporting codes within the club. Hence, the quiet trip to the airport.

The theme for the conference was 'Coaching Young Athletes in a Changing World'. It was an apt title given a couple of recent stories in the media, which were giving conference attendees plenty to talk about during conference down time. One 'hot topic' of conversation focused on the exploits of 17-year-old sprint phenom Edward Osei-Nketia, who at that time was the subject of a tug of war between New Zealand and Australia and was also being scouted by rugby union, rugby league, and Australian rules football. These sports coveted his physical presence and speed (1.90 m (6'3"), 95 kg (209 lbs); and 10.9 s for 100 m) and felt they could coach the skills once he had 'signed on'. Another 'hot topic' during conference breaks was the recent release of data by New Zealand's Accident Compensation Corporation (ACC operates NZ's no-fault accident insurance scheme) that identified injuries in children (10–14 years) in all sports had risen 60% between 2008 and 2017. Fuelled by media speculation, there was plenty of debate by conference delegates over this figure; was this just clever manipulation of statistics, or was it a problem with the children or sports they played? Others blamed intensive training regimes, or the emphasis that some sports placed on early specialisation that often shepherded children into sport-specific academies. Some felt that the increase in injury rates were a consequence of children no longer having sufficient exposure to fundamental movement skills through play.

The complexities around these debates were further highlighted by some of the keynote conference presentations. One presenter described a model that tennis adopted for early talent identification and engagement with a tennis-specific academy. Yet another speaker championed Sport New Zealand's position that 'Balance is better' (Sport NZ, 2019a, 2019b) and attempted to debunk the commonly held belief amongst many parents and coaches that early specialisation would set up children to be great athletes in the future. This speaker pointed out that, in the New Zealand context, most top athletes grew up playing multiple sports, and most delayed specialising until they were well into their teens. Sport New Zealand urged administrators of sports to focus on keeping 'young athletes enjoying their sport, developing their skills and staying healthy' (ACC, 2019). Consistent with their position, Sport NZ had been supportive of national sporting organisations who had abandoned provincial representative teams for young athletes under age 14, replacing them with development opportunities for more youngsters.

During the conference, Joan, Charlie and Ivan did gravitate to colleagues from their respective sports, but true to the assurances they had given to their club's governing board, they met for breakfast each day to share their views on what they had heard and seen. At their first meeting, they turned to the topic of the sprinter Osei-Nketia. Ivan wondered how rugby had missed noticing his talent at a younger age – did a major sport like rugby not have a talent identification programme? Charlie knew there were active rugby recruiters working in all levels of the high school game, as well as looking at athletes from other sporting codes. Their aim was to recruit potential talent into rugby, often through provincial age group academies. Even though Charlie loved rugby, he was concerned that the recruiters seemed to focus only on selecting big physiques, 'I don't think that many of those academy players go on to be elite rugby players. Somehow, we are missing some very good prospects, the ones who are late developers or have smaller physiques, but excel once they mature.'

Joan chimed in with, 'Rugby and rugby league are always scouting our track and field athletes' and supported Charlie's concern about the limitations associated with recruiters privileging large physiques. From her perspective, this was a short-term solution to a perceived problem and did not support long-term athlete development. Joan said, 'You know I was watching skateboarders out in the hotel carpark [parking lot] last night. Just hanging out and perfecting their tricks. No formal instruction, just encouragement and sarcastic feedback from their mates [friends]. They seemed to be videoing themselves attempting different tricks. I just marvel at the tenacity, durability, and skill of those kids performing all sorts of amazing stunts – no organisation and not a parent or adult coach in sight. I've often wondered how we would use that level of athleticism in track and field.' Mumbling his assent, Charlie also wondered how the degree of body awareness and control of the skateboarders would assist rugby players to become better performers. Ivan said what seems strange to him was that 'the big-time sports seem to invest heavily in talent identification and development yet they wouldn't even give those skateboarders a second look'.

Turning her attention to Ivan, Joan said 'there are obvious similarities in athleticism between skateboarders and gymnasts. I've got to say that you've got a great programme running back home – those children seem so enthusiastic. I've been watching that young girl Collette. So athletic. I think she would make a great jumper – long or triple! I'd love to get her out on the track with us.' To which Ivan responded with a wry grin: 'Good luck with that – her parents are highly invested in her being an elite gymnast, but I don't think she's actually enjoying gym anymore. I wish they'd let her try some other sports as well.' The mention of parents got Charlie animated. 'I've got parents hounding me about getting their sons and daughters into weight training for rugby – they're afraid that they are going to get left behind if they are not big and strong. I am in a bit of a bind because, after all, I am an SCC but I've also read the NSCA guidelines for youth resistance training (Faigenbaum et al., 2009; Haff & Triplett, 2015), and it seems to me that the guidelines are just a watered-down version of the adult recommendations. That doesn't seem right to me – kids are not simply small adults – so I don't think getting involved in youth resistance training is worthwhile. Some parents are placing their children in commercial sport performance programmes. Those programmes claim to be helping kids to become more athletic, and while I understand that there is no harm with a well-supervised programme, I ask – why would you bother? I can't see gym training being that motivating for kids – surely there's better things they could be doing at younger ages?'

To Charlie's surprise, Ivan agreed, explaining that 'I've seen some of those coaches with the younger rugby teams and for goodness sake, it's like some kind of boot camp out there. What we try and do in gymnastics is link everything we do into a skill and we use a lot of bodyweight, and repetition rather than external loads. Sometimes we use light sand bags or elastic "bungy cords" to help them to isolate an area for specific strengthening so that they can build up to a skill. But, by and large, it is all functional, and we progress the conditioning as we progress each skill. From what I've seen, Joan does the same with her athletes.' 'That's right,' Joan said. 'Our throwers might be learning how to perform a few lifts under supervision, but we also use bodyweight and repetition. We use quite a bit of plyometrics, but again as long as it is tied into the discipline and the skill drills that we have them do, we always try to keep it pretty functional. I don't think our young athletes would recognise it as conditioning, it's just track and field training to them.'

'Exactly – my gymnasts would think the same,' exclaimed Ivan. 'When the kids are young, if the conditioning is too disconnected from the skills of the sport, you're going to lose them. Besides, they have plenty of time to get into strength training more as they get older – what's the rush?'

Throughout the conference Joan, Charlie and Ivan continued to meet up daily to share thoughts on, and experiences of, the conference. In contrast to the quiet trip going to the conference, travelling back home was full of lively discussion as they drew on their understanding of SCC practices to discuss, and debate, their thoughts on talent identification in their respective sports and how they would manage strength and conditioning for their developing athletes. They agreed that their club's governing board would be very happy with their investment in the conference.

Part 2: commentary

Acknowledging the complex environment of talent identification and development

Talent identification and development practices are employed by many sports organisations with the primary aim of accelerating and maximising the development of sporting talent. Yet, there is little consensus as to what constitutes talent or what conceptual framework is most appropriate to inform research and practice relating to talent identification and development (Trankle & Cushion, 2006; Vaeyens et al., 2008; Wiseman et al., 2014). Cassidy et al. (2016) observed that sport sociologists have, somewhat surprisingly, had little appetite for exploring the complexities surrounding talent identification and development. To begin exploring the complexities, Cassidy et al. (2016) discussed talent identification and development from historical, cultural, structural and critical perspectives. They noted that many of the ideologies, practices and practitioners from the former Eastern Bloc had found welcoming 'new homes' in the Western world with the Eastern Bloc's demise. These ideologies have been accepted and adopted in the absence of research-based evidence and with little critical evaluation. This commentary seeks to explore some of the challenges associated with talent identification and development.

It is within these dynamic and strategic contexts that S&C professionals have been tasked with contributing to both the identification of future elite performers, and the nurturing and development of the identified athletes; all to ensure that promise translates into performance. The rhetoric at least is that SCCs are valued by sports organisations as key contributors to the health and wellbeing of young athletes as they progress through developmental pathways.

Sporting performance is acknowledged to be multidimensional (e.g. Johnston et al., 2018). Combined with this, the dynamic environment in which the practices of talent identification and development occur creates one of the greatest challenges for SCCs. Namely, how do they frame the question (talent identification) they are seeking to answer? It appears that SCCs often default to the easily measurable markers of talent: the physique and physiological fitness of individuals as categorised by standardised fitness tests. But to base talent identification on a limited selection of physical factors means that the subsequent contributions that SCCs can make to the talent identification and development process will by definition also be limited.

How many SCCs reflect on what physical attributes and capabilities are important to successful performance in the selected sport? As part of their academic preparation, SCCs are taught to conduct a thorough needs analysis for the sport or athlete with whom they are working (Haff & Triplett, 2016). While previous knowledge of a sport and time-motion analyses may go some way to determining needs, the many nuances of sport performance are often more difficult to elucidate. Furthering understanding may require SCCs to explore work outside of their domain of comfort. For example, the work that sport psychologists have conducted on talent identification and development offers additional insights into some of the 'difficult to measure' determinants of performance. As Polman et al. (2004) elegantly pointed out, we can identify key elements of sporting performance and then track those elements, but that quantitative data will rarely reveal anything about the quality, need for or timing of those actions.

Despite these challenges, SCCs are in a position to make positive contributions to the processes associated with talent identification and athletic development and to lead the way in challenging flawed practices. For example, any fitness testing situation presents as an educational opportunity to help a young athlete understand more about their physical capabilities and offer some guidance on how to safely enhance some of those qualities. Aside from the numbers that describe a youngster's physique and physical abilities, a competent SCC can offer sport coaching staff additional perspectives to contribute to an individual's profile. For example, they may be able to provide coaches with additional commentary on the quality of movements, the individual's responses to instruction and coaching information, their motivation and the sense of effort and confidence that they may observe during testing.

Additionally, SCCs are in a position to point out some of the associated issues; e.g., the of commonly used fitness tests. Given the unpredictability around maturation and the progression of fitness, test sensitivity is arguably one of the most important considerations that coaches and SCCs need to consider to ensure that their talent identification and development processes do not unwittingly exclude individuals who may in fact mature into excellent athletes (Vaeyens et al., 2009).

Talent identification

Talent identification is a blunt instrument, particularly when it comes to team sports (Pearson et al., 2006), and there are growing debates as to the merits of the processes associated with it. Sport talent identification programmes and practices have been identified as generally costly and largely ineffective (e.g. Bailey et al., 2010; Johnston et al., 2018). What is more, many successful athletes were not even identified as talented in their youth (DiFiori et al., 2017; Martindale et al., 2007). Further, Cumming et al. (2017) argued that it may be unwise to invest so heavily in physically capable youths at the expense of others who may in fact turn out to be outstanding adult performers. We contend that there are three key reasons that talent identification lacks utility: (1) there is a lack of understanding of what constitutes talent; (2) experts are uncertain about what general markers of talent correlate with successful performance and what talent actually looks like for a given sport (Johnston et al., 2018); and (3) experts are often 'blinded' by the stereotypes of particular sports and how the game is to be played.

Drawing on the work of prominent psychologists, Trankle and Cushion (2006) described talent as a 'label of approval we place on traits that have a positive value in the particular context in which we live' (p. 266). Gagné (1993) also recognises the multifaceted nature of talent. He described talent as the 'superior mastery of systematically developed abilities (or skills) and knowledge in at least one field of human activity to a degree that places an individual within at least the upper 10% of age peers' (Gagné, 1999, p. 230). So, learning to run fast(er), or learning how to visually track different baseball pitches based on the pitcher's motion, would be examples of talents that have been developed.

A possible reason for the uncertainty surrounding the identification of markers of talent that correlate with successful performance is that those working in talent identification confuse talent with giftedness. According to Gagné (2000), giftedness is the use of natural abilities, or aptitudes individuals display, in either the creative, intellectual, socio-affective or sensorimotor domains, that enable them to be ranked in the top 10% of their peers. Being able to naturally run very fast, or having the visual acuity to 'see' a baseball travelling at high speed, are gifts. By confusing giftedness with talent, there is potential for those working in the talent development area to focus on some things while overlooking others. We all know of people who were considered 'gifted' but never 'made it', and others who worked hard with the abilities they had to achieve success in ways that many people would not have predicted. A very good example of the latter is former All Black (NZ national rugby team) Richie McCaw. McCaw captained the team, achieved 100 test caps (international test matches played), won two Rugby World Cups, and was named the World Rugby player of the year three times. He is considered by some to be the greatest of all time; yet, his high school rugby coach said while he was a good player at school 'you wouldn't have picked what he would have done' (Hepburn, 2011).

Lewis (2003) placed the utility of talent identification under the public microscope by describing some of the biases perpetuated with physique stereotypes in Major League Baseball documenting the success of the Oakland A's baseball organisation at looking beyond the obvious. His later discourse on former NBA star Shane Battier provided further evidence that the so-called 'scholars of a sport' might often observe and measure certain things but may overlook other skills that are equally relevant to successful sporting performance (Lewis, 2009). Battier was initially recognised as 'at best, a replaceable cog in a machine driven by superstars', but when a more nuanced look was taken, it was realised that 'every team he has ever played on has acquired some magical ability to win'. Lewis (2009) provided an account of how easy it is for those looking for talent to look at the wrong things. He explained that in 2005, the Houston Rockets' owner said that he wanted somebody to look at the players, but not in the 'normal way'. Despite this desire, when the owner was given the proposal to recruit Shane Battier, he said, 'All I knew was Shane's stats . . . [and] they weren't great.' Moreover, it was obvious '[h]e can't dribble, he's slow and hasn't got much body control'. Hardly a ringing endorsement! However, when Battier's game was analysed in a way that was not considered 'normal' (i.e. not based on the typical statistics that focused on shots made, rebounds or assists), it highlighted that '[w]hen he is on the court, his teammates get better, often a lot better, and his opponents get worse – often a lot worse' (Lewis, 2009).

Lewis (2009) also highlighted how the urban/suburban divide, as well as cultural identity, can influence how an individual plays the game and how we judge who is talented or not. Battier grew up in the suburbs with a Black father and a White mother. He revealed that when playing at high school, the urban-based teams treated him like 'a suburban kid with a white game', whereas his regular teammates treated him as a Black person with, we can assume, a black game. Battier went on to say,

> *Everything* I've done since then is because of what I went through with this. . . . What I did is alienate myself from everybody. I'd eat lunch by myself. I'd study by myself. And I sort of lost myself in the game.
>
> (Lewis, 2009, *emphasis in original*)

By not fitting the 'norm', Battier's talent went unrecognised for a long time and highlights one of the reasons that talent identification lacks utility and can mislead the unaware.

Talent development

Another possible reason why talent identification lacks efficacy is because the experts lack knowledge on how talent markers will evolve with maturation and developmental input.

Over the decades, a number of player/talent development models have been promoted in the English-speaking world (see Bailey et al., 2011). Some of these models provide 'descriptive' accounts of sports development, while others provide 'prescriptive' accounts. Descriptive models attempt to 'provide an accurate description of an event and its variables', while prescriptive models 'focus on the values or principles that *ought to* characterise the event' (Bailey et al., 2011, p. 39, *emphasis added*).

Interestingly, it is a prescriptive model that has become possibly the most recognised and widely promoted talent development model and that has had a 'profound influence on how coaches and sports are advised to develop athletic talent and skill' (Gilbert, 2017, p. 112). The Long Term Athlete Development (LTAD) model, conceptualised by Istvan Balyi (Balyi & Hamilton, 2004), prescribes early and late specialisation pathways, with suggested windows of optimal trainability and accelerated adaptability that are based on age and maturation. Some of the critiques of the model include that: it is predominantly based on physiological paradigms; there is an absence of supporting empirical evidence; it creates anxiety in parents, young athletes and coaches with its suggested windows of opportunity; and the unashamed attempts by Balyi and others to commercialise an important life event (Côté & Hancock, 2016; Ford et al., 2011). Despite its considerable shortcomings, Day (2011) observed that LTAD has become viewed by some as a 'global law that must be adhered to for athletes to be internationally competitive' (p. 181). Yet Côté and Hancock (2016) argue that absence of research around the LTAD reinforces its focus as a commercial product that is not supported by any significant line of evidence.

Lloyd and Oliver (2012) proposed an alternative approach to youth strength and conditioning with their Youth Physical Development (YPD) model. This prescriptive model is largely based on empirical physiological research but challenges the LTAD model's identification of key periods for emphasising training for different fitness variables. The YPD acknowledges the need for individualisation and advocates conditioning for all physical qualities throughout childhood. Based on maturation of the endocrine system, the YPD model emphasises fundamental movement skills, strength, speed and agility prepuberty, with the expectation that adaptations will be largely neural. The authors of this model place a greater emphasis on strength, with power and hypertrophy recommended as more appropriately introduced with adolescence.

A model that has been also been described as prescriptive, but nonetheless provides evidence for the key role psychology plays in an athlete's development, is the Psychological Characteristics of Developing Excellence (Abbott & Collins, 2004). A feature of that model is the emphasis it places on the developing athlete's ability to successfully negotiate the transition between developmental stages. As such it recognises the importance of focusing on the ability of a young athlete to get there, as well as to already be there – the capacity to develop, and not just the capacity to perform. The development of physical and sporting abilities is unpredictable and biological maturation is not linear, so the development of athletic abilities should be expected to be dynamic, atypical and marked by spurts and bursts followed by variable periods of latency. Another model that is informed by descriptive and prescriptive accounts of athletic development is Bailey and Morley's (2006) Model of Talent Development. The model was initially based on empirical research into talent development in school physical education, before its authors added a 'prescriptive account of effective practice' (p. 49). This model recognises that physical abilities and dispositions, personal characteristics, environmental factors, access and opportunity, and indeed chance, can all potentially influence the development of talent.

For the strength and conditioning coach, the above prescriptive models for talent development provide a range of generic frameworks that are largely theoretical. Given the practical and ethical challenges of conducting training research with youth, such frameworks could be described as prudent rather than proven. Fears of potential harm to children as a consequence of intensive training, and in particular the inclusion of resistance training, have largely been dispelled (Faigenbaum et al., 2009; Lloyd et al., 2016). Indeed, development guidelines for youth athletes (Lloyd et al., 2016) and age-appropriate conditioning guidelines (Faigenbaum et al., 2009) propose that conditioning modes can be complementary to 'organic' adaptations during periods of growth and maturation – so-called 'synergistic adaptations' (Lloyd et al., 2016). However, as Charlie observes in the pedagogical case, just because we can do something does not mean that we should.

There is value in competent strength and conditioning professionals giving thought to factors other than the physical and drawing on the full range of competencies described in our professional competence framework (Chapter 2). These factors were identified by Bailey and Morley (2006) as dispositions, and personal, social and environmental contexts that will each contribute with different weightings to physical activity and sporting outcomes. Exposing young athletes to adult forms of training and preparation could risk introducing them to some of the problematic adult behaviours regarding training volume, training effort and training with pain and injury (Myer et al., 2016).

The Developmental Model of Sport Participation (DMSP; Côté et al., 2012; Côté & Vierimaa, 2014) is a descriptive model, which was informed by a large body of psychological empirical evidence and proposed multiple pathways for youth sporting development. The empirical data was gained from retrospective interviews conducted with elite Canadian and Australian athletes in a range of sports that included gymnastics, basketball, netball, hockey, rowing and tennis. From the interview data it was found that most of the elite athletes went through three developmental phases, the sampling phase (6–12 years), the specialising phase (13–15 years) and the investment phase (16-plus years), and there had also been opportunities to transition across pathways (Bailey et al., 2011). Key concepts and the importance of the sampling phase – deliberate practice and deliberate play – were discussed in Chapter 10. In the specialising phase, the young person normally reduces the number of sports they participate in, and sport specificity increases, yet there is still a focus on fun and enjoyment. As the name suggests, in the investment phase the young person begins to commit to achieving at a high level in a specific sport and skill development assumes even greater importance (Bailey et al., 2011).

While Joan, Charlie and Ivan had attended several sessions in the Connecting Coaches conferences that encouraged them to question the dominant ideologies driving youth athlete development, they were not sure where to start, and they certainly were not aware of the talent development models outlined in this chapter. Most approaches to youth training that they had encountered and been involved with inevitably focused on remediating deficiencies; deficiencies that were based on adult reference points (Kochanek et al., 2019). The contribution of SCCs to youth athletic development generally focuses on two interrelated areas, conditioning and fundamental movement skills, for which the term integrative neuromuscular training (INT) has been coined (Myer et al., 2016). While INT has been designed to target both health and skill-related fitness through strategic mastery and progression of movements, it still offers primarily adult structured experiences.

In our pedagogical case, Charlie voices reservations about S&C for children and he wonders if developmental S&C for children and youth could step away from traditional models (Lloyd et al., 2016) and possibly reimagine conditioning to accommodate children's physical activity preferences. One such way could be through applying Burton et al.'s (2011) conceptual model that was developed to enhance children's sporting experiences. Based on Coakley's (1980) observations on children's experiences and points of enjoyment when engaging in informal and formal sporting activities, Burton et al. (2011) sought to make systematic environmental changes to optimise sporting experiences. In the absence of adult organisation, it has been noted that children enjoy playing with friends (Coakley, 1980) and enjoy interacting with and testing themselves with older and more physical individuals (Coutinho et al., 2016). When they are playing, children seek to maximise their time on task and resent stoppages and standing around (Coakley, 1980). Coakley (1980) also observed that children are motivated by their perceived competence and the freedom to experiment, problem solve and try different strategies without consequence.

While specific exercise techniques, increased loading and an organised structure of repetitions and sets may be one of the ultimate objectives of youth conditioning, children could be scaffolded towards a similar outcome, but with more enjoyable and motivating experiences. Involving friends, partner exercises and activities, and providing the opportunity to experiment, are some elements that could easily be given a subtle conditioning emphasis. As Myer et al. (2016) state, children are able to, and do tend to, self-regulate their physical activity if left to their own devices. However, traditional strength and conditioning ideologies may inadvertently be teaching youth to adopt adult-like attitudes to intensity, effort and exercise volume. Persson et al. (2019) explored reasons for youth opting out of sport, finding that there were reasons that had to do with the sport structure (e.g. training times, time commitment and nature of training) and interpersonal reasons (e.g. having fun, sense of belonging, sense of capability, pressure from coaches). Through sharing some of their ideas and experiences, the three colleagues in our pedagogical case are considering their practices and making progress towards reframing youth conditioning, in the process rewarding the investment of their Sports Club. As competent SCCs, they have scope to reimagine how they structure S&C for developing athletes, and how those youth athletes feel engaging in that environment.

Summary

The importance accorded sport by society has fostered significant interest in identifying and developing the next sporting talent. In this chapter we note the influence that programmes from the former Eastern Bloc have had on contemporary interpretations of, and preoccupation with, ways of nurturing, progressing and accelerating athletic talent. Various talent identification and development models are discussed and critiqued, primarily on the basis that early ability does not accurately predict the potential for later ability. The chapter describes differences between giftedness and talent, a distinction that we suggest underpins the potential disconnect between 'being at' and 'getting to' a level of sporting ability. SCCs' involvement with talent identification and development are often driven by sport-specific norms, and a focus on physique and physiology, and the measurement and conditioning of these attributes. As there are multiple apparent pathways to sporting excellence, we argue that a deficit approach to athlete development may not be helpful, and we suggest that SCCs have the ability to offer far more insight and professional input into the nurturing of athletic abilities.

End of chapter tasks

1   Much of today's S&C is conceptualised as a means to enhance athletic performance, i.e. S&C builds better athletes. However, S&C without sport is also an option. Engage in a

2   Imagine you're the SCC for an elite-level youth athlete, or a youth, who consistently outperforms his or her peers. Would, and should, their early success affect how you consider coaching them in S&C activities?
3   Talent identification, talent development, giftedness, skills, intelligence, cognitive, affective and physical domains – some of these terms are used in this chapter whereas others are not, and more still could be brought into this discussion. Create a typology (e.g. a table) that lists these constructs and relevant information such as when the word was first used, became popularised and key theorists or researchers who studied it; biological, psychological, social qualities (i.e. how race, gender, socioeconomic class, geography, are used); how it has been measured; changes in meaning over time, etc.
4   Strength and conditioning practices are often implemented in rigid, prescriptive ways. Indeed, S&C coach education specifically states how to design a programme, the order of exercises, how to prescribe specific intensities, rest. Yet, youth, and often adults too, are motivated by fun, exploration, play, social relations. Discuss these intersecting biopsychosocial demands. Can we, as SCCs, maximise all of these concerns, or do we need to emphasise some over others, and should the emphasis change over time?

(Note: item 1 appears at top: "discussion about how we could use the principles and practices of S&C to enhance the lives of young people without the emphasis on sport.")

References

Abbott, A., & Collins, D. (2004). Eliminating the dichotomy between theory and practice in talent identification and development: Considering the role of psychology, *Journal of Sports Sciences*, 22(5): 395–408.

Accident Compensation Corporation. (2019). Significant surge in Kiwi kids side-lined by sports injuries. www.acc.co.nz/newsroom/stories/significant-surge-in-kiwi-kids-side-lined-by-sports-injuries/ (accessed 13 February 2020).

Bailey, R., Collins, D., Ford, P., et al. (2010). *Participant Development in Sport: An Academic Review*, Leeds: Sports Coach.

Bailey, R., & Morley, D. (2006). Towards a model of talent development in physical education, *Sport, Education and Society*, 11(3): 211–230.

Bailey, R., Toms, M., Collins, D., Ford, P., MacNamara, A., & Pearce, G. (2011). Models of young player development in sport. In I. Stafford (ed.), *Coaching Children in Sport*, London: Routledge.

Balyi, I., & Hamilton, A. (2004). *Long-Term Athlete Development: Trainability in Childhood and Adolescence – Windows of Opportunity – Optimal Trainability*, Victoria: National Coaching Institute British Columbia & Advanced Training and Performance Ltd.

Burton, D., Gillham, A.D., & Hammermeister, J. (2011). Competitive engineering: Structural climate modifications to enhance youth athletes' competitive experience, *International Journal of Sports Science & Coaching*, 6(2): 201–217.

Cassidy, T., Jones, R., & Potrac, P. (2016). *Understanding Sports Coaching: The Pedagogical, Social, and Cultural Foundations of Coaching Practice* (3rd ed.), London: Routledge.

Coakley, J. (1980). Play, games and sport: Developmental implications for young people, *Journal of Sport Behavior*, 3: 99–118.

Côté, J., & Hancock, D.J. (2016). Evidence-based policies for youth sport programmes, *International Journal of Sport Policy and Politics*, 8(1): 51–65.

Côté, J., Murphy-Mills, J., & Abernethy, B. (2012). The development of skill in sport. In N. Hodges & A.M. Williams (eds.), *Skill Acquisition in Sport: Research, Theory and Practice*, New York: Routledge, pp. 269–286.

Côté, J., & Vierimaa, M. (2014). The developmental model of sport participation: 15 years after its first conceptualization, *Science & Sports*, 29: S63–S69.

Coutinho, P., Mesquita, I., Davids, K., et al. (2016). How structured and unstructured sport activities aid the development of expertise in volleyball players, *Psychology of Sport and Exercise*, 25: 51–59.

Cumming, S.P., Lloyd, R.S., Oliver, J.L., et al. (2017). Bio-banding in sport: Applications to competition, talent identification, and strength and conditioning of youth athletes, *Strength and Conditioning Journal*, 39(2): 34–47.

Day, D. (2011). Craft coaching and the 'discerning eye' of the coach, *International Journal of Sport Science and Coaching*, 6(1): 179–195.

DiFiori, J.P., Brenner, J.S., Comstock, D., et al. (2017). Debunking early single sport specialisation and reshaping the youth sport experience: An NBA perspective, *British Journal of Sports Medicine*, 51(3): 142–143.

Faigenbaum, A.D., Kraemer, W.J., Blimkie, C., et al. (2009). Youth resistance training: Updated position statement paper from the national strength and conditioning association, *Journal of Strength & Conditioning Research*, 23(5): S60–S79.

Ford, P., De Ste Croix, M., Lloyd, R., et al. (2011). The long-term athlete development model: Physiological evidence and application, *Journal of Sports Sciences*, 29(4): 389–402.

Gagné, F. (1993). Constructs and models pertaining to exceptional human abilities. In K.A. Heller, F.J. Mönks, & A.H. Passow (eds.), *International Handbook of Research and Development of Giftedness and Talent*, Oxford: Pergamon Press, pp. 69–87.

Gagné, F. (1999). Gagné's differentiated model of giftedness and talent (DMGT), *Journal for the Education of the Gifted*, 22(2): 230–234.

Gagné, F. (2000). Understanding the complete choreography of talent development through DMGT-based analysis. In K.A. Heller (ed. & trans.), *International Handbook of Giftedness and Talent* (2nd ed.), Oxford: Elsevier Science, pp. 67–79.

Gilbert, W. (2017). *Coaching Better Every Season: A Year-Round System for Athlete Development and Program Success*, Champaign, IL: Human Kinetics.

Haff, G.G., & Triplett, N.T. (eds.). (2015). *NSCA Essentials of Strength Training and Conditioning* (4th ed.), Champaign, IL: Human Kinetics.

Haff, G., & Triplett, N.T. (2016). *Essentials of Strength Training and Conditioning* (4th ed.), Champaign, IL: Human Kinetics.

Hepburn, S. (2011). Local heroes: Nurturer of OBHS rugby, *Otago Daily Times*. www.odt.co.nz/sport/rugby/local-heroes-nurturer-obhs-rugby (accessed 5 Dec. 2019).

Johnston, K., Wattie, N., Schorer, J., et al. (2018). Talent identification in sport: A systematic review, *Sports Medicine*, 48: 97–109.

Kochanek, J., Matthews, A., Wright, E., et al. (2019). Competitive readiness: Developmental considerations to promote positive youth development in competitive activities, *Journal of Youth Development*, 14(1): 48–69.

Lewis, M. (2003). *Moneyball: The Art of Winning an Unfair Game*, New York: W.W. Norton.

Lewis, M. (2009). The no-stats all-star, 13 Feb. www.nytimes.com/2009/02/15/ (accessed 22 July 2019).

Lloyd, R.S., Cronin, J.B., Faigenbaum, A.D., et al. (2016). National strength and conditioning association position statement on long-term athletic development, *Journal of Strength & Conditioning Research*, 30(6): 1491–1509.

Lloyd, R.S., & Oliver, J.L. (2012). The youth physical development model: A new approach to long-term athletic development, *Strength and Conditioning Journal*, 34(3): 61–72.

Martindale, R.J.J., Collins, D., & Abraham, A. (2007). Effective talent development: The elite coach perspective in UK sport, *Journal of Applied Sport Psychology*, 19(2): 187–206.

Myer, G.D., Jayanthi, N., DiFiori, J.P., et al. (2016). Sports specialization, part II: Alternative solutions to early sport specialization in youth athletes, *Sports Health*, 8(1): 65–73.

Pearson, D.T., Naughton, G.A., & Torode, M. (2006). Predictability of physiological testing and the role of maturation in talent identification for adolescent team sports, *Journal of Science and Medicine in Sport*, 9: 277–287.

Persson, M., Espedalen, L.E., Stefansen, K., et al. (2019). Opting out of youth sports: How can we understand the social processes involved? *Sport, Education and Society*. DOI:10.1080/13573322.2019.1663811.

Polman, R., Walsh, D., Bloomfield, J., & Nesti, M. (2004). Effective conditioning of female soccer players, *Journal of Sports Sciences*, 22(2): 191–203.

Sport New Zealand. (2019a). Balance is better. https://sportnz.org.nz/assets/Uploads/SportNZ-BalanceIsBetter.pdf (accessed 5 Dec. 2019).

Sport New Zealand. (2019b). Why we need to tackle early specialisation. https://sportnz.org.nz/news-and-events/media-releases-and-updates/articles/why-we-need-to-tackle-early-specialisation-2 (accessed 5 Dec. 2019).

Trankle, P., & Cushion, C. (2006). Rethinking giftedness and talent in sport, *Quest*, 58(2): 265–282.

Vaeyens, R., Gullich, A., Warr, C.R., et al. (2009). Talent identification and promotion programmes of Olympic athletes, *Journal of Sports Science*, 27: 1367–1380.

Vaeyens, R., Lenoir, M., Williams, A., & Philippaerts, R. (2008). Talent identification and development programmes in sport: Current models and future directions, *Sports Medicine*, 38(9): 703–714.

Wiseman, A.C., Bracken, N., Horton, S., & Weir, P.L. (2014). The difficulty of talent identification: Inconsistency among coaches through skill-based assessment of youth hockey players, *International Journal of Sport Science and Coaching*, 3: 447–455.

12 Older and wiser?

Introduction
Part 1: pedagogical case
Part 2: commentary
Pressures
Ageing and athletic performance reviewed
Negotiating flexibility
Strength and conditioning strategies
Summary
End of chapter tasks
References

Introduction

Just as sporting talent is being 'realised' at younger ages, athletes are also continuing to compete for longer at elite levels (Weir et al., 2010). This chapter explores how SCCs might approach the challenge of managing the fitness needs of motivated athletes with ageing physiological and musculoskeletal systems, as well as understand some of the social and socioeconomic influences associated with being an older athlete. In the chapter we discuss some of the pressures facing veteran athletes, discuss their expectations around S&C, and critique some assumptions regarding ageing bodies. Like many challenges, we suggest that the ageing athlete presents an opportunity for professional development, and we suggest S&C strategies that could provide some flexibility around training to accommodate the needs of the older athlete.

Part 1: pedagogical case

Carl is enjoying a relaxing coffee with Jenna, a close friend from high school. Jenna plays professional basketball in the Australian Women's National Basketball League (WNBL). With busy schedules, the two friends rarely catch up. This coffee meeting will be their last opportunity for a while, as Jenna will fly back to Melbourne tomorrow for the start of preseason training. When Jenna asked to meet, she was a little cryptic suggesting that she wanted to 'pick Carl's brain'. Given that Carl knows very little about basketball, he's assuming that Jenna wants to glean some of his expertise as an S&C professional. Carl completed a sport science degree and was drawn to S&C as a career path. He interned with a sports conditioning company and has since completed terms as an S&C coach with women's field hockey and with rugby league. He has been in his current role as head SCC with a local professional rugby club for the past five years.

Carl was, of course, looking forward to seeing his old school friend – the sports star – but felt a little unsure about how he could possibly help her. He knows that Jenna has always been conscientious about her fitness work, has remained in great shape for basketball and has remained relatively injury free. He considers that her discipline around her fitness probably had a lot to do with her remarkable career in the sport, having represented Australia at two Olympics and three World Championships. When Jenna arrived, and after the obligatory catching up on their respective partners and Jenna's children (6- and 4-year-olds), Carl casually asked about Jenna's fitness and the state of her body, heading into yet another gruelling season.

As it turned out, that wasn't an ideal or sensitive thing to ask – luckily, they were long-term friends! At 35 years of age, Jenna has been playing high-stakes basketball for 18 years. She went from high school directly into a four-year basketball scholarship at a US college. At the completion of her final college season, she joined her first WNBL team at age 21. As well as playing in the WNBL, Jenna has been doubling up with Australian National Team (Opals) commitments for 14 of those 18 years.

'To be honest,' she responds, 'while I'm loving the idea of getting back into the team environment and playing again, I'm a bit over the thought of another season of high-pressure fitness training.' Jenna explains that a new coach is leading the organisation this season and he has brought along a number of his own staff, including a new SCC with a reputation for being a hard task-master. This strength coach worked with the Tall Ferns (New Zealand's women's basketball team) a few seasons ago, and some of Jenna's teammates who had played on that team didn't enjoy his approach at all.

'I just don't need to be training another coaching group at this stage of my career!' was Jenna's attempt at making light of her fears. 'I went into college basketball not really understanding what it took to prepare physically for the sport; I mean really prepare! In high school we kind of just played basketball to give us our fitness, and simply concentrated on loving the game. So, at college the strength coaches we had were really invaluable in teaching me how to train and condition myself properly. I really appreciated and enjoyed the guidance and foundation that they gave me. But since then there have been training ups and downs, and it's an ongoing challenge of being accountable to both a WNBL team strength coach and a national team strength coach, who are sometimes on completely different pages. When I was with the Vikings [another WNBL team], they somehow decided I would be more effective 5 kg lighter. That was just a horrible off-season trying to lose that weight! It was only a year after I had Brianna [her 6-year-old daughter] and look what it did to my game. I was dropped to the bench for the national team. I was slower on the court and I just didn't feel right all season. Then I managed to dislocate my shoulder and lost most of that WNBL season. Thankfully with a new team and coaches, that 5 kg obsession disappeared and I managed to play my way back into the game and regained my position on the starting line-up. Strange, but I think that shoulder injury might have saved my career! During rehabilitation, I got back to what I think is my normal weight and I developed a new understanding of how my body responds to training. When I damaged my anterior cruciate ligament four seasons ago, I was better prepared for the rehabilitation process and had no real difficulty working my way back into the starting line-up. Part of it is the experience you gain. Once you have had a few injuries, you get better at "listening" or paying better attention to how your body feels.

'What I'm trying to say is when I was starting out and didn't know any better, the strength and conditioning coaches were helpful – a godsend, really – they made a huge difference to how I trained and looked after myself as a professional athlete. But for the last half of my career, I've found that those strength coaches have really just become "noise"! As far as I am concerned now, they are just distractions from actually working on my fitness and my game. I'm not convinced there is really anything to be gained from constantly thrashing myself in training. I get it that it's a team thing and as a senior player I need to be seen to be leading and setting good examples for my teammates in training, but surely I can do that in other ways than pushing weights in a gym. I understand my body better than anyone and I know what works for me. I know my injuries and weaknesses, and I know what keeps me sharp and out there on the court performing. You're the strength coach Carl! What I'm after are ideas for approaching this new strength coach in a way that I can get across some of those thoughts without coming across as being a slacker.' Still 'bruised' from his earlier question, Carl asked a little more subtly this time, 'So you say that you are fit for basketball. What are your main concerns then?'

Jenna replies that she knows that she can still play the game at the WNBL level, but realises that she is no longer the 17-year-old kid that they both knew back in high school. 'I'm 35 now, Carl. I have two kids. I'm not in denial here. I'm certainly not as quick and explosive as I was in college, but I still have good strength and a good base fitness; still better than most in the league. But if I'm honest, I find all of those weights sessions really fatiguing and boring – I don't believe that I really need to be any stronger in the gym. I also don't want to clock up lots of meters running aimlessly around cones on the court. I'd rather be running a drill and looking after my knees and legs a bit better. I think that I can gain a lot more useful fitness being in games and team sessions, rather than through the ongoing in-season gym work. I am finding that I am more tired after the league games than I used to be, and definitely have more soreness following games. I simply don't recover as quickly from games or heavy trainings as I used to. But I am expected to be there in the gym and out there on the floor, lining up with everyone else – even though they could be 15 years younger than me – conditioning day in and day out!'

She continued by saying, 'I can still see and understand the game well. I can read the court, the ebb and flow of the game and it all still seems to slow down for me, so that I have time to make the right move or a pass. As a guard that's always been my game and that skill set has seemed to have improved with experience. So, yes, I might have lost a step, but I've gained a second in other ways. I'm still in love with basketball, Carl! I wouldn't carry on doing this if I didn't. I'm still motivated to compete to start, and I think I can still be a major contributor for this team. I know that these strength coaches all claim to understand that we are all individuals, yet all I see is all 14 of us training the same! I get it that for the sake of the team that there have to be standards and consistency. I also understand that as a senior player I need to be a role model for the younger players coming in to our team environment. The last thing I want is for any of this to be perceived as special treatment or favouritism. What my 35-year-old body needs is a whole lot different from what I needed coming in as a 17-year-old! Also, I have a young family and a fair bit going on in my life outside of basketball. I'd be happy if they just left me, and some of the other senior players, to take more responsibility for our own training. I really don't need that training volume that I'm sure that they are going to throw at us and I certainly don't need someone screaming at me, pumping me up to squeeze out just one more rep. I think I've become immune to those attempts at motivation. So, how can I have a good conversation with this new S&C and get him to understand and agree to some kind of compromise? I'm asking for 'friend help' here, Carl – you're an experienced strength coach and I respect your perspective.'

Part 2: commentary

Carl is an experienced S&C professional, but this conversation with Jenna proved unsettling for him. Despite his years of experience, Jenna's situation is something that he had not encountered, or at least hadn't contemplated before. If anything, it got him thinking about his own coaching ideology and whether he had been missing key signs along the way. As such, he could really only provide Jenna with a couple of seemingly vague suggestions, but he promised to get back to her when he'd had time to think through a more reasoned response. Carl was a little embarrassed that he hasn't really reflected on the training needs of some of his older athletes, or considered the nature or ramifications of any training allowances. Listening to Jenna's story, he immediately recalled that American swimmer Dara Torres won a relay silver medal at the 2008 Olympics at age 41. He thought too of Jaromir Jagr, who had played contact sport in the National Hockey League until age 45. Carl also found an online article on basketball legend Tim Duncan, who had played in the physical National Basketball Association until age 40. His long-time coach Gregg Popovich had commented:

> if you see him walk, that one leg doesn't even straighten out (because of knee injuries). Obviously, he doesn't have the athleticism he used to have. But the guy is uniquely intelligent as far as knowing what his strengths and weaknesses are.
>
> (Amick, 2013)

Clearly, many athletes have had long and successful careers competing at the highest level. In starting to think his way through Jenna's request for help, Carl resolved to approach this by revisiting his strength and conditioning ideologies. To do this he opted to:

- contemplate some of the physical, social and psychological pressures facing the older athlete and consider those in light of the needs of the organisation and team management.
- revisit and update his understanding of the physiology of ageing and its likely impact on sport performance, and implications for traditional S&C methods.
- consider strategies to manage an older athlete's conditioning effectively and to the satisfaction of all parties.

Pressures

When thinking about the rugby context, where Carl was currently working, he decided that there were two main external social pressures on older athletes: the 'sports habitus' and normative expectation that most rugby players tend to retire in their early 30s (Smith, 2019). While many players continue to play social rugby beyond the age of 30, it is widely presumed that their performance declines, and this perception tends to be reinforced by media speculations on players retiring from the sport (Cosh et al., 2013). A recent example of this perception, and how it was challenged, came after an Australian newspaper headlined a story with 'Wallabies warned not to take All Blacks' senior citizens lightly' and listed the names, along with their ages, of nine current All Blacks (New Zealand national team) who were 30 years or older (New Zealand Herald, 2019). In riposte, Smith (2019) pointed out that the author of the Australian newspaper article had conveniently overlooked the fact that the All Blacks' 2015 Rugby World Cup winning squad contained 11 players aged 30 or over. Eight of those 11, including Richie McCaw (34), Dan Carter (33) and ancient hooker Keven

Mealamu (36), had played in the convincing 34–17 grand final win over the Wallabies (the Australian national team).

Reflective of the rugby example, Carl remembered that he had worked with 'older' athletes during his career, and he recalled these athletes continuing to perform at the highest level well into their 30s. Players often retired because they had lost the battle with recurrent injuries or non-selection (NZRPA, 2009), so it was difficult to discern whether retirements occurred because of age or injury. He was also aware that some older athletes faced different distractions or circumstances as they got older, with relationships and families affecting sleep and available training time, along with business and career development roles. Yet, having other commitments does not automatically impair performance. For example, 20-time tennis grand slam champion Roger Federer travels the world tennis circuit with his family of six.

> So as long as the kids have a good time on Tour, it's also okay for me to keep playing. The moment I will feel that they are not happy travelling anymore, I will not want to leave them at home alone. My family is my No. 1 priority, it's always been clear for me. I do not know when it's gonna end.
>
> (Gatto, 2019)

As a professional working in such high-stakes sport settings, Carl is mindful that most sport organisations seek to present themselves as meritocratic, certainly in the eyes of players and supporters. Consequently, there is a view by some that a team dynamic could be negatively affected if the coaching staff is perceived to demonstrate favouritism by, for example, allowing a loyal and 'older' athlete to take up a roster spot, or to keep a younger, and by implication a supposedly better player, on the bench. As Carl reflected on his experiences of working with older athletes, he came to the realisation that he had relied on, and expected, veteran athletes to assume stereotypical leadership roles and adopt 'warrior' like attitudes to S&C. But after listening to Jenna, he was beginning to ask – was that the right approach? Were his expectations and assumptions placing undue pressure on an athlete who may have other life priorities, or who would perhaps prefer to be 'just' another team member. He was hearing what Jenna was saying and was now starting to wonder whether he had in the past been an 'irritant' for some of his squad. Could there be other ways that Carl could manage his older athletes?

Ageing and athletic performance reviewed

Although there is a large body of research investigating the links between physiological adaptations and sport performance, the majority of research explores performance development, with very little attention paid to performance of the older athlete. In fact, there is a paucity of research on athletes between ages 30 and 50, making it difficult to identify the nature of the relationship between ageing physiological function, skill, performance and training loads. Peak physiological function is suggested to occur around 30 years of age, whereas decision making and cognitive skills will continue to evolve well beyond that age (Allen & Hopkins, 2015). Allen and Hopkins (2015) point out what we have all observed: successful performance in some sports and activities requires different mixes of skills, physiology and physical attributes. We would also contend that psychological skills such as decision making and social skills such as interpersonal communications and leadership are also important.

Due to the dominance of physiological knowledge in the SCC community and the importance of muscle powering sport performance, the physiology of ageing has tended to focus primarily on muscle. It has been shown that with increasing age, motor units are affected by changes in the nervous system, with type II fibres losing innervation and some of those being re-innervated by slower type I fibre motor nerves (Faulkner et al., 2008). These changes in fibre properties help explain age-related reduction in maximum force and rate of force development capacity that in turn affect power, acceleration and speed abilities. Changes in muscle architecture and muscle-tendon mechanical properties, in combination with reduced neural activation, are likely to contribute to altered musculotendinous stiffness. These changes can compromise force generation and transmission, and the ability to store and return energy in stretch shortening cycle movements.

Yet, for many sports, objectively measuring the physiological contribution to success is rarely as straightforward as measuring muscle strength, or other fitness measures. Arampatzis et al. (2011) submit that the plasticity of the neuromuscular and musculoskeletal systems provides adaptability that enables older athletes (and others) to compensate for physiological changes and maintain optimal performance. Further, while there is some speculation that ageing participants' ability to physiologically recover from fatiguing exercise may be compromised (e.g. Fell & Williams, 2008; Mitsumune & Kayashima, 2013), there have been other observations that suggest oestrogen provides some protection from muscle damage. Therefore, it could be that female athletes may differ from men in their responses to resistance training load (Fell & Williams, 2008; Fernandez-Gonzalo et al., 2014).

It is commonly assumed that both aerobic and anaerobic power decline with age. This was illustrated by Kostka et al. (2009) when they tested a cohort of *untrained* males. They found that aerobic power and anaerobic power decreased 7.5% and 11% respectively per decade in this cohort. Yet, when Nybo et al. (2014) tracked one *competitive* athlete from ages 19 to 40, they found that that athlete's VO2max was relatively unaffected by their advancing age; so training appeared to have a relatively potent ability to negate ageing effects on aerobic fitness. Given the influence of ageing on the musculoskeletal system, the greater decline in anaerobic performance is not unexpected. However, Capelli et al. (2016) found that well-trained cyclists were able to maintain their mean aerobic power without any noticeable decline until age 40, and their anaerobic capacity appeared to be similarly well maintained until age 49. Different training modes may offer advantages for older elite athletes. For example, high-intensity training is thought to be effective at maintaining VO2max (Nybo et al., 2014; Foster et al., 2007) and has the added benefit of providing some stimulus to recruit type II fibres and help retain muscle mass. In summary, despite the negative 'spin' that is often given to physical fitness and ageing, research on well-trained athletes engaging in intensive training into their 40s appears to indicate that most elements of fitness can be relatively well maintained.

To further retain their competitive edge, ageing elite athletes may also consider emphasising and improving on other aspects of performance that may be more resistant to age-related decrements. Faulkner et al. (2008) illustrated this point using Jenna's sport of professional basketball. Using individual statistics on free throw (an uncontested and highly controlled static skill) shooting percentage, and points scored per game (a contested skill with high physical demands) of three elite professional athletes who played beyond age 40, they were able to demonstrate that while the free throw shooting was consistent across careers, their points scored per game declined significantly after age 30. This suggests that there will be elements of a sport where any physical decline has little to no influence, and there will be other ways for athletes to contribute to team performance.

Other aspects of performance that S&C coaches could account for when working with older athletes include the role psychology and social factors play in performance. Callary et al. (2018) discussed the importance of coaches recognising psychosocial behaviours and characteristics that they could adopt for their coaching practice to cater for their athletes' matured self-concept. We believe there would be merit in SCCs also recognising some of these changes and accommodations. The collective findings of Callary and colleagues suggest that hallmarks of a quality sport experience for a coached older adult include; sport mastery, meaningful competitive and personal endeavours, fun, fitness, quality relationships, feelings of empowerment and validation, as well as intellectual stimulation (Callary et al., 2015, 2017; MacLellan et al., 2019; Rathwell et al., 2015).

In our pedagogical case, Jenna may be more comfortable if she knew that her new SCC was cognitively competent and was capable of thinking and contemplating situations in context. From her description, Jenna wants to be treated as a knowledgeable veteran athlete who also has an extensive and well-established life outside of basketball. She feels that she knows how her body responds to different training modes, and as such she would prefer to know why her SCC is recommending that a particular mode is for her. In her team setting, Jenna would really like the SCC to relinquish his normal 'SCC control' and share some of his 'power' with her (Callary et al., 2018). The benefit for her SCC is that in giving up a little, he is going to gain a lot. He is not only going to have a happier and more settled training room, but he will also be learning more about how to coach and gain the trust and respect of older athletes.

Negotiating flexibility

After due consideration, Carl has ideas about how he might manage Jenna's conditioning, but the challenges are ultimately ones that have to be faced by Jenna and her team (i.e. coaching staff, the medical and SCC). As a starting point, he thinks that Jenna could seek to review her individual needs analysis with the SCC. The aim of these discussions for Jenna would be to have her programme adjusted in order to shift focus from fitness development and progression towards more of an emphasis on fitness maintenance and keeping her healthy. If this came to pass, then Jenna and the SCC could jointly identify key areas and methods for maintenance, and discuss training modes and exercises that may not be well tolerated by Jenna, along with substitutes or compromises.

As a prelude to the meeting of the wider coaching group, it would be advantageous for a meeting to educate of the coaching staff to facilitate their understanding that Jenna is not an injured athlete trying to keep up, but an older athlete trying to adjust to changes in her body and the busyness of her life- someone still capable of competing at the highest level. Moreover, there may be some value in Jenna bringing pertinent game statistics to help support this explanation of her continuing ability to perform. When meeting the wider coaching team, Jenna would need to explain, with the support of the SCC, that her ability to complete physical training will be influenced by her day-to-day soreness, pain and fatigue; and subsequently her motivation. A desired outcome from this meeting would be that the group reach an accord on any non-negotiable team training participation expectations. What Jenna is asking for is individualised, not special (read easier or softer), programmes to enable her to remain healthy, focused and productive. Focusing on her training being individualised, and not reduced, would enable her to still be an active part of the team culture and continue as a role model. What she is seeking is a mutually trustworthy environment in which she will agree not to shirk any responsibilities, and in turn, the coaching team will not expect her to complete any training that is not essential for her or the team. Carl thinks that it would be wise to schedule periodic reviews of Jenna's progress and to ensure that things are proceeding satisfactorily for all parties.

Strength and conditioning strategies

The process of physical adaptation is the fundamental focus of S&C and ultimately results from any interactions between work (training) and recovery. These variables will need to be reconsidered and manipulated to suit Jenna's training tolerance, injury history and training preferences. The challenge for her SCC will be to find the optimal balance for Jenna between loading and recovery. Overall the total training volume will need to be reduced and this may mean more individualised management of her load through briefer exposures to high-intensity/high-load training. Her lower-intensity periods may need to be lower than what she previously performed or that her teammates completed. Given the expected slower recovery response, the number of higher-intensity sessions may need to be reduced over the training week, and there may be a need for a planned or unplanned recovery week within the periodised plan. Jenna's programme would benefit from built-in flexibility, so that sessions can be switched out to suit her training and game responses. Regular monitoring of Jenna's responses will be essential, and this may be preferable more through daily conversations than through monitoring training metrics. For example, knowing that at home there is a sick child, which has resulted in disrupted sleep for Jenna, may be more relevant information than GPS data. In this case the SCC needs to avoid the temptation to default to multiple and frequent measures, and instead have regular and frank conversations with Jenna about her subjective and objective responses to training.

Carl considers the experience of coaching an older athlete would be a welcome challenge for an S&C professional. Even though he is not involved, he is excited at the prospect of learning and experimenting with an experienced and authentic veteran athlete – it has made him rethink some of his S&C practices. He thinks, for example, that at a 'micro' level, there are a number of things that Jenna's SCC could explore during the preseason when training is generally less pressured. For example, he may look at how Jenna responds to, and recovers from, eccentric loading, and it may be that this element needs to be minimised or removed from her conditioning. In that respect, cross training could be considered as a means of reducing orthopaedic loading. The SCC could also spend time analysing Jenna's stretch shortening cycle capabilities. Given that stiffness and musculotendinous elasticity is affected by age (and injury), there may be alterations in Jenna's jumping and landing strategies that could be incorporated into her training regime. Together, the athlete and SCC could experiment with different preparatory and recovery strategies. There may also be ways to disguise Jenna's reduced training loads from the team by having her complete extended warm-ups and cool-downs during team training sessions.

Summary

In this chapter we contend that a number of S&C strategies could be negotiated for older athletes who continue to seek to compete at the elite level. Assumptions around the age threshold for optimum performance are constantly being challenged, and an SCC is likely to encounter athletes who have had lengthy exposures to S&C practices – their needs and expectations are therefore likely to be different. We argue that competent S&C professionals should approach this challenge with inquisitiveness and curiosity, recognising that this presents a valuable and unique professional development opportunity. The research literature tends to focus on the physiology of ageing with the implication that physical capabilities deteriorate to a point where excellent performance will no longer be possible. Our pedagogical case suggests that this perspective ignores many of the psychosocial capabilities and skills that enable older athletes to continue to compete at the highest levels. An enlightened sport coach would hopefully recognise the value of having the services of an elite, highly experienced player who is healthy and contributes to team culture. Similarly, we encourage SCCs to continue to treat each athlete as an individual, seek to understand each athlete's unique contexts, and find ways to accommodate and manage their ongoing S&C needs.

End of chapter tasks

1 Identify some of the biological, psychological and socio-pedagogical considerations of S&C for older athletes.
2 Reflect on a hypothetical case where an athlete reports to you some psychosocial concerns around, for example, weight gain, stress, perception of pain, that seem to conflict with your desire to implement a biologically informed S&C programme. What would you do? What knowledge informs your decision making, and theirs? Hypothesise several scenarios and what outcomes might occur.
3 Create a chart that identifies some of the biological, psychological and socio-pedagogical aspects of performance for older athletes; you may want to start with a single sport rather than aggregating all sports. You could also create a chart that maps the development of these aspects from youth to masters and note the changes that occur over time (i.e. noting how the social skills and cognitive development of an older athlete might explain their high performance at an advanced age).
4 Imagine we took a rigorous and comprehensive developmental approach to S&C for older athletes. What would we need to do make such a vision a reality? How might we change the current way we practice S&C for youth through adulthood?

References

Allen, S.V., & Hopkins, W.G. (2015). Age of peak competitive performance of elite athletes: A systematic review, *Sports Medicine*, 45: 1431–1441.
Amick, S. (2013). Tim Duncan discovers the cure for aging, *USA Today Sports*, 1 Apr. www.usatoday.com/story/sports/nba/spurs/2013/04/01/tim-duncan-san-antonio-ageless-tony-parker-gregg-popovich/2040251/ (accessed 5 Sept. 2019).
Arampatzis, A., Degens, V., Baltzopoulos, V., et al. (2011). Why do older sprinters reach the finish line later? *Exercise and Sport Sciences Reviews*, 39(1): 18–22.
Callary, B., Rathwell, S., & Young, B.W. (2015). Masters swimmers' experiences with coaches: What they need, what they want, what they get, *Sage Open*. DOI:10.1177/2158244015588960.
Callary, B., Rathwell, S., & Young, B.W. (2017). Coaches' report of andragogical approaches with masters athletes, *International Sport Coaching Journal*, 4: 177–190.
Callary, B., Rathwell, S., & Young, B.W. (2018). Coach education and learning sources for coaches of masters swimmers, *International Sport Coaching Journal*, 5: 47–59.
Capelli, C., Rittveger, J., Bruseghini, P., Calabria, E., & Tam, E. (2016). Maximal aerobic power and anaerobic capacity in cycling across the age spectrum in male master athletes, *European Journal of Applied Physiology*, 116: 1395–1410.
Cosh, S., Crabb, S., & Le Couteur, A. (2013). Elite athletes and retirement: Identity, choice, and agency, *Australian Journal of Psychology*, 65: 89–97.
Faulkner, J.A., Davis, C.S., Mendias, C.L., et al. (2008). The aging of elite male athletes: Age-related changes in performance and skeletal muscle structure and function, *Clinical Journal of Sport Medicine*, 18(6): 501–507.
Fell, J., & Williams, A.D. (2008). The effect of aging on skeletal-muscle recovery from exercise: Possible implications for aging athletes, *Journal of Aging and Physical Activity*, 16: 97–115.

Fernandez-Gonzalo, R., Lundberg, T.R., Alvarez-Alvarez, L., et al. (2014). Muscle damage responses and adaptations to eccentric-overload resistance exercise in men and women, *European Journal of Applied Physiology*, 114: 1075–1084.

Foster, C., Wright, G., Battista, R.A., et al. (2007). Training in the aging athlete, *Current Sports Medicine Reports*, 6: 200–206.

Gatto, L. (2019). Roger Federer: 'Travelling with wife and children is a massive task'. www.tennisworldusa.org/tennis/news/Roger_Federer/78504/roger-federer-travelling-with-wife-and-children-is-a-massive-task-/ (accessed 6 Dec. 2019).

Kostka, T., Drygas, W., Jegier, A., et al. (2009). Aerobic and anaerobic power in relation to age and physical activity in 354 men aged 20–88 years, *International Journal of Sports Medicine*, 30: 225–230.

MacLellan, J., Callary, B., & Young, B.W. (2019). Adult learning principles in master's sport: A coach's perspective, *Canadian Journal for the Study of Adult Education*, 31(1): 31–50.

Mitsumune, T., & Kayashima, E. (2013). Possibility of delay in the super-compensation phase due to aging in jump practice, *Asian Journal of Sports Medicine*, 4(4): 295–300.

New Zealand Herald. (2019). Bledisloe cup: Aussie media poke fun at all Blacks veterans. www.nzherald.co.nz/sport/news/article.cfm?c_id=4&objectid=12258306 (accessed 14 Dec. 2019).

Nybo, L., Schmidt, J.F., Fritzdorf, S., et al. (2014). Physiological characteristics of an aging Olympic athlete, *Medicine & Science in Sports & Exercise*, 46(11): 2132–2138.

NZRPA. (2009). Retired player survey. www.nzrpa.co.nz/pdf/NZRPA-Retired-Player-Survey-FINAL.pdf (accessed 1 Sept. 2019).

Rathwell, S., Callary, B., & Young, B.W. (2015). Exploring the context of coached masters swim programs: A narrative approach, *International Journal of Aquatic Research and Education*, 9(1): 70–88.

Smith, T. (2019). Bledisloe cup: Age should not hurt weary 'Old Blacks' despite Australian media jibe. www.stuff.co.nz/sport/rugby/all-blacks/114985843/bledisloe-cup-age-should-not-hurt-weary-old-blacks-despite-australian-media-jibe (accessed 6 Dec. 2019).

Weir, P.L., Baker, J., & Horton, S. (2010). The emergence of masters sport: Participatory trends and historical developments. In J. Baker, S. Horton, & P.L. Weir (eds.), *The Masters Athlete: Understanding the Role of Sport and Exercise in Optimizing Aging*, London: Routledge, pp. 7–14.

Part 5
Health, injury and wellbeing

13 Conditioning for protection?

Introduction
Part 1: pedagogical case
Part 2: commentary

    Injury prevention
    Strength and conditioning and prehabilitation

Injury causation and the web of determinants

    Injury prevention initiatives
    Transferability of movement control training initiatives to prevent injury

Tensions within strength and conditioning

    Deficit model
    Attitudes
    Ecological validity considerations

Summary
End of chapter tasks
References

Introduction

In this chapter we question the premise that conditioning helps keep athletes healthy and injury free. While it is generally accepted that participation in resistance training strategies can help protect athletes from musculoskeletal injuries (e.g. Faigenbaum et al., 2016), injury rates in sport continue to rise (e.g. Caldwell, 2017). There are of course many plausible explanations for this observed trend (e.g. improved injury awareness, reporting and recording, better medical support and changes in sport tactics and play). In this chapter we engage with some of the biophysical arguments, strength and conditioning techniques, and ideologies that are promoted to prevent injury and keep athletes healthy. In addition, we note some of the behavioural challenges for injury prevention and address commonly held assumptions about what constitutes a 'healthy' athlete.

Part 1: pedagogical case

Laura had been feeling really energised at the prospect of a project assigned for her Sports Writing and Reporting course, a final requirement for her journalism degree. She had decided to write a piece on concussion in football (American) and was looking forward to researching the topic and hopefully getting to interview a few key individuals for her project. She had settled on concussion partly based on personal interest, but primarily because her roommate's father was the head coach for a local college's Division II football programme. Recently, when Laura had been at dinner at her roommate's family home, the conversation had turned to the hot topic of football concussions. Coach Bill mentioned that his players were part of a concussion study being conducted by the university's Kinesiology Department and they were trialling a neck strengthening regimen to help prevent concussion. Picking up on her interest, Coach Bill had offered Laura full access to the team's training sessions, and to the players and staff in his programme.

A few weeks after that dinner conversation, Laura met with Colin, the team's head strength and conditioning coach, and they organised for her to spend a week embedded within the football programme. Arriving at her first early morning conditioning session, Laura was a little surprised to find the entire squad sprawled across the gym floor, lying and rolling on rubber balls and foam rollers. Colin explained that this routine was a relatively new practice called self-myofascial release (SMR); this had become a popular way of encouraging athletes to take responsibility for the care of their own bodies. SMR was supposed to improve joint mobility by helping to relax muscles, and was also claimed to help facilitate recovery from previous exercise. Each day, the squad spent their first 20 minutes stretching and 'rolling' various muscles using the foam rollers. As this foam rolling session wrapped up, Colin reminded the players they were all required to work through the neck strengthening programme before they moved on to their lifting session. Laura immediately noticed a few rolling eyes and sensed a general air of reluctant discontent. Colin caught her look and acknowledged the players' responses with a shrug of his shoulders.

The neck strengthening exercises consisted of partnered resisted exercises using rubber bands and body balls (Swiss balls). It seemed to Laura that the exercises progressed nicely from basic neck strengthening, to partner exercises where the neck was carefully loaded, to more dynamic loading exercises. Although sport science was not her thing, as a layperson she could appreciate the apparent logic of strengthening the neck in multiple planes of movement to help control head movement during tackles and collisions, and therefore prevent the brain from being concussed. Once the players were engaged in their neck exercises, Colin wandered over to Laura and explained that the players had not really 'bought into' the neck strengthening regime because the exercises took 30 minutes out of their daily training time, and the guys don't think that it is time well spent. 'You've got to realise', he said, 'every player here is seeking to get bigger, stronger, and faster for the football season, and spending 30 minutes on neck exercises is not contributing to that'. He also explained that, in the players' minds, because they could not measure individual progress with the neck exercises – being in the gym was often all about 'seeing their numbers going up' – they were genuinely reluctant to get excited about neck exercises. Colin admitted to Laura that he was 'kind of sympathetic to the players' lack of compliance'. Indeed, Laura noticed that many of the players seemed to hurry through the neck exercises with little apparent effort, and as soon as practicably possible started moving on to the other exercises for their session.

During breaks in their exercise routines, Laura was able to talk with several players. One explained that every Monday, before they did their heavy upper body routine, they had a series of balance and prehabilitation exercises to complete before going onto a lower body strength session. He clearly took these 'prehab' exercises seriously, yet he confirmed Colin's suspicions, suggesting that he and his teammates did not really value the neck exercise session. 'Doing all of those neck exercises takes too long, and I'm not convinced that they are going to make any difference to concussion. The head impacts in football happen so quickly and unexpectedly, so I don't think there's any way a few slow strength exercises are really going to protect me. Our prehab routine makes far more sense for injury prevention and I find it's a great warm-up before I start lifting heavy.'

One of the team's athletic trainers, Shelly, entered the weight room to observe a couple of players working through their routines. After being introduced, Shelly explained to Laura the shoulder prehabilitation routine the players were doing. 'We have a lot of shoulder injuries in football, mainly shoulder separations and dislocations, but sometimes it's a pectoralis major tear or a rotator cuff injury. The thing is that these guys often have a history of lifting a lot of heavy weights, so they've become very strong in the major muscle groups but they've neglected other areas. Their stabilising muscles haven't been strengthened in parallel with those big muscles. We've added in these prehabilitation exercises to try and help prevent some of those shoulder injuries. I think most teams are doing some form of prehabilitation these days, so presumably it works. We also have some of our players working on knee and hamstring prehab exercises. I really wish they would put more effort into the neck exercises though. A couple of our players here, have a history of 'stingers' (a nerve injury caused by compression or elongation of the shoulder) and a few others have other recurrent neck problems. Those players in particular could really benefit from more neck strengthening. The trouble is that the neck muscles are not 'show muscles' and aren't strength tested, so they are not as interested in them.

Later that morning, Laura was out on the field observing the different position groups moving through their training drills. She was surprised by the intensity of the training and high impact collisions. One of the assistant coaches remarked to Laura: 'Man, I can't believe I once played this sport. These guys are spending so much time in the weight room these days, and have so much better nutrition than we had. They seem to be bigger, faster, and stronger each year. Some of those collisions out there are scary, and that's scrimmaging against teammates!'

After the lunch break, Coach Bill invited Laura up into the observation tower with him, and they chatted as he continued to cast an observant eye over the scrimmages. 'A lot of the players on our roster have come to us as "single-sport" athletes, meaning that they were "encouraged" to specialise and focus only on football from a young age (see Chapter 10, 'Early sampling and deliberate play'). So they've been lifting weights and playing football, but many of them haven't really benefitted from playing a range of different sports that would have developed different body parts, involved different movement patterns, and required different types of fitness. I'm really not a great believer in this prehab thing – I'm not convinced that you can really prevent the injuries that occur in many of those collisions out there. I think it is largely down to luck sometimes. But, I don't tell the players that and I certainly don't give that impression to our strength and conditioning coaches or our athletic trainers. They believe in this preventive stuff, and the players believe in it, and I think that as long as that's the case, there is no harm in the player's being encouraged to look after their bodies. This is a brutal sport and the sad reality is that many of these players will be hurt over the season – but if we have a run of injuries and drop a few key games, you can bet that questions will be asked of me and our injury prevention programme.'

For Laura, the training day concluded at 4 p.m., leaving her with time to collect her thoughts and review her notes from her first day with the programme. It was early days, but she was mightily impressed with the structure and organisation of the programme. She sat for a while and reflected on all that she had observed and heard. The word that leapt out at her was 'contradictory'! Already she was thinking of changing the topic of her writing piece. Sure concussion was topical and, thanks to the media, in the public consciousness – but it had been written about a lot. Laura was feeling that the apparent conflicting ideologies she was discovering might be more interesting to explore through further research and interviews. The team had a neck strengthening regime that no one really wanted to do and yet it could help. They had a rehabilitation programme that everyone completed diligently that could have tenuous links with injury prevention. The head coach didn't appear to value or believe that the injury prevention initiatives were effective, but liked the structure and discipline that these initiatives provided. In all of this, player compliance appeared to be in a delicate balance. The team appeared to be going to great lengths to prevent injury, yet they still spent the bulk of their training trying to enhance the size of the players. As she thought it through, this gym conditioning would ultimately result in bigger bodies at higher speeds producing massive collisions; collisions that were bound to injure. On the surface, things appeared well reasoned; yet with a deeper level of scrutiny, it seemed to Laura that there were so many apparent contradictions.

Part 2: commentary

Injury prevention

Historically, sport and physical activity have been embraced and promoted positively by governments and sporting organisations as being health promoting and broadly beneficial to society (e.g. van Mechelen, 1992). There has been, however, a growing awareness of the concomitant potential for injury, pain and harm – harm that can continue to follow participants into their later lives. Research suggests that approximately every fifth unintentional injury in the developed world is associated with sports or physical exercise (Timpka et al., 2006), a statistic that is difficult to reconcile with wellbeing, particularly when the latter is viewed in a holistic fashion. Unresolved musculoskeletal injury and joint deterioration can restrict habitual physical activity and lead to various comorbidities, compromising health (Golightly et al., 2009). Aside from threats to participant welfare, a high rate of injury can significantly affect sport and athletic performance outcomes. From a public relations perspective, the apparent injury risk can also be a disincentive to commencing or continuing sport participation (Boufous et al., 2004). These concerns have prompted intensified efforts around injury prevention.

Preventing or minimising injury risk, and its associated after-effects, can be approached from multiple perspectives. Interestingly, most contemporary research has addressed injury prevention from the standpoint of the 'vulnerable athlete' and has explored ways to make individuals more resilient to identified inciting or injury-provoking events within their respective sports. Little research has, however, questioned the structure of individual sports and explored the effect of rule changes, or the effect of officiating and individual behaviours with respect to those rules (McBain et al., 2012; Micheo, 2019). Indeed, most injury prevention research has focused on protective equipment or the physical training of individuals. Consequent to this emphasis, injury prevention has become a significant part of athlete preparation and management.

Strength and conditioning and prehabilitation

In recent times, the evaluation of the performance and effectiveness of S&C professionals has included their ability to prevent and rehabilitate injury. We routinely hear that S&C is in and of itself an injury prevention strategy (Faigenbaum et al., 2016); the logic being that by increasing strength or, for example, improving range of motion, we are in turn adding to the 'natural' protective function of muscle and other elements of the musculoskeletal system. While historically rehabilitation has not been a major focus of SCCs, the resistance training knowledge and skills of SCCs and their expertise with conditioning methods have been recognised to be a key part of injury prevention and rehabilitation. With the professionalisation of sport and an increased emphasis on, and time dedicated to, S&C, the relationship between physical training and injury incidence has been increasingly placed 'under the microscope'. The concept of prehabilitation has emerged in recent times as part of the routine practice of a competent S&C professional. Prehabilitation is a term adopted from medicine and has potentially been misinterpreted by the S&C community. The concept of prehabilitation originated with the American military's desire to increase military draft suitability by 'remediating defects' that had been identified in individuals prior to their military medical examinations (Rowntree, 1942). Prehabilitation in turn was adopted and became commonplace in general and orthopaedic medicine (e.g. Asoh & Tsuji, 1981), where it was recognised that various forms of conditioning, undertaken prior to surgery, typically resulted in better treatment outcomes.

Injury causation and the web of determinants

Given that the term prehabilitation has become synonymous with S&C contexts, it is timely to reflect on the interpretations and appropriateness of the prehabilitation concept. The historical premise of prehabilitation is that defects or problems are clearly identifiable, that those defects are remediable and that appropriate remedial action will then remove or negate the problem or subsequent risk. Prehabilitation as an injury prevention strategy in S&C contexts appears to be 'drawing a long bow' in assuming the potential for injury prevention. As a hypothetical solution to injury, prehabilitation is a premise that cannot be easily proven or discounted. The causes of athletic injuries are multifactorial and complex, with both identified and unknown factors interacting in nonlinear and unpredictable ways. These erratic interactions will typically confound attempts to anticipate and prevent injury (Bittencourt et al., 2016). Philippe and Mansi (1998) described such nonlinearity as representing a web of determinants. By this, they meant that various factors can be interlinked in ways such that small changes could accumulate and combine to produce large and unexpected consequences. In that respect, Bittencourt et al. (2016) used the term 'equifinality' to describe the potential for many alternate pathways to lead to a given injury, confounding attempts to anticipate and avoid injury. Conceptually, the web of determinants is at odds with the traditional reductionist approaches that are commonly employed to inform the development of injury prevention strategies. Put simply, reducing injury to one or more putative 'known' causes will likely result in other potential causes being overlooked and the importance of the 'known' factors being overestimated. Bittencourt et al. (2016) hasten to emphasise that informed reductionist views still have a place in injury prevention practice. It is, however, important to heed the observation of Cameron (2010), who suggested that while some injury risk factors may be perceived to be non-modifiable (not influenced by S&C methods), we should avoid the temptation to discount these factors as unimportant and unworthy of pursuit. Gaining an understanding of all potential risk factors could prove to be crucial for contextualising ostensibly modifiable risk factors.

Injury prevention initiatives

The identification of intrinsic and extrinsic risk factors for injury have given rise to multicomponent programmes, such as those observed by Laura in this chapter's pedagogical case.

These have been supported by the findings from numerous intervention studies (e.g. Attwood et al., 2018), yet theoretical challenges can be mounted about the true modifiability of some of the identified risk factors. For example, Alentorn-Geli et al. (2014) stated that many of the anatomical and biomechanical risk factors associated with injury may not in fact be relevant to athletes; in reality the evidence for neuromuscular and biomechanical risk factors for athlete injury are often assumed rather than proven. Although there have been promising findings from prevention programmes, the evidence base remains limited, and conclusions are often constrained by the research designs employed, the variability in programme adherence (Andrews et al., 2013) and a heavy reliance on seeking to 'normalise' biomechanical movement patterns (Ardern et al., 2018). Some of these factors could account for the equivocal findings from injury prevention programmes. For example, Kristenson et al. (2013) found that novice professional football (aka soccer) players had a lower rate of injury than the established, and presumably better conditioned, athletes. Similarly, Brown et al. (2016) obtained a reduced serious injury rate in junior, but not senior, rugby union players following an intervention programme. In both cases the more advanced athletes are assumed to be better physically conditioned and more skilful. By asking the 'why' questions around these mixed results, practitioners could begin to identify that other factors such as differences in injury exposure, level of medical support, willingness to acknowledge and report injury, and style and level of play, potentially influence overall injury risk. In other words, by narrowing our focus, we may be overlooking important aspects of injury incidence.

Recently, other injury prevention initiatives have come to the fore in the context of the New Zealand All Blacks rugby union team. Arguably these initiatives have come about as a result of viewing health more broadly than just the physical ability to play. Days before the naming of the 2019 World Cup squad, Liam Squire, a player widely considered to be a certain selection to make the team, communicated to the head coach that he wanted to withdraw from consideration. He explained why:

> After what has been a really tough year for me mentally and physically, and after speaking with people I trust on whether I should make myself available again for the All Blacks, I felt I wasn't ready just yet physically or mentally for the pressures of test match rugby. . . . As Steve [the coach] said yesterday, if the All Blacks do get injuries, and I'm performing well enough, then I'm 100% available. The decision has been bloody hard but I feel it's the best one for me and the All Blacks. I wish the team every success and am behind them 100%. I have never been one to speak a lot publicly so I hope people can respect my privacy and decision on this and I can move forward and keep enjoying my rugby. For me mental health is a lot more important than playing rugby.
> (NZ Herald, 2019)

Increasingly, mental health is being discussed in society and in the context of sport. There are numerous plausible reasons for this. For example, former National Hockey League goalie Clint Malarchuk has recently gone public with his daily struggle with depression, anxiety and obsessive compulsive disorder (Boren & Gutierrez, 2019). Malarchuk made headlines for the terrifying moment in 1989 when a skate slashed his jugular during a game.

> TV viewers watched in horror as his throat was cut during a Buffalo Sabres game. He grabbed his neck as blood spurted onto the ice. Malarchuk thought he was going to die and told one trainer to call his mother. He didn't die, of course, and was back on the ice not long after being stitched back together. The wound healed, but the mental

devastation was only starting.... 'With athletes, we're kind of depicted as really tough. We do not want to admit that we are struggling in any way because of the stigma. Mental illness is real, and it's out there.'

(Boren & Gutierrez, 2019)

Although he soon returned to the ice after this horrific neck injury, Malarchuk dealt with post-traumatic stress disorder as a consequence of the injury, along with the aforementioned ailments. If we accept that the causes of athletic injuries are multifactorial and complex, with both identified and unknown factors interacting in nonlinear and unpredictable ways, then we can assume that poor mental health is a factor in some athletic injuries (e.g. Ivarsson & Johnson, 2010). Many SCCs are with athletes for several hours a day, so if they are encouraged to become informed about viewing health and wellbeing more holistically, then they may be able to identify indicators of poor, or ill, mental health and be able to support the athlete to seek help. If an athlete is having issues with mental health, then it is fair to assume that other parts of their lives and training, which assist in injury prevention, are possibly also being neglected. The NSCA has creditably published a position statement on supporting athletes with mental health issues (Gearity & Moore, 2017) but has stopped short of considering the links with conditioning and performance alluded to in this chapter.

Transferability of movement control training initiatives to prevent injury

We question here the assumptions made concerning movement control training programmes and the transferability of those learned movement skills to sport. In sport, multiple unanticipated injury-provoking incidents are encountered during training or game events. Most preventative programmes target improved movement control, raising the question: Can preventative biomechanical re-education strategies afford actual protection from injury? (Hewett & Bates, 2017). Prevention programmes are usually introduced and completed in controlled settings where an individual performs selected movement tasks in a preplanned and unimpeded environment. However, if these programmes are to replicate reality, then the movements need to be performed in settings where attention is not focused solely on those movements. In competition, athletes have to make adjustments to their own movements, the actions of opponents and the ways in which game play organically evolves (Almonroeder et al., 2018). Furthermore, athletic actions are usually conducted at high velocities and under high loads (Ekstrand et al., 2013). Motor learning and motor control fundamentals were highlighted by Benjaminse (2015) in her critique of preventative strategies, where she pointed out that the internal instructional focus adopted in such programmes may be counterproductive to the development of movement patterns with the necessary sensorimotor adaptability that is vital to athletic performance. This fundamental criticism could be levelled at most injury prevention programmes that involve standardised exercises and movement patterns practised in highly controlled settings. An SCC could consider complementing such programmes using cognitive distractors and more authentic sport specific movement patterns and tasks.

Tensions within strength and conditioning

As Laura identified in the pedagogical case, for the reflective practitioner it is apparent that numerous contradictions are evident in the work of the SCC. There is a need to provide individual training loads that provoke positive adaptations, yet these training loads also introduce fatigue and repetition through deliberately constrained movement patterns (Gabbett et al., 2016). The SCC is constantly trying to measure and balance the need for, and the risk of, increased load (Windt et al., 2017). If that training 'dose' is misjudged, an overuse injury or an increased risk of traumatic injury can result. We could also argue that S&C places a significant emphasis on developing strength and enhancing force production. Given that the musculoskeletal system in effect produces, controls, absorbs and senses force, it could be argued that a force production emphasis may not stimulate parallel improvements in those other capabilities. The structural adaptations of the musculoskeletal system and the neuromotor adaptations to S&C could affect those structures' protective functions and predispose athletes to injury (Cochrane et al., 2010).

Laura also notes the rather obvious paradox with a collision sport such as football, where the athletes are being conditioned to develop higher forces, move at faster speeds and often with added body mass in order to excel in their sport. Yet those higher forces, velocities and masses are inevitably going to result in bigger collisions and higher-impact forces. We train athletes to get stronger, stronger and stronger without considering that by helping them to throw harder or jump higher, we may be encouraging injury – particularly if we are not concomitantly training them to decelerate their throwing arm or to land better.

Deficit model

A deficit approach is often adopted for injury prevention interventions, highlighting another tension for the SCC. Adopting such approaches assume that helping to convert an individual to being an 'ideal normal' will somehow provide protection from injury, and that screening will help identify those who fall short of an ideal norm and therefore are supposedly at increased risk. This is another example of not adequately framing one's question (Chapter 3). SCCs are often socialised into believing that there is an ideal normal, but framing the problem by questioning some of those assertions can help. For example, an SCC may notice that athletes who correspond with the ideal normal still get injured, just as some with the non-ideal profile have managed to escape injury.

The deficit model assumes that a putative deficit is the cause of a problem, whereas often that level of causative association has not been supported by research findings. Van Mechelen's (1992) sequence of prevention model should help eliminate this problem; establish the extent of the problem, identify injury mechanisms, introduce preventive measures and then assess effectiveness by revisiting the extent of the problem. However, injuries addressing theoretical imbalances and movement imbalances are commonly promoted in sport through sport-specific injury prevention programmes, yet these have seldom demonstrably reduced injury incidence. A good reality check for the strength and conditioning professional contemplating injury prevention programmes is to recognise that an athlete with risk factors will not necessarily get injured (Howe et al., 2017), and that other athletes without risk factors will.

Attitudes

Laura's placement permitted her to observe first-hand the attitudes of the coaching staff and athletes to injury prevention programmes. As Donaldson et al. (2016) have observed, some sport coaches have voiced concern that preventative programmes offer little in the way of performance enhancement, yet appear to contribute in their own way to athletes' overall fatigue, muscle soreness and an increased injury risk exposure. Exercise-induced fatigue contributes to alterations in proprioception and exercise technique, with changes in movement control and efficiency likely (Hooper et al., 2013). Fatigue-related interference with neuromuscular control can in turn affect joint dynamic stability (Ribeiro et al., 2008). While much attention is directed to tissue failure through maladaptation as an injury etiology, an alternative explanation is that fatigue-related 'failure' of musculotendinous units to protect musculoskeletal structures can also lead to injury. Gabbett (2016) highlights the quandary facing S&C professionals: realising the objective of developing athlete resilience without at the same time exposing them to greater injury risk. He notes the 'inverted U' relationship between training load and soft tissue injury risk, and the difficulty of finding the optimal individual load.

Ecological validity considerations

In keeping with Laura's observations, Donaldson et al. (2016) maintain that successful interventions need to account for the contexts in which they will be implemented. The perspectives of coaching staff and athletes need to be carefully considered, along with the regular demands on the time and energies of the athletes, and the positional and individual differences in fitness and commitment to conditioning. If, as has been suggested, programme compliance is important, coaches and athletes will need to be educated not only about the benefits but also about the practicalities of integrating preventative exercises and patterns into existing training routines. In this respect the long-term attractiveness and suitability of programmes need to be contemplated, and if the fidelity of technique is crucial (Frank et al., 2015), the importance of correct technique needs to be clearly conveyed to the individuals involved.

Any prevention programme needs to consider the practical challenges of introducing activities for injury prevention that will not conflict with other training needs and that will not impose on limited training time. Most injury prevention programmes appear to be one-size-fits-all, and the wisdom of such a scattergun approach is questionable. Acevedo et al. (2014) were supportive of preventive programmes but made the case for interventions to target individuals with identified modifiable risk factors, and to be individually tailored to the sport and the athlete.

In the process of researching her project, Laura has demonstrated insightful reflections from her week imbedded with the football squad. While it could be easy for her to have been overawed by the nature and extent of a programme, Laura said 'Wait, What?' (Ryan, 2017) and 'How can that be?' She noticed apparent discrepancies between theory and practical application and sensed the lack of enthusiasm and buy-in from the coaching staff and athletes around some practices. These attitudes may be indicative of the lack of faith in the programme efficacy, the provision of insufficient educational information or a lack of understanding of the pressures and nuances of a football training week on behalf of the programme sponsors/advocates. She has sensed that within the programme, it is convenient to accept some 'truths' and reject others. She also hinted at questions concerning whose interests were being best served and taken care of (athlete, coach, researchers or SCCs) with the various initiatives and processes within the football programme. A competent SCC would hopefully be considering all of these potential messages and seeking to improve the implementation of this important aspect of S&C.

Summary

This chapter examines two relatively recent additions to S&C scope of practice: prehabilitation and injury prevention focused movement competency programmes. We discuss the potential for reducing injury in sport and the various strategies that have been adopted. There is a sense that certain preventive strategies may be privileged by specific sports because they are more convenient and less disruptive for that sport. The concept of prehabilitation is unpacked and examined on the basis of our ability to accurately identify and remediate causes of injury. The web of determinants concept was used to emphasise that the multiple causative factors of injury are interrelated in nonlinear and unpredictable ways. We also question the concept of non-modifiable injury factors which may be interpreted to mean that a given factor is of lesser importance. This chapter examines the rationale of injury prevention programmes that target modifying basic strength, range of motion and biomechanics of movement, with some success but overall equivocal findings. We note that our pedagogical case highlights some of the issues with injury prevention programmes, namely athlete and management acceptance, compliance and exercise fidelity. We also argue in this chapter that prevention strategies should be inclusive of mental wellbeing in athletes, who may be dealing with various challenging aspects of sport, particularly injury and its consequences.

End of chapter tasks

1 Evidence-based practice (EBP) has become a popular buzzword in today's age. In short, it means using science and research to guide one's practice. Scientists claim that without EBP, you're just guessing. However, some EBP models do acknowledge the clinician's, or in this case the SCC's, clinical judgment and the client's or patient's, or in this case an athlete's, preferences and desires. Consider, on your own or with a group, the following questions:

   - What evidence counts, and what's excluded?
   - Does it make sense to use knowledge obtained in a lab, or artificial setting, when working in the complex, messy reality of athletic performance and coaching?
   - Do clinicians or coaches actually consider the preferences and desires of their clients or athletes?
   - Have you ever used EBP, but things did not resolve or perhaps even got worse?

2 Consider the issue of *modifiability* recognised in the chapter. Pick a topic, such as muscle strength, connective tissue remodelling, or alignment of bones and joints, and research how modifiable it is. Can change occur? If so, how much, and importantly, what practical difference does this change make? How much time is needed to cause this change? How long does the change last? Do you think this is essential and meaningful?

3 Watch an elite sporting match and question the logic of that sport's contributing to health. Next, watch youth sport, perhaps a contact or collision sport like rugby or American football, hockey or even boxing or MMA. Why do we subject youth to these sports when there are other, safer sports that arguably develop the same qualities without the risk of injury?

4 An SCC often helps athletes become stronger and gain body mass (often muscle and sometimes fat). Greater strength and mass can mean greater forces are produced, which can increase, not decrease, injury. Discuss this paradox and the SCC's role and ethics of developing elite athletes and healthy people.

5 Read a book or an article by, or about, an athlete or coach discussing mental health (see the following list for some examples). Consider the individual and social forces acting

upon this person and how it affected their mental health. How could you become aware of how sport generally, and SCC specifically, positively and negatively effects mental health? What could you do to develop a mentally healthy S&C environment? Where, and to whom, will you refer athletes for proper mental healthcare?

- *All Blacks Don't Cry: A Story of Hope* by John Kirwan (2010)
- *Inside Out Coaching: How Sports Can Transform Lives* by Joe Ehrmann (2011)
- https://nypost.com/2019/05/29/metta-world-peace-i-wish-i-had-trusted-more-people-with-my-mental-health-struggle/
- www.theplayerstribune.com/en-us/articles/kevin-love-everyone-is-going-through-something
- Gearity, B.T., & Moore, W.G. (2017). Mental health best practices: Inter-association consensus document: Best practices for understanding and supporting student-athlete mental wellness. *Strength and Conditioning Journal*, 39(4): 1–3.

References

Acevedo, R.J., Rivera-Vega, A., Miranda, G., et al. (2014). Anterior cruciate ligament injury: Identification of risk factors and prevention strategies, *Current Sports Medicine Reports*, 13(3): 186–191.

Alentorn-Geli, E., Mendiguchia, J., Samuelsson, K., et al. (2014). Prevention of anterior cruciate ligament injuries in sports. Part I: Systematic review of risk factors in male athletes, *Knee Surgery, Sports Traumatology, Arthroscopy*, 22: 3–15.

Almonroeder, T.G., Kernozek, T., Cobb, S., et al. (2018). Cognitive demands influence lower extremity mechanics during a drop vertical jump task in female athletes, *Journal of Orthopaedic & Sports Physical Therapy*, 48(5): 381–387.

Andrews, N., Gabbe, B.J., & Cook, J. (2013). Could targeted exercise programmes prevent lower limb injury in community Australian football? *Sports Medicine*, 43: 751–763.

Ardern, C.L., Ekås, G.R., Grindem, H., et al. (2018). 2018 international Olympic committee consensus statement on prevention, diagnosis and management of paediatric anterior cruciate ligament (ACL) injuries, *British Journal of Sports Medicine*, 52: 422–438.

Asoh, T., & Tsuji, H. (1981). Preoperative physical training for cardiac patients requiring non-cardiac surgery, *The Japanese Journal of Surgery*, 11(4): 251–255.

Attwood, M.J., Roberts, S.P., Trewartha, G., et al. (2018). Efficacy of a movement control injury prevention programme in adult men's community rugby union: A cluster randomised controlled trial, *British Journal of Sports Medicine*, 52: 368–374.

Benjaminse, A. (2015). *Motor Learning in ACL Injury Prevention*, Groningen: University of Groningen.

Bittencourt, N.F.N., Meeuwisse, W.H., Mendonça, L.D., et al. (2016). Complex systems approach for sports injuries: Moving from risk factor identification to injury pattern recognition – narrative review and new concept, *British Journal of Sports Medicine*, 50: 1309–1314.

Boren, C., & Gutierrez, M. (2019). This former NHL star 'almost died three times': Now he's speaking out about mental illness. www.washingtonpost.com/sports/2019/11/07/this-former-nhl-star-almost-died-three-times-now-hes-speaking-out-about-mental-illness/ (accessed 7 Dec. 2019).

Boufous, S., Finch, C., & Bauman, A. (2004). Parental safety concerns: A barrier to sport and physical activity in children? *Australia and New Zealand Journal of Public Health*, 28(5): 482–486.

Brown, J.C., Verhagen, E., Knol, D., et al. (2016). The effectiveness of the nationwide BokSmart rugby injury prevention program on catastrophic injury rates, *Scandinavian Journal of Medicine and Science in Sports*, 26: 221–225.

Caldwell, O. (2017). Sport injury costs soar to $542m – that's more to ACC than road crashes. www.stuff.co.nz/sport/94891232/sports-injuries-cost-nz-500m-more-than-road-carnage (accessed 7 Dec. 2019).

Cameron, K. (2010). Commentary: Time for a paradigm shift in conceptualizing risk factors in sports injury research, *Journal of Athletic Training*, 45(1): 58–60.

Cochrane, J.L., Lloyd, D.G., Besier, T.F., et al. (2010). Training affects knee kinematics and kinetics in cutting maneuvers in sport, *Medicine and Science in Sports and Exercise*, 42(8): 1535–1544.

Donaldson, A., Lloyd, D.G., Gabbe, B.J., et al. (2016). Scientific evidence is just the starting point: A generalizable process for developing sports injury prevention interventions, *Journal of Sport and Health Science*, 5: 334–341.

Ekstrand, J., Hägglund, M., Kristenson, K., et al. (2013). Fewer ligament injuries but no preventive effect on muscle injuries and severe injuries: An 11-year follow-up of the UEFA champions league injury study, *British Journal of Sports Medicine*, 47: 732–737.

Faigenbaum, A.D, Lloyd, R.S., MacDonald, J., et al. (2016). Citius, Altius, Fortius: Beneficial effects of resistance training for young athletes: Narrative review, *British Journal of Sports Medicine*, 50: 3–7.

Frank, B.S., Register-Mihalik, J., & Padua, D.A. (2015). High levels of coach intent to integrate a ACL injury prevention, *Journal of Science and Medicine in Sport*, 18(4): 400–406.

Gabbett, T.J. (2016). The training-injury prevention paradox: Should athletes be training smarter and harder? *British Journal of Sports Medicine*, 50: 273–280.

Gabbett, T.J., Hulin, B.T., Blanch, P., et al. (2016). High training workloads alone do not cause sports injuries: How you get there is the real issue, *British Journal of Sports Medicine*, 50: 444–445.

Gearity, B., & Moore, E.W.G. (2017). National strength and conditioning association's endorsement of the national collegiate athletic association sport science institute's 'mental health best practices inter-association consensus document best practices for understanding and supporting student-athlete mental wellness', *Strength & Conditioning Journal*, 39(4): 1–3.

Golightly, Y.M., Marshall, S.W., Callahan, L.F., et al. (2009). Early-onset arthritis in retired National Football League players, *Journal of Physical Activity and Health*, 6(5): 638–643.

Hewett, T., & Bates, N. (2017). Preventive biomechanics: A paradigm shift with a translational approach to injury prevention, *American Journal of Sports Medicine*, 45(1): 2654–2664.

Hooper, D.R., Szivak, T.K., DiStefano, L.J., et al. (2013). Effects of resistance training fatigue on joint biomechanics, *Journal of Strength and Conditioning Research*, 27(1): 146–153.

Howe, L.P., Waldron, M., & Read, P. (2017). A systems-based approach to injury prevention for the strength and conditioning coach, *Strength and Conditioning Journal*, 39(6): 60–69.

Ivarsson, A., & Johnson, U. (2010). Psychological factors as predictors of injuries among senior soccer players: A prospective study, *Journal of Science and Medicine in Sport*, 9(2): 347–352.

Kirwan, J. (2010). *All Blacks Don't Cry: A Story of Hope,* Auckland: Penguin Books.

Kristenson, K., Waldén, M., Ekstrand, J., et al. (2013). Lower injury rates for newcomers to professional soccer: A prospective cohort study over 9 consecutive seasons, *American Journal of Sports Medicine*, 41: 1419–1425.

McBain, K., Shrier, I., Shultz, R., Meeuwisse, W., Klügl, M., Garza, D., & Matheson, G. (2012). Prevention of sport injury II: A systematic review of clinical science research, *British Journal of Sports Medicine*, 46(3): 174–179.

Micheo, W. (2019). Physical and rehabilitation medicine in health care systems: Prevention and prehabilitation in physical and rehabilitation medicine – the example of musculoskeletal and sports injuries, *Journal of International Society of Physical and Rehabilitation Medicine*, 2: S76–S80.

New Zealand Herald. (2019). Rugby world cup: Liam Squire reveals why he turned down all Blacks. www.nzherald.co.nz/sport/news/article.cfm?c_id=4&objectid=12263276 (accessed 7 Dec. 2019).

Philippe, P., & Mansi, O. (1998). Nonlinearity in the epidemiology of complex health and disease processes, *Theoretical Medicine and Bioethics*, 19: 591–607.

Ribeiro, F., Santos, F., Gonçalves, P., et al. (2008). Effects of volleyball match-induced fatigue on knee joint position sense, *European Journal of Sport Science*, 8(6): 397–402.

Rowntree, L.G. (1942). Rehabilitation and prehabilitation, *JAMA*, 119(15): 1171–1175.

Ryan, J.E. (2017). *Wait, What? And Life's Other Essential Questions*, New York: HarperCollins Publishers.

Timpka, T., Ekstrand, J., & Svanstro, L. (2006). From sports injury prevention to safety promotion in sports, *Sports Medicine*, 36(9): 733–745.

van Mechelen, W., Hlobil, H., & Kemper, H. (1992). Incidence, severity, aetiology and prevention of sports injuries: A review of concepts, *Sports Medicine*, 14(2): 82–99.

Windt, J., Gabbett, T.J., Ferris, D., et al. (2017). Training load – injury paradox: Is greater preseason participation associated with lower in-season injury risk in elite rugby league players? *British Journal of Sports Medicine*, 51: 645–650.

14 Return to play following injury

Introduction
Part 1: pedagogical case
Part 2: commentary
Strength and conditioning ideologies
Injury prevention paradigms
Return-to-play decisions
Pain and sport injury
Acting ethically
Summary
End of chapter tasks
References

Introduction

Injury prevalence in sport is highly topical, generating significant pressure for researchers and sport administrators to improve methods of preventing and managing injury. We argue in this chapter that another approach might be to examine the cultures surrounding sport and how players, coaches and management respond to injury. Premature return to competition from injury has been identified as a preventable cause of injury, yet many coaches are prepared to start a player who may only be 90% fit. In this chapter we examine some of the apparent contradictions between strength and conditioning objectives, caring for athletes and injury management.

Part 1: pedagogical case

After paying his dues as a volunteer strength and conditioning coach (SCC) at a local rugby club, Paullu (aka Paul to everyone outside his family) is seeking full-time employment as an SCC. Although he currently earns his living as a personal trainer, his five years working with the St Kilda premier rugby team have convinced him that strength and conditioning (S&C) is his real passion. Paul has worked his way up through the club by helping with the club's age-group (i.e. youth) teams running fitness sessions and game-day warm-ups. For the past three years he has worked alongside coach Bodie Murray, and, with Bodie projected to be the next regional (read provincial/state) coach, Paul is hoping that if Bodie takes on that role, he will be included as part of his coaching/management team. Coach Bodie has been great to work with, operating what Paul perceives to be a really 'professional' programme and setting high expectations for the players as well as for the rest of his management and support team. Even though it is only an amateur club team, Paul feels that he is operating pretty much as he would if he was an SCC with a professional rugby team. During the last off-season, nearly half the premier squad completed weights and conditioning programmes. As a way of recognising Paul's good work, the club sponsored six players to have paid personal training sessions with him during the off-season. That endorsement encouraged a few other players to pay their own way for extra training sessions. For Paul, the experience of working over the summer with a committed group of players was a great opportunity, not only for developing his conditioning repertoire but also for building good rapport with many key squad members.

Paul lives with his partner Leanne, a final-year (i.e. senior) nursing student. He describes her as a very caring person who will make a great nurse. Leanne likes to constantly test and challenge Paul's knowledge about anatomy and physiology. This often occurs as she is preparing to write an assignment or take an examination. Her latest assignment required her, as a student nurse, to reflect on an ethical dilemma. Leanne chose to discuss the dilemma she would face if her personal values conflicted with the values of the nursing profession, her employer (the hospital board) or a patient. She really struggled to think her way through how she would deal with such a situation. Not only did every stakeholder in the scenario have the right to be treated fairly, but she was also about to join a profession where practices were very rule-based and organisations had definite standards of practice. Leanne got very upset when Paul suggested that she should follow the rules and just do her job. She accused Paul of having no empathy for the players he worked with and challenged him on the role ethics played in his work as an SCC, in the S&C profession and the sport of rugby in general.

Leanne's challenge and assertions upset Paul. His initial irritation gave way to his reflecting on the points that she had made. What did he actually know about ethics and acting ethically? He certainly hadn't been taught much about that at university! Later that week he swallowed his pride and asked if he could read one of her articles on ethics and values in the nursing profession. She gave him a 2011 article by Sellman on professional values and nursing. After reading this, he didn't have to think too hard to find some parallels between nursing and his work with rugby. In fact, the Sellman paper made him think about a current 'situation' that he realised he was wrestling with. Callum, one of the team's veterans at 35 years of age, had played premier rugby for 15 years. As the team's first choice blind-side flanker, he was considered an integral part of the team's success. Paul's concern was that four weeks earlier, Callum had separated his acromioclavicular (AC) joint and had been sidelined since. The team physiotherapist considered the injury to be a relatively minor grade II separation that would typically require about six weeks for the ligaments to heal. However, the common thinking around rugby circles was that if you waited for the AC joint pain to disappear completely, you would be needlessly wasting nearly half of the season. So, most of the people playing, coaching or managing rugby would be comfortable with players returning to play before an injury like this was fully pain-free. With this 'common-sense' view in mind, the physiotherapist, and Paul, had progressed Callum through running drills for the past two weeks, but they had not exposed him to any sprinting, heavy weights or contact drills.

This season the St Kilda premier team was close to making the playoffs for the first time in seven years. With three games remaining, they needed only one more win to secure a place in the playoffs (finals rounds). The coach has let team management know that he wants Callum back playing for the next game as he wants to secure a playoff spot early and avoid the risk of elimination. Coach Bodie considers Callum to be his 'kind of player; a warrior not a worrier', and he appreciates having players like Callum who will play on, even when it hurts. He believes that this type of player inspires others to work and play hard. Coach Bodie claims you can't teach that kind of toughness. While the coach maintains that he would not want to risk the long-term health of any of his players, he views an AC joint injury as being commonplace and therefore easy to recover from. The physiotherapist believes that Callum should be 'OK' to play this Saturday; after all, it will be five weeks between the initial injury and the upcoming game. He believes that the AC region might still be a little tender, but Callum is highly unlikely to do any further damage. Paul wonders whether this physiotherapist, in his first year with any premier rugby team, is a little intimidated by Callum and the coach's insistence that he must be fit to play!

Coach Bodie pulled Paul aside at the beginning of the week prior to Callum's return and made it very clear to him that he was to take special care of Callum this week. The coach not want Callum to aggravate the AC injury or incur another injury. Paul perceives Callum to be a bit of an 'old-school' rugby player who doesn't appear to have much respect for his body. The guy loves to play but doesn't really seem to value fitness training. Paul suspects that Callum has not been doing his therapeutic modalities and rehabilitation exercises, and he certainly hasn't sought out any fitness maintenance advice or guidance from Paul. While Callum claims that 'he is good to go' for Saturday, he doesn't like anyone else wearing his number, even if it is just for a few games. Paul is not convinced that Callum has given any real thought to the possible consequences of playing and further damaging his shoulder. This is bewildering to Paul as Callum already has a noticeable limp, has to avoid any jumping drills and definitely has chronic pain in other parts of his body. These ailments are from previous rugby injuries.

A few weeks ago, Paul would have done exactly what Coach Bodie asked of him – no questions asked. But since the discussion with Leanne about ethics and values in the nursing profession, and reading that article, he is having second thoughts. He is less confident that Coach Bodie and the physiotherapist are acting ethically by declaring Callum fit to play the next game. It seems that they are putting the team's, and their career, interests ahead of Callum's. Paul accepts that Coach Bodie would not want any harm to come to Callum, but his focus is firmly on what he thinks a club championship would mean to the club, the players, the community and potentially his future coaching career.

As Paul ruminates on his dilemma around Callum, he considers how much time, effort and money he and the club invested during the off-season in getting players like Callum fit to play for the season. Yet, now they want to play him at maybe 90% readiness, having not trained with rugby-specific intensity for the previous five weeks because of his injury. When Paul reflects on this situation, he begins to ask himself ethical questions. What was the point of all those sweaty summer sessions? How much does the coach really value the players' fitness, or for that matter, Paul's S&C input? And what about Mike, who's been filling in at blind-side while Callum has been sidelined? Mike is fit and healthy and doing an excellent job on the field, but Coach Bodie is now going to bench Mike in favour of the less fit, more experienced Callum. Callum will be playing hurt, short on fitness, and may not even last the game. Where is the logic in that? Paul is also having trouble believing that Callum is really fit enough and that it is safe for him to return to play (RTP). If the coach is worried about Callum getting injured in training this week, then surely he's signalling he too doesn't really believe that Callum is recovered. Paul is feeling like he, the coach, the physiotherapist and Callum are not on the 'same page' when it comes to conditioning, injury and rugby.

Paul is increasingly conflicted about Callum playing on Saturday and his role in helping that to happen. One more week away from the game would be consistent with the RTP guidelines for this injury. One more week would give them a chance to put Callum through some contact progressions and test the injury in a controlled setting. He can't stop asking himself – how would he feel if he did not at least raise the question with Coach Bodie and the physiotherapist and Callum was to reinjure himself because of prematurely returning to play. What if he was left with a permanently damaged shoulder? What if he changed his tackling technique and suffered a serious head injury as a consequence? What if his inability to perform endangered a teammate? Maybe ethics is important for SCCs to consider after all!

Part 2: commentary

It is heartening that Leanne and Paul's conversations have stimulated him to re-examine some of his team's practices. He has the benefit of growing experience, and he is demonstrating several professional competencies with his critical thinking. He is concerned about how S&C is valued, and at the same time he is considering his personal and professional values and the pedagogy of relationships. As a caring exercise professional, he is thinking beyond any possible short-term benefits to the athletes and team, and considering potential harm to their sporting success and career longevity. He is also aware of potential effects on long-term health and wellbeing. These ethical choices can be a challenge for SCCs who are typically educated and prepared for their careers through predominantly biophysical curricula and professional development that ultimately influences their thinking and decision making. While this educational grounding is appropriate and, at times, emphasises athlete health and safety, some of the consequences of sport participation and S&C are often overlooked in traditional exercise science curricula. With a biophysical mindset, decisions can often come down to theoretical arguments, and in many cases this reasoning may not be sufficient.

In the pedagogical case, Paul is facing a web of professional dilemmas, with apparent pressures from different directions. There is the coach who, while he claims to have the player's long-term health and wellbeing at heart, has other personal and team goals that are dependent on player availability. There is an injured player, Callum, who has not been compliant with the rehabilitation processes and who is likely unaware of, or chooses to discount, the potential harm from returning prematurely. Paul is working with the team physiotherapist, who he perceives as feeling professionally vulnerable, and Paul is seeking a solution that will not undermine him and damage their working relationship. Then there is the issue of RTP readiness and Paul's overarching S&C and fitness ideologies. The 'sporting ethic' and the social aspects of pain and injury are hinted at in Paul's descriptions and undoubtedly provide another sociocultural influence on all of these issues. Hughes and Coakley (1991) were among the first contemporary researchers to explore attitudes to pain and injury in sport. They described a 'sport ethic' as being characterised by individuals (i.e. athletes, coaches) willing to make sacrifices for their sport, overlook risks, play through pain and willingly push themselves beyond perceived limits.

Strength and conditioning ideologies

Paul's reflections in the pedagogical case highlight some apparent contradictions surrounding injury, RTP in sport and S&C, and illustrate many ideological issues with injury prevention and injury resolution. When an injury occurs, by necessity the primary focus becomes the 'injury'; logically, the injury pathology and the time frame for healing need to take precedence. However, as an injured athlete progresses through the stages of rehabilitation, the focus shifts towards the demands of the sport. While RTP decision making may not fall within the SCC's scope of practice, we contend that an SCC is probably the most knowledgeable in terms of sport-specific physical demands, especially force production and force absorption requirements. In the scenario that Paul describes, Callum's AC joint injury became, and remained, the focus up until his RTP. In the above pedagogical case, Paul highlights that rugby union, and the position that Callum plays (blind-side flanker), necessitates numerous high-speed impacts, tackling and grappling, and grappling to gain or maintain control of the ball. In Paul's mind, the focus appears to be injury and healing centred. Maybe questions need to be asked about Callum's ability not only to perform the requisite tasks of the game, but also to endure the random events of an open skilled sport such as rugby. If Callum wants to RTP, and contribute effectively, he needs to be able to participate in the impacts and the grapples without giving a second thought to his injury. To do these things on the field, Paul needs Callum to have progressed through a graded RTP exercise protocol that would require him to encounter increasingly greater forces in a controlled setting. Instead, Paul is working with a coach who does not want Callum to be exposed to those movement patterns and forces prior to game day; presumably because he is fearful that his injury may recur or regress! The obvious paradox is, if Callum is considered 'fit' to play, should he not also be 'fit to train'?

The pedagogical case highlights another apparent tension. Sport covets and privileges physiques and physical abilities, yet in the injury context these emphases can be overlooked by the coach, player and physiotherapist. In this case, if the coach is prepared to start a key, but injured player, who has deconditioned for five weeks, ahead of a healthy and presumably fully fit substitute, the coach is intimating that fitness is less important than other playmaking skills. In a sense, starting this key player at, let's say 90% of his peak fitness, ahead of a less experienced but 100% fit player, appears to contradict the large emphasis on fitness for the sport. Paul could consider that the work that he and the players have put in to fitness development during the off-season and preseason, and his professional contribution is not really valued.

These attitudes may not be lost on the athletes because they often do not comply with structured and progressive rehabilitation programmes. Levy et al. (2006) suggest that rehabilitation adherence rates could be as low as 40%, arguably because 'mentally tough' athletes may perceive their injury to be trivial and unlikely to be problematic. The actions of both athletes and coaches would appear to challenge the concept of prehabilitation and rehabilitation. How is an SCC likely to feel emphasising prehabilitation in his programme, but then witnessing coaching staff and athletes discounting it during the season? If his professional values emphasise caring for players, he is unlikely to view athletes as just biophysical apparatus, but as individuals with thoughts and feelings, and futures.

Injury prevention paradigms

Injury research has generally focused on two key outcomes: preventing injury and accelerating the healing and resolution of injuries, with the latter influencing readiness to RTP. Van Mechelen et al.'s (1992) model for injury prevention provides a framework for identifying injury etiologies and risks, with multiple factors acknowledged as adding significant complexity to any prevention challenge (Meeuwisse, 1994). As these models have guided most injury prevention research, the key research drivers have typically been medical and paramedical professions, and sport scientists with interests in injury prevention. The resulting research findings have in turn reflected those researchers' biophysical backgrounds. Based on the identification of putative risk factors for injury, protective equipment has been added or redesigned, rules have been modified and preventive conditioning regimes have been developed. For example, screening procedures (e.g. Bushman et al., 2015) and prehabilitation exercises (e.g. Meir et al., 2007) are two common injury intervention trends in S&C.

Both of these strategies are theoretical, rather than experimentally grounded or substantiated, and effectively reinforce a collective confidence that specific intervention and conditioning strategies can help mitigate injury risk.

The multifactorial nature of injury etiology has meant that strategies to reduce injury have not always met with universal success. Certainly, there have been some notable injury prevention 'wins', for example, with catastrophic neck (e.g. Quarrie et al., 2007) and dental injuries (e.g. Knapik et al., 2007) in contact sports being meaningfully reduced. But there have also been apparent fails, particularly for contact sports where the prevalence of injuries such as concussion and anterior cruciate ligament disruption have continued to rise, particularly in elite sport.

Return-to-play decisions

Several studies (e.g. Creighton et al., 2010; Fulton et al., 2014) have demonstrated that the strongest predictor of injury is previous injury. Whether individuals reinjure the same body part or suffer a remote injury due to movement dysfunction or fatigue, secondary injuries are arguably the most preventable of athletic injuries. For example, if secondary deficits in proprioception, range of motion, strength and movement control are not adequately addressed, returning athletes may be exposed to traumatic or atraumatic injury (Fulton et al., 2014). The RTP decision making is, however, a fraught process influenced by numerous factors.

Anatomical recovery (i.e. optimal tissue healing) will often proceed at a faster pace than functional (i.e. sport skills) recovery, yet if deficits in strength, proprioception or movement control persist, the ability to absorb and respond to forces may be compromised (Marshall & Golightly, 2007). If these variables are not specifically addressed in a RTP process, the potential for a subsequent injury or re-injury may be elevated. From an SCC perspective, the injured tissue structures have been identified and the positional demands of the sport are known, so there is no reason why Callum's injury in our pedagogical case cannot be progressively and comprehensively tested before a RTP is sanctioned.

In a consensus statement on RTP decision making, the American College of Sports Medicine list several criteria for RTP that include anatomical healing and recovery, restoration of sport-specific skills, and psychosocial readiness (Herring et al., 2002). While those criteria are clearly important, RTP processes are rarely standardised, well structured, detailed or communicated within a team or across a sport (Beardmore et al., 2005). By default, the decision-making process is often left to the discretion of medical support staff, and as such exposes RTP decision making to external pressures and the taking of shortcuts.

Noting the inconsistency of RTP practices, Creighton et al. (2010) developed a decision-based model designed for use by medical practitioners, which has relevance for SCCs. The first step of their model evaluates an athlete's health status considering individual factors and the nature, signs and symptoms of the injury. The next step evaluates the future risk to the athlete based on factors such as the nature of the sport (collision versus endurance), position played, level of competition and capacity to use products to protect the injured part. The final step includes what they term 'decision modifiers'. These might include elements such as the time of the season, importance of the game, pressure from the athlete, external pressures and any legal or insurer constraints. The model provides opportunities for all stakeholders involved in the injury to input into the decision-making process.

If Paul was to use this model, he could provide his views and integrate them with expertise of other stakeholders, such as the team physiotherapist and coach, with the aim of working towards developing a standardised RTP process that emphasises athlete wellbeing, as well as the ability of support staff to withstand the coercive elements of the sport. By clearly communicating such a process to everyone involved with the team, the process would be transparent and hopefully less vulnerable to manipulation.

Pain and sport injury

While injury preventive and treatment strategies are strongly influenced by biophysical knowledge, individual responses and attitudes to pain and injury, and to fear of injury, are all rooted in the psychosocial domain. Finch (2006) extended Van Mechelen's (1992) model, noting that intervention strategies often failed to adequately consider the context of the intervention and the important role that behaviour played in the prevention of injuries. While her model emphasised the need to consider the psychology of behaviour change and prevention strategy implementation, it fell short of including social determinants of behaviours.

Nixon's (1996) finding that many (94% in one study) athletes play hurt, and are encouraged to do so, supports an earlier claim by Hughes and Coakley (1991) that a particular 'sport ethic' exists. In explaining what this looks like, Nixon (1996) said that most athletes are surrounded by a social network that explicitly, or tacitly, reinforces that athletes can play when they are hurt, and they are to ignore pain and injury. Athletes are more likely to mask injuries and hide pain if they fear judgments from significant others like coaches and selectors (Charlesworth & Young, 2006). Moreover, as pain is a subjective construct, it tends to be marginalised within discussions of sports injuries, which reinforces the practice of viewing the body as a machine (Howe, 2004).

Howe (2004) referred to the subculture within, and around, specific sports and sports clubs as the 'sporting habitus'. Here he describes sporting habitus as the subtle, but deeply ingrained, messages that are conveyed about what it means to be the 'right' sort of athlete in that sport and that club. As illustrated in the pedagogical case, a sport such as rugby and its associated social networks offer messages about how pain and injury should be endured. In describing a rugby club subculture that made decisions around the acceptable risks and losses, Howe (2004) explains how a 'good team player' didn't complain, willingly played hurt, and was able to ignore their body's pain and discomfort. Howe's observations still hold true 15 years later. This was illustrated at the 2019 Rugby World Cup where All Black Beauden Barrett was a starting player despite carrying a persistent injury (Napier, 2019). When Indianapolis Colts (American football) Pro Bowl quarterback Andrew Luck retired suddenly at age 29 – for the sake of his injury-racked body and long-term health – fans reportedly booed his decision (Zirin, 2019). These examples of cultural norms or sporting habitus show some of the influence on the decision-making process of players, coaches and support staff when deciding when to RTP. Furthermore, coaches reinforce these cultural norms when they pick the right sort of player, ignore or deliberately make life miserable for injured players. Within such a sporting habitus it may be preferable for someone like Callum to play hurt than to be isolated and described as 'not a team player', or to risk derailing his sporting career. The paradox here is that athletes who play while injured or in pain will likely reduce their chances of performing well.

Coaches can unintentionally get caught up in their own pressures and put team success ahead of an athletes' wellbeing, tacitly pressuring them to play. With respect to injury, coaches normally seek to present themselves as responsible individuals who are behaving appropriately for their coaching role (Chesterfield et al., 2010). This impression management is particularly evident when communicating about injuries, where they are generally eager to reassure any audience that athlete beneficence is their priority (Beardmore et al., 2005). Yet, as Nixon (1994) notes, coaches may communicate that they care for the athletes' health and wellbeing, while at the same time they are paradoxically encouraging and expecting athletes to take risks with their bodies. There is a need to understand that with injury, the risk can endure, and consequences can follow athletes into later life.

This is a difficult dilemma for Paul to confront. It is very likely that the coach understands some of the long-term risk associated with playing hurt, but this 'knowing' is vague and likely being suppressed or trivialised in favour of short-term gains. The influences of the habitus of the sport are often deeply ingrained. Paul could informally present the coach with summaries of some of the research on the health and wellbeing of retired athletes and subtly work towards moving the coach's behaviour to align more closely with his presented, idealised self.

Acting ethically

The questions Paul asked himself at the end of the pedagogical case highlight some of the challenges SCCs face when it comes to acting ethically in contested environments. Some of the challenges can come from unexpected sources. For example, in high-performance sport the competition schedule can require athletes, coaches and, to a lesser extent, administrators to be away from their families and their communities for extended periods. Being away from a 'home' environment, where one is more readily accountable, may provide opportunities for unethical action to occur. The prevalence of this occurrence is illustrated by the commonly heard saying 'what goes on tour stays on tour'. Making decisions about return to play is another practice that requires coaches to act ethically.

The following section illustrates how Paul's response to Coach Bodie's request to have Callum ready to RTP, *prior* to the recommended date in the RTP protocols, could vary depending on what ethical perspective guides his decision-making process. Here we only draw on a normative ethical framework to illustrate the potential for variance. We use this framework because of its dominance in discussions of ethics in the Western world. In Chapter 3 we discuss the normative ethics in more detail, as well as provide an overview of some of the critiques of such a framework.

If Paul's response to Coach Bodie was informed by a 'contractarian' ethical perspective, we would see Paul seeking the advice of various stakeholders involved in the situation (e.g. Callum, Coach Bodie, the medical staff, and management) on Callum making an early return to play. When forming his decision, Paul would consider all stakeholders' views equally and objectively, which would inform discussions so they could come to a shared agreement. It is possible that upon consulting with the stakeholders, Paul decides to support Callum's early RTP. While this decision may not be one that Paul would have initially suggested, having discussed the situation with the stakeholders, it is a decision he believes is fair as it has been made with the co-operation of all the stakeholders.

If Paul's response to Coach Bodie was informed by a 'deontological' (non-consequential) ethical perspective, it would be based on what he thought was the right thing to do, regardless of the consequences, even if that action could cause harm. The drivers of Paul's decision-making process and response would be obligation and duty. Furthermore, if he was like his parents, who were practicing Catholics, he may also appeal to divine commands (aka rules) written in the Bible, thereby reflecting a rule-based deontological perspective. Paul could explain to Coach Bodie that it was his duty and obligation, as an ethical SCC, to abide by objective assessments and as such he would not support an early RTP. He would not be swayed from his decision, even if a veiled threat was made that his contract may not be renewed the following season.

Another interpretation of the deontological perspective is that that moral obligations can change depending on circumstances, which has been termed an act-based deontological perspective (Morgan, 2007). In this case he would account for the context in which the decision was being made. For example, St Kilda was only one win away from the playoffs, and if they lost the next game it could potentially be Callum's final game of the season and his career. If the team won, Callum could have a few games off to further recover from his injury in preparation for the playoffs. Also, Callum is adamant he is healthy enough to play on Saturday, and after all these years playing, he claims he knows the limitations of his body and likely long-term consequences – he is prepared to play even if his return is considered too early. Given these specific circumstances, Paul is willing to be more flexible in his interpretation of the RTP protocols and may support Callum's return.

If Paul's response to Coach Bodie was informed by a utilitarian (consequentialist) perspective, it could be based on the focus of getting 'the greatest good for the greatest number of people'. Like the previously described deontological perspective, the utilitarian perspective on ethics also has act- and rule-based perspectives. If Paul was informed by an act-based utilitarian perspective, he would consider the benefits of Callum playing, and if the benefits 'outweighed any suspected harmful effects' (DeSensi & Rosenberg, 2003, p. 64), then he would support the coach's request. If the team was successful (i.e. won the game and reached the playoffs), but Callum incurred further injuries, Paul would be able to justify the outcome as being the consequence of achieving the 'greatest good for the greatest number'. That is, the club would avoid the risk of elimination, which would provide job security for all the players as well as coaching and management staff, which in turn would have benefits for businesses and fans in the community. If Paul's response to Coach Bodie was informed by a rule-based utilitarian perspective, he would not support an early return as Callum would at best be only 80% fit. Informed by this perspective, Paul would view the most ethical action to be to continue playing the fully fit player who had been standing in for Callum during his recovery period. Taking this action would mean there would be a higher probability that there would be no injury-related substitution in that position during the game, which would enable the players to further develop their combinations, and in doing so potentially produce a win. While adopting a rule-based utilitarian perspective meant a different decision from that reached when using an act-based utilitarian perspective, the consequences of the decision were still the same. That is, the club would avoid elimination, and job security would be provided for all the players as well as coaching and management staff and supporters.

If Paul's response to Coach Bodie was informed by a virtue ethical perspective (which has become a popular perspective when discussing ethics in sports coaching contexts; see McNamee, 1998, 2008, 2011; Fernandez-Balboa, 2000; Cassidy et al., 2016), then his focus would be on him *being* good rather than simply *doing* right, and he would make a conscious choice to act with moral intent. Paul's actions would be judged to be virtuous if they were 'what a virtuous agent would, characteristically, do in the circumstances' (Driver, 2007, p. 138). Paul has been raised with family values that include belief in the virtues of honour, integrity and dignity, as well as the Christian virtues, specifically, diligence, patience, kindness and humility. As a consequence, Paul attempts to incorporate these values into his S&C work. If influenced by a virtuous perspective, Paul would not support an early RTP. Paul may explain that doing so would threaten his integrity as an ethical SCC because it would go against his moral principles by being dishonest, which in turn would decrease the chance of others viewing him with respect or being held in high esteem. Also, Paul viewed himself as a kind person, and he did not believe that knowingly supporting Callum to RTP earlier than was recommended was a kind thing to do, especially in consideration of his long-term wellbeing.

Our pedagogical case hints at the ethical dilemma being contemplated by Paul. As an SCC he has to navigate the potential conflict between his personal values, the values and ethical code of his profession, and the values of the organisation as represented by the player, coach, club and community.

Summary

This chapter introduces and discusses several ethical challenges and considerations around injury and return-to-play, elements that are often overlooked in S&C signature pedagogies. The drivers of coach and athlete behaviours in response to injury are examined in the context of Hughes and Coakley's (1991) 'sport ethic' and the 'sport habitus' (or culture of the sport). We discuss the capacity and ability of SCCs to contribute to various stages of injury treatment and management. We note several apparent contradictions that relate to a professed ethic of care, particularly with respect to the amount of physical and physiological recovery considered necessary for a safe return to play. We comment on the RTP decision-making processes in sport; for the often highly detailed and controlled environments of sport, the RTP process appears to be surprisingly ad hoc and inconsistent. Attitudes to injury and pain by athletes, coaches and interested observers are discussed for their contribution to how injuries are framed and the complexity of injury recovery. We close the chapter by discussing the tension around the ethics of RTP decision making and in particular the challenge of reconciling personal, professional and organisational values.

End of chapter tasks

1 Identify ways that orthodox S&C practices might be contributing to the injury of athletes.
2 Outside pressure can put pressure on coaches to push athletes to return to play before they've recovered from an injury. Create a plan for this ethical issue at the individual level (yourself) and/or your organisation.
3 Describe the messages you have observed being delivered in sport, and in S&C settings, that seem to encourage risky behaviour that likely contributes to injury.
4 Consider the S&C coach in relation to the Sports Medicine Team or Healthcare System within your context. How much breadth and depth in the care and prevention of athletic injuries do key stakeholders (e.g. physicians, physiotherapists, athletic trainers, SCCs) possess? What is the scope of each practitioner (i.e. legally permissible conduct based on competence), and what are the implications of this on decision making?

References

Beardmore, A.L., Handcock, P.J., & Rehrer, N.J. (2005). Return-to-play after injury: Practices in New Zealand rugby union, *Physical Therapy in Sport*, 6(1): 24-30.
Bushman, T.T., Grier, T.L., Canham-Chervak, M., et al. (2015). The functional movement screen and injury risk association and predictive value in active men, *American Journal of Sports Medicine*, 44(2): 297–304.
Cassidy, T., Jones, R., & Potrac, P. (2016). *Understanding Sports Coaching: The Pedagogical, Social, and Cultural Foundations of Coaching Practice* (3rd ed.), London: Routledge.
Charlesworth, H., & Young, K. (2006). Injured female athletes: Experiential accounts from England and Canada. In S. Loland, B. Skirstad, & I. Waddington (eds.), *Pain and Injury in Sport: Social and Ethical Analysis*, London: Routledge, pp. 89–106.

Chesterfield, G., Potrac, P., & Jones, R. (2010). 'Studentship' and 'impression management' in an advanced soccer coach education award, *Sport, Education and Society*, 15(3): 299–314.

Creighton, D.W., Shriner, I., Shultz, R., et al. (2010). Return-to-play in sport: A decision-based model, *Clinical Journal of Sport Medicine*, 20: 379–385.

DeSensi, J., & Rosenberg, D. (2003). *Ethics and Morality in Sport Management* (2nd ed.), Morgantown, WV: Fitness Information Technology.

Driver, J. (2007). *Ethics: The Fundamentals*, Malden, MA: Blackwell.

Fernandez-Balboa, J-M. (2000). Discrimination: What do we know and what can we do about it? In R.L. Jones & K.M. Armour (eds.), *Sociology of Sport: Theory and Practice*, London: Longman.

Finch, C. (2006). A new framework for research leading to sports injury prevention, *Journal of Science and Medicine in Sport*, 9: 3–9.

Fulton, J., Wright, K., Kelly, M., et al. (2014). Injury risk is altered by previous injury: A systematic review of the literature and presentation of causative neuromuscular factors, *The International Journal of Sports Physical Therapy*, 9(5): 583–595.

Herring, S.A., Bergfeld, J.A., Boyd, J., et al. (2002). The team physician and return-to-play issues: A consensus statement, *Medicine & Science in Sports & Exercise*, 34: 1212–1214.

Howe, P.D. (2004). *Sport, Professionalism and Pain: Ethnographies of Injury and Risk*, London: Routledge.

Hughes, R., & Coakley, J. (1991). Positive deviance among athletes: The implications of overconformity to the sport ethic, *Sociology of Sport Journal*, 8: 307–325.

Knapik, J.J., Marshall, S.W., Lee, R.B., et al. (2007). Mouthguards in sport activities: History, physical properties and injury prevention effectiveness, *Sports Medicine*, 37: 117–144.

Levy, A., Polman, R., Clough, P., et al. (2006). Mental toughness as a determinant of beliefs, pain, and adherence in sport injury rehabilitation, *Journal of Sport Rehabilitation*, 15: 246–254.

Marshall, S.W., & Golightly, Y.M. (2007). Sports injury and arthritis, *North Carolina Medical Journal*, 68(6): 430–433.

McNamee, M. (1998). Celebrating trust: Virtues and rules in the ethical conduct of sport coaches. In M. McNamee & J. Parry (eds.), *Ethics and Sport*, London: E and FN Spon.

McNamee, M. (2008). *Sports, Virtues and Vices: Morality Plays*, London: Routledge.

McNamee, M. (2011). Celebrating trust: Virtues and rules in ethical conduct of sports coaches. In A. Hardman & C.R. Jones (eds.), *The Ethics of Sports Coaching*, London: Routledge.

Meeuwisse, W.H. (1994). Assessing causation in sport injury: A multifactorial model, *Clinical Journal of Sport Medicine*, 4: 166–170.

Meir, R., Diesel, W., & Archer, E. (2007). Developing a prehabilitation program in a collision sport: A model developed, *Strength and Conditioning Journal*, 29(3): 50–62.

Morgan, W. (2007). *Ethics in Sport*, Champaign, IL: Human Kinetics.

Napier, L. (2019). All Blacks star Beauden Barrett reveals he's been battling leg injury at tournament. www.nzherald.co.nz/sport/news/article.cfm?c_id=4&objectid=12274415 (accessed 8 Dec. 2019).

Nixon II, H.L. (1994). Social pressure, social support, and help seeking for pain and injuries in College Sports Networks, *Journal of Sport and Social Issues*, 18(4): 340–355.

Nixon II, H.L. (1996). Explaining pain and injury attitudes and experiences in sport in terms of gender, race, and sports status factors, *Journal of Sport and Social Issues*, 20: 33.

Quarrie, K.L., Gianotti, S.M., Hopkins, W.G., & Hume, P.A. (2007). Effect of nationwide injury prevention programme on serious spinal injuries in New Zealand rugby union: Ecological study, *British Medical Journal*, 334: 1150–1153.

Sellman, D. (2011). Professional values and nursing, *Medicine, Health Care and Philosophy*, 14: 203–208.

van Mechelen, W., Hlobil, H., & Kemper, H.C. (1992). Incidence, severity, aetiology and prevention of sports injuries: A review of concepts, *Sports Medicine*, 14: 82–99.

Zirin, D. (2019). Andrew Luck and the NFL's looming crisis of race and class. www.thenation.com/article/andrew-luck-nfl/ (accessed 11 Sept. 2019).

15 Looking after yourself as a strength and conditioning coach

Introduction
Part 1: pedagogical case
Part 2: commentary
Educational and professional preparation
Negotiating work settings
Adopting personal protection strategies
Preparing for crises
Summary
End of chapter tasks
References

Introduction

Having a career as an SCC can be all-consuming, stressful and competitive, often with anti-social work schedules and in many cases inadequate remuneration. Aside from work conditions, employment can be precarious. This chapter discusses strategies that support SCCs to attempt to modify their work environment so they are able to take time out, moderate their stress and continue to develop professionally. In particular this chapter examines negotiating work settings, and developing personal protection strategies as ways of insulating oneself from the potential negative aspects of being an SCC.

Part 1: pedagogical case

The Voice: University Blue's Student Newspaper since 1908
TROUBLED IN THE GYM
By BEN DWIGHT
October 17 2019 in OFF THE RECORD: Columns

A recent spate of coach firings in collegiate sports has been portrayed in national media as yet another example of the callous and cutthroat underbelly of collegiate sport. Scant attention is paid to the plight of the numerous support staff who get caught up in the fallout of coach sackings. 'Off the Record' reporter Ben Dwight spoke, unsurprisingly, off the record, with an anonymous veteran collegiate strength and conditioning coach (SCC).

Ben Dwight (BD): Coach Anonymous, you've been with University Red for three years now, but you also worked in professional sport. I know a lot of college students aspire to careers in sport, but it seems to be a pretty ruthless environment. When a head coach gets fired there can often be a 'domino effect' with the likes of assistant coaches, athletic trainers and SCCs also being shown the door. Is this an accurate observation, and is this fair?

Coach Anonymous (CA): Accurate, yes, but fair – NO! Never fair, Ben – well, hardly ever. But that's the unfortunate reality in our world of elite sport. It's often dismissal by association, rather than anything that the staff may or may not have done. SCCs have significant involvement in a programme – we probably spend more time with the athletes than anyone else on the coaching staff, but we don't recruit the athletes, we don't select the starters and we certainly don't develop the game plans. Yet, somehow, we are often held accountable when athletes don't perform or win.

BD: So, true, we often report that our college athletes and teams are the fittest that they've ever been, and then next week a loss is blamed on poor fitness. Surely things can't change that much from week to week?

CA: No, and that's the bit that hurts, Ben! But you know, SCCs are often part of that problem. I get really annoyed when some of my S&C colleagues, those who crave the spotlight, 'loudly and proudly' claim credit for their role in a team's win. To me that just draws undue attention to S&C, especially when then that team then turns around and loses. Before coming here, I had a really good run with a highly successful women's football (soccer) club. I was the head SCC and we had several good seasons, as well as a few not so good ones. From the outset, I decided to never claim credit for good team performances. I think an SCC's contribution goes well beyond wins and losses. Sure, we all like winning, but there are so many other factors that determine successful performance. I found that I got more satisfaction from focusing on developing individual athletes and helping to get them prepared to be independently motivated to train effectively and perform to the best of their ability. Pragmatically, I also figured that if you don't stick your head up claiming credit, you're also less likely to have the finger pointed in blame.

BD: Hmm, that's an interesting protective strategy. But tell me, people generally aim for their career to track from collegiate sports to the professional domain. Why did you leave professional sport for a job in collegiate sports? Wasn't that a bit of a comedown for you?

CA: No, not really. There were many factors. The Women's football league was struggling financially and the club that I was working with was no exception. To reduce costs, the club had gradually moved to using interns and volunteers to complete some of the core work. I don't think that ever works well. The other thing was that I was only ever on a one-year contract, so that financial uncertainty made it difficult for my partner and I to plan for our future.

For example, we could not see our way clear to make the break from renting and commit to taking out a mortgage on a home. We've also got a young family and S&C is not a family-friendly sort of occupation. Apart from a select few, most women footballers are not fully professional, so training sessions had to fit around their paid work, which meant trainings were early mornings and evenings. You can appreciate that a lot of S&C work must take place during what we consider other people's leisure time. That would normally be our leisure time also! When our children were younger and not at school, those hours worked well for family time, but once they were at school, that was no longer the case and I was never there for them.

BD: So has being in the collegiate sport environment improved those things?

CA: Sure – coming from a head S&C role to an assistant's role in college has meant better resourcing, more staff to spread the work around, and to provide cover for the work that really has to be done. That roster meant that I was not away from the family every evening and every weekend. But it wasn't just those things. As an SCC, I felt as though the work demands were constantly expanding and the more I did, the more was expected – I called it expectation creep – not only because it continued to grow but it also because it crept up on you! I was the only full-time SCC for my previous football club; other clubs had at least two SCCs. I was expected to run the programme with a couple of part-time staff, which with budget cuts became a couple of interns. Those interns often had variable skill sets and work ethics, and with my work schedule, I didn't really have the time to adequately mentor or supervise them. I still feel bad that we really did nothing for the career development of those interns. I also felt conflicted about some of the practices within the club. For example, I was fortunate to have worked under three different and very good head coaches, but you were really at the mercy of the pressures that they faced and their whimsical approaches. Even though these sport coaches had little to no specialist conditioning knowledge or understanding, I ultimately had to comply with whatever fitness or conditioning strategy the next coach seized upon. I could try and explain why a particular method might be flawed and may not work, but the head sport coach ultimately had the final say.

BD: We don't really hear or read much about S&C in sport except when something new and unusual is being praised!

CA: Yeah, on the one hand I get that mentality. The buck stops with the head coach and they are under immense pressure to get results. So I understand why they grasp at any possibility of gaining a competitive edge. But! I've had seasons where my time was soaked up managing recovery methods, heart rate training or GPS monitoring. To me, those things just all became 'noise' that took me away from doing the simple things, and doing them well. In my current role, we have a better S&C infrastructure that lets us evaluate new techniques and really work on educating the sport coaches as to why we should or shouldn't follow particular practices.

But the thing that really pushed me out the door of professional sport and into collegiate sports was that I had a good friend and colleague, a head SCC at another club, who was fired for basically doing a great job. His head coach had insisted that the players had not been aerobically fit enough the previous season and the coach wanted a huge emphasis on aerobic conditioning – long runs and the like. My buddy tried to explain that that would take them away from a lot of the higher-intensity work pieces and they'd probably lose some speed, acceleration and agility. Also, with so much time on their feet, the players would likely be a lot more fatigued or suffer from chronic or overuse injuries. The coach wouldn't hear of it, and sure enough they ended up having a miserable season. His players had superb endurance but lots of soft tissue injuries, struggled to match the speed of other teams, and the club ended up narrowly missing relegation [Note: in some competitions bottom-placed teams can face relegation to a lower division. To return to that competition level, the team would need to be the top team in lower-level competition to win promotion back to the higher division]. Come review time, instead of taking ownership, the head coach 'threw my friend under the bus'. The head coach claimed that the team wasn't explosive enough and that the high injury rate had destroyed their season. My buddy was devastated at the mendacity, self-preservation and lack of accountability from the head sport coach and indeed the whole organisation. He's out of S&C now and doing OK, but that was a great SCC's career needlessly destroyed.

BD: Are conditions really any better in the collegiate environment, or is this just another set of challenges for you?

CA: Yes and no! I'm loving the different environment, the variety of young athletes that I get to work with, and the influence that you can have on their lives. I'm also really valuing the collegiality of our S&C team. While I'm no longer heading a programme, I'm learning new things. I've got more professional development opportunities and I get to see more of my family. There are times, however, when I struggle with what's right. I think my values are very much about the wellbeing of the student athlete and sometimes I do question the values of my profession and the values of the Athletic Department. Some of these young athletes are 'broken' and we keep putting them out there to break themselves some more – all for what?

I realise that my job could end tomorrow. I know that if the teams start to flounder and a sport coach gets let go, I and my colleagues could just as easily be collateral damage. There's usually plenty of blame going around in these situations, and the finger often settles on fitness. We are an easy scapegoat! The next coach coming in might strike a deal with the university to bring in their own people, so I could lose my position very easily. The reality is that there are plenty of people out there who want my job and will be prepared to do it for less pay and will be willing to work longer hours. Some of them are genuinely good and capable people, but so many of them are what we derisively call S&C fans. They simply crave association with elite sports people and often do not treat themselves or the field as professionals. Don't get me wrong, this is the best job and I love it, but sometimes it's a lousy career!

Part 2: commentary

The story recounted by the anonymous SCC in this pedagogical case will resonate with many professionals who have worked with sport through various roles and settings. The opportunity to be associated with high-level athletes and elite sport is perceived by sports enthusiasts to be glamorous and therefore highly coveted as a career path. Indeed, many would consider it a privilege to secure paid employment working within sport. The economic and cultural capital of elite sport produces the impression of desirability, whereas we don't hold non-elite coaches and sport settings in the same high regard. Apparent allure aside, the reality is that sporting organisations will often mirror the unpredictability of both sporting performances and competitive outcomes. This organisational inconstancy can make employment within sports precarious. While there is no recasting the uncertainty of sporting outcomes, and improving employment conditions and the infrastructure of sports organisations is beyond the scope of this book, the wellbeing of SCCs within these settings, and all settings more generally, warrants our attention.

Our pedagogical case reinforces the reality that it is common for SCCs to become highly invested in the day-to-day demands of being an S&C professional and to affiliate and commit strongly to the athletes they work with, the team and the organisation (Gilmore et al., 2018). As the boundaries between work and non-work lives have blurred (Colbert et al., 2016), being happy in the workplace and having good relationships has become increasingly important for personal health and wellbeing. The salient points identified in the pedagogical case we will discuss include: educational and professional preparation, negotiating work settings, adopting personal protection strategies and preparing for crises.

Educational and professional preparation

Most professional educational processes focus on providing knowledge and fostering skilled performance (Cruess et al., 2016) but are less likely to adequately prepare aspiring professionals for the micro-politics (Cronin et al., 2019) and other 'bumps and setbacks' that will likely be encountered in the workplace. SCCs are expected to provide professional services and to act ethically, but there is usually very little offered in the way of training or professional development on these aspects of practice (Dawson et al., 2013), or indeed how to negotiate and thrive in the workplace. Indeed, whilst the US-based National Strength and Conditioning Association has produced documents on professional standards and guidelines, codes of ethics, and an education recognition program and a recently released accreditation plan, there is currently no required coursework for SCCs to learn how to practice ethically (NSCA, 2019). Beddoe et al. (2013) argue that professional resilience training should be part of professional development. Such training should continue to help aspiring professionals to develop their own professional identity, yet provide appropriate reality checks that will help apprise them of the potential professional perils that may be encountered, all without destroying their professional optimism and inherent altruistic leanings (Beddoe et al., 2013).

In the neoliberal environment (i.e. profit-based, free market economies), many organisations have reportedly become increasingly dependent on part-time, casual and unpaid internships, or casualised entry-level positions to undertake functions that may be core and important to an organisation's operations (Baines et al., 2017). Young, enthusiastic individuals who identify strongly with sport are often prepared to work long hours performing mundane work (Dawson et al., 2013) and offer solutions to some of the economic pressures faced by sporting organisations. A willingness to undertake such work, under often highly stressful and demanding conditions, is often motivated by the intense competition to gain an experience edge and a 'desperation' to secure paid employment within sport. Baines (2004) used a compulsion-coercion continuum to show how people are influenced into volunteering or interning roles. Similarly, those influences are seen in the sporting environments in which SCCs work. Pressures can come from compulsion, where the SCC may feel compelled by their intrinsic motivation or sense of being a good team member (Tonurist & Surva, 2017), or coercion driven by a fear of negatively influencing their future employability and their perceived value to an organisation. Regardless of the source of pressures, these experiences can leave individuals naive to, and unprepared for, some of the challenges of the work environment.

Negotiating work settings

The work environment is acknowledged to be a crucial determinant of personal wellbeing. We discuss it here, fully cognisant that there is often limited opportunity for employees to have a major influence on their working conditions. Rather than implying that these things are easily manipulated, we present a summary of suggestions for identifying a suitable work setting.

Although limited positions exist, an SCC seeking employment may find it useful to conduct personal due diligence on the sports organisation and its management and leadership structure. Enquiring about the values and the ideologies of the organisation and the coaching hierarchy (Orvik et al., 2015) can help with anticipating future compatibility. It may be possible, for example, to discover how interprofessional communications occur within the organisation, the nature of the information that is shared and how that information is processed (Quinn et al., 1996). For example, an organisation may favour shared values and open communication across professions and roles, and it may emphasise seeking mutually acceptable solutions (Quinn et al., 1996). On the other hand, there may be external professional influences on the role and work of the SCC, which may be unwelcomed and could contribute to a loss of professional flexibility and options for creativity. For example, an organisation may place primary responsibility for managing workload and preventing injuries on SCCs. As there are many influences on workload and injury that may be beyond the control of an SCC, making SCCs fully accountable could be conceived as abrogating responsibility for what should be shared care. Organisationally, this could foster a risk avoidance culture for the SCC team (Ponnert & Svensson, 2016). A propensity to try new things and take 'risks' may be primarily influenced by internal factors, but external factors such as organisational consequences can negate those influences. How new initiatives are framed organisationally may influence whether the prevailing culture is 'risk averse' or 'risk seeking' (Hill et al., 2019).

Strength and conditioning (S&C) has been described as a process-based profession, operating within outcome-based settings (Watts, 2016). Therefore, there may be an inevitable mismatch between the aspirational progressive and sustained campaign of S&C, and a 'this season must count' mindset of the athletes and coaches. As described in our pedagogical case, the unpredictable employment situation in sport places additional pressures on the SCC's work. Ideally, an SCC would be able to negotiate a contract with a term that provides some stability, the freedom to be creative, and ample opportunity for the SCC's processes to be realised (Wagstaff et al., 2016). Given the intense competition for S&C roles and the seasonal cycle of position vacancies, writing an acceptable notice period into contracts could also provide the SCC with a greater sense of security and ongoing employability (Gilmore et al., 2018).

'Knowing how' and many of the other relational aspects of S&C (see 'Professional competence framework'; Chapter 2) can only be developed through repeated exposure to authentic professional problems (Quinn et al., 1996). As part of researching a prospective employer, it may be useful for the SCC to also identify professional responsibilities, the scope for exposure to a variety of training methods, professional development opportunities, including mentoring, and the presence of a support network. In summary, researching an employment opportunity should help an SCC to focus not only the contribution that they can make to an organisation, but also their professional development and professional and personal wellbeing.

Adopting personal protection strategies

As highlighted in our pedagogical case, the hypercompetitive environment of sport can foster work settings that may be fickle, reactive and that privilege a 'success now' ethos (Gilmore et al., 2018). Organisational micro-politics can mean that some individuals will become adept at presenting themselves positively, covering their shortcomings and finding ways to appear indispensable to an organisation. This may come at the expense of organisational and professional values and collegiality (Gilmore et al., 2018). One proactive protective action for S&C professionals is to seize every opportunity to educate colleagues on S&C and the knowledge, skills and attributes of SCCs. Through education, SCCs have opportunities to determine their preferred methods of working, establish realistic outcome objectives and have some influence on how they are professionally evaluated. For example, there are collective misunderstandings about the magnitude and rate of change possible for a fitness parameter, how those changes will likely translate into performance, and the influence that fitness really has on injury prevalence. The more that misunderstandings such as these become entrenched, the greater the pressure on, and vulnerability of, the SCC. These are perceptions that can be modifiable through knowledgeable explanations; thus it is important that SCCs educate and correct misunderstandings.

A challenge when joining any organisation may be protecting and sustaining one's personal integrity. Integrity has been described as taking a stance and being committed to maintaining and acting on a set of personal values (Banks, 2010). At times, one's values could extend beyond, or be in conflict with, the existing values of the profession, or the implicit values and expectations of the organisation (Banks, 2010). To practice with integrity, Orvik et al. (2015) suggest that individuals need to remain true to their personal values within their practice, and to be willing to negotiate their practice within the work context by seeking ways to practice without compromising personal values. As an individual is integrated into a given work setting, it should be possible for them to make explicit their values by the ways in which they communicate and act.

Sport tends to expect a strong sense of shared purpose and 'oneness' (Roderick, 2006), including close affiliations with the athletes and wider team. It is therefore common for professionals operating within sport to connect strongly to their work and subsequently find themselves in many ways defined by their roles and interactions (Reay et al., 2017). Hings et al. (2018) describe sport as having an instant culture, meaning that there is a constant search for an immediate competitive edge and success (Gilmore et al., 2018). As such, it is expected that 'loyal employees' will do everything in their power to make everything possible – and as soon as possible – for the benefit of the team. Such approaches can become a major drain of time and energy for those involved, including the athletes. The perceived need to constantly comply with organisationally determined professional expectations will likely come with a personal cost (Hings et al., 2018). A plausible protective strategy is to seek to extricate oneself from those potentially problematic mindsets by establishing and maintaining a healthy life balance. Interpretations of 'healthy' will vary greatly, but clearly the key message is to keep one's work engagement, in terms of the hours and emotional investment involved, in check. With the assistance and understanding of colleagues, professional role identity and work boundaries can be reimagined (Reay et al., 2017). This might consist of collectively conducting reality checks to ensure that identified actions are indeed necessary and/or critical. A collaborative approach can also assist in protecting time and energy for family, friends and other pastimes or hobbies.

The growing awareness and concerns around mental health and wellbeing have increased the attention given to the concept of resilience. According to Kegelaers et al. (2019), resilience can be described as an inherently optimistic construct that is argued to be a positive adaptation within everyone's reach. Resilience captures several personal attributes and behaviours that include the likes of optimism, confidence and emotional regulation (Wagstaff et al., 2016; Gonzalez et al., 2016). A key part of resilience would appear to be one's mindset, which Dweck (2017) has defined as fairly stable beliefs that are amenable to modification.

Dweck dichotomised mindsets into two categories: 'fixed' and 'growth'. An individual with a fixed mindset would tend to see their abilities as stable and with fixed traits that are largely resistant to any attempted modification. In contrast, someone with a growth mindset would view their abilities as cultivatable and responsive to different experiences. As mindsets are considered to vary with different traits, rather than representing a generic attitude (Caniëls et al., 2018), the professional mindsets of interest here may not be the dominant mindset for an individual. From the pedagogical case, our anonymous SCC's colleague, who had lost his position, would benefit from having a growth mindset that would help that individual avoid catastrophising their job loss and instead begin to explore possible learnings and opportunities. In that respect, Kegelaers et al. (2019) view resilience as being an effective buffer against many professional threats (robust resilience), and that mindset may help individuals move forward after professional setbacks.

An SCC with a fixed mindset would be likely to have a predominantly transactional approach to their work. From our professional competence framework (Chapter 2), a fixed mindset in S&C would be more likely to emphasise their knowledge and functional roles, focusing on their ability to write training prescriptions and coach exercise techniques. A professional with a growth mindset would be more likely to demonstrate a transformational approach. This SCC would likely emphasise other elements from the professional competence framework, such as behavioural and ethical competence, and would pay more attention to the relational aspects of S&C coaching. The effectiveness of this coach could, for example, be evaluated based on their athletes' experiences in the coach-led training environment, the return to play practices following injury and the relationships that the SCC has with the athletes and coaching and managerial staff (Gillham et al., 2017). A key difference is that an SCC with a fixed mindset may be more likely to think that they simply need more practice in order to perfect their craft and improve their employability, whereas a growth mindset approach may lead the SSC to constantly seek to discover and redefine S&C and their role within the profession.

Schroder et al. (2017) suggest that mindsets become more relevant in times of challenge, with growth mindsets helping individuals adjust in response to perceived threats. Strategies to foster the development of a growth mindset include attempting to create a growth environment within the workplace that responds positively to perceived work challenges. A growth mindset will also be facilitated by SCCs being self-reflective and humble. Workplace humility would be characterised by being open and willing and able to assess one's characteristics, strengths and weaknesses (Watkins et al., 2019).

Robust resilience can be bolstered by building a professional network of supporters and colleagues that can be trusted. As coaching is a social undertaking (e.g. Rynne et al., 2017), the ability to share, learn from and be supported by others helps contribute to resilience. As discussed in Chapter 9, interprofessional rounds can help foster shared interests, identify common values and generate satisfying solutions (Quinn et al., 1996). Given the job loss scenario described in our pedagogical case, the mindset of the SCC and the strength of their work support network would be unlikely to prevent their sacking but may help them rebound and face their immediate future positively.

Preparing for crises

The nature of organisations is that change cycles are inevitable, so it is important to be preemptive and establish some rebound resilience to help minimise emotional commitments to work and to help circumvent organisation cynicism when changes do occur. Some measure of employment satisfaction will no doubt depend on the approach that the SCC adopts to S&C coaching. From SCC Anonymous's self-description, they appear to have adopted a transformational approach to their role. Coach Anonymous is making the most of the collegiality of the S&C team by adopting a growth mindset in terms of professional development opportunities and their own evolution as an SCC, and they have placed a major emphasis on family and having an appropriate work–life balance.

Developing and maintaining a supportive network of trustworthy individuals who understand you and your professional role and work is highly recommended for any SCC. Such a network should include people who care for you as well as care about you (Cronin et al., 2019). The network could extend wider than the organisation and the S&C profession to include contacts who could provide connections for further training opportunities and (if necessary) future employment opportunities. While it is great to have mentors who inspire you and contribute to your professional development in terms of knowledge and functional competence, it is equally important to seek out supervisors or mentors for professional support. Professional supervision could help an SCC, like Coach Anonymous, to deal with some of the personal and professional issues that arise; a friendly sounding board who will help conduct reality checks and provide reassurances that you are not misinterpreting things or overreacting.

Of course, no reassurances can be given that these strategies will help to completely mitigate work-related stressors, but they'll likely help soften the blow and reduced the duration of distress. As S&C continues to evolve as a profession, hopefully organisational and social understandings of the SCCs' abilities (and limitations) will be more universally understood and recognised; recognised as one of many cogs in contributing to athletic performance. Until then, coping strategies can provide some protective mechanisms to insulate oneself from the potentially negative aspects of the work and provide options for reacting to those problematic situations when they do arise.

Summary

Through our pedagogical case we open up discussion on personal and professional wellness in the workplace. Given the context and positioning of sport, we recognise that SCCs are often situated in highly competitive workplaces where pressures may be coming from multiple directions. We also acknowledge that sport is a precarious and vulnerable work environment, where the line between one's work and one's life often becomes blurred. The signature pedagogies of S&C and professional development rarely prepares SCCs for the challenges of the organisational micro-politics, or provides them with the tools for personal and professional resilience. We argue that competition for work within sport allows for coercion and individual compulsion to be leveraged to produce unhealthy work situations. We suggest various strategies to help SCCs to preemptively prepare for workplace issues by, for example, clarifying one's scope of practice, schedule of expected duties and expectations around hours of work, and conducting due diligence on the working environment. We also contend that SCCs should adopt personal protection strategies by striving for a growth mindset, developing a supportive network of trusted colleagues and possibly organising to engage professional supervision.

End of chapter tasks

1   Imagine you're getting to interview for an S&C job. You want to understand how the organisation supports its employees. Write a few questions down that you could ask during an interview that would tap into how the organisations value and support its staff;

for example, what opportunities exist to practice self-care, professional development or work–life balance?

2   S&C coaches often work odd (e.g. early morning, late evening, weekends) and long hours. Describe some ways you can practice self-care to cope with the rigors of coaching and develop your resilience. Consider multiple aspects of wellbeing such as physical, social-relational, mental, financial, etc.

3   In the chapter it was suggested that educating others on their misunderstandings of S&C, and providing them with realistic outcomes, could help alleviate SCCs' stress and problems in the workplace. Create a list of the top 10 misunderstandings that co-workers might believe about S&C. Next, drawing on the research, create something concise and effective (e.g. infographic, flyer, video or cartoon, etc.) that might address this misunderstanding.

4   It's been said that there are only two guarantees in life: death and taxes. At some point in your coaching career, you're going to experience a crisis, trauma or similar severe event. For example, you or somebody in your care, or organisation, suffers from loss of a job, partner/spouse troubles, serious illness or death, physical or mental injury, financial hardship, etc. Develop a crisis management plan for yourself; consider what's likely to happen and how you could develop the tools now in order to mitigate negative effects. To enlarge your world view, ask other coaches what's happened to them that they were or were not prepared for and how it affected them.

References

Baines, D. (2004). Caring for nothing: Work organization and unwaged labour in social services, *Work, Employment and Society*, 18(2): 267–295.

Baines, D., Cunningham, I., & Shields, J. (2017). Filling the gaps: Unpaid (and precarious) work in the nonprofit social services, *Critical Social Policy*, 37(4): 625–645.

Banks, S.J. (2010). Integrity in professional life: Issues of conduct, commitment and capacity, *British Journal of Social Work*, 40(7): 2168–2184.

Beddoe, L., Davys, A., & Adamson, C. (2013). Educating resilient practitioners, *Social Work Education: The International Journal*, 32(1): 100–117.

Caniëls, M., Semeijn, J., & Renders, I. (2018). Mind the mindset! The interaction of proactive personality, transformational leadership and growth mindset for engagement at work, *Career Development International*, 23(1): 48–66.

Colbert, A.E., Bono, J.E., & Purvanova, R.K. (2016). Flourishing via workplace relationships: Moving beyond instrumental support, *Academy of Management Journal*, 59(4): 1199–1223.

Cronin, C., Knowles, Z.R., & Enright, K. (2019). The challenge to care in a premier league football club, *Sports Coaching Review*. DOI:10.1080/21640629.2019.1578593.

Cruess, R.L., Cruess, S.R., & Steinert, Y. (2016). Amending Miller's pyramid to include professional identity formation, *Academic Medicine*, 91: 180–185.

Dawson, A.J., Leonard, Z.M., Wehner, K.A., et al. (2013). Building without a plan: The career experiences of Australian strength and conditioning coaches, *Journal of Strength and Conditioning Research*, 27(5): 1423–1434.

Dweck, C. (2017). *Mindset: Changing the Way You Think to Fulfil Your Potential*, London: Brown Book Group.

Gillham, A., Doscher, M., Fitzgerald, C., Bennet, S., Davis, A., & Banwarth, A. (2017). Strength and conditioning roundtable: Strength and conditioning evaluation, *International Journal of Sports Science and Coaching*, 12(5): 635–646.

Gilmore, S., Wagstaff, C., & Smith, J. (2018). Sports psychology in the English premier league: 'It feels precarious and is precarious', *Work, Employment and Society*, 32(2): 426–435.

Gonzalez, S.P., Detling, N., & Galli, N.A. (2016). Case studies of developing resilience in elite sport: Applying theory to guide interventions, *Journal of Sport Psychology in Action*, 7(3): 158–169.

Hill, T., Kusev, P., & van Schaik, P. (2019). Choice under risk: How occupation influences preferences, *Frontiers in Psychology*. DOI:10.3389/fpsyg.2019.02003.

Hings, R.F., Wagstaff, C.R.D., & Anderson, V. (2018). Professional challenges in elite sports medicine and science: Composite vignettes of practitioner emotional labor, *Psychology of Sport & Exercise*, 35: 66–73.

Kegelaers, J., Wylleman, P., Bunigh, A., & Oudejans, R. (2019). Mixed methods evaluation of a pressure training intervention to develop resilience in female basketball players, *Journal of Applied Sport Psychology*. DOI:10.1080/10413200.2019.1630864.

NSCA. www.nsca.com/professional-development/professional-development-overview/ (accessed 3 Dec. 2019).

Orvik, A., Vagen, S.R., & Axelsson, S.B. (2015). Quality, efficiency and integrity: Value squeezes in management of hospital wards, *Journal of Nursing Management*, 23: 65–74.

Ponnert, L., & Svensson, K. (2016). Standardisation – the end of professional discretion? *European Journal of Social Work*, 19(3–4): 586–599.

Quinn, J.B., Anderson, P., & Finkelstein, S. (1996). Managing professional intellect: Making the most of the best, *Harvard Business Review*, Mar.–Apr.: 71–80.

Reay, T., Goodrick, E., Waldorff, S.B., et al. (2017). Getting leopards to change their spots: Co-creating a new professional role identity, *Academy of Management Journal*, 60(3): 1043–1070.

Roderick, M. (2006). A very precarious profession: Uncertainty in the working lives of professional footballers, *Work, Employment and Society*, 20(2): 245–265.

Rynne, S.B., Mallett, C.J., & Rabjohns, M.W.O. (2017). High performance coaching: Demands and development. In R. Thelwell, C. Harwood, & I. Greenlees (eds.), *The Psychology of Sports Coaching: Research and Practice*, Abingdon: Routledge, pp. 114–126.

Schroder, H.S., Yalch, M.M., Dawood, S., et al. (2017). Growth mindset of anxiety buffers the link between stressful life events and psychological distress and coping strategies, *Personality and Individual Differences*, 110: 23–26.

Tonurist, P., & Surva, L. (2017). Is volunteering always voluntary? Between compulsion and coercion in co-production, *Voluntas*, 28: 223–247.

Wagstaff, C.R.D., Gilmore, S., & Thelwell, R.C. (2016). When the show must go on: Investigating repeated organizational change in elite sport, *Journal of Change Management*, 16(1): 38–54.

Watkins Jr., C.E., Hook, J.N., & Mosher, D.K. (2019). Humility in clinical supervision: Fundamental, foundational, and transformational, *The Clinical Supervisor*, 38(1): 58–78.

Watts, M. (2016). The evaluation of a strength and conditioning coach: A process-based profession in an outcome-based system. www.elitefts.com/education/the-evaluation-of-a-strength-and-conditioning-coach-a-process-based-profession-in-an-outcome-based-system/ (accessed 14 Oct. 2019).

Index

adaptation 22, 25, 59, 61, 62, 73, 134–135, 144, 147, 149, 159–160, 183; general adaptation syndrome 59, 62, 64; maladaptation 73, 161; neuromotor 160; structural 160; synergistic 135
adult 123, 125, 130, 132, 135–136, 146, 149, 163
Akkerman, S.F.: and Bakker, A. 108, 112; and Bruining, T. 110, 112
American College of Sport Medicine 171
anatomy 7, 167; functional 11
andragogy 11
athlete-centered 59, 64, 74, 104, 108
athletic injury rehabilitation 6
athletic training 7, 82, 164
Australasian College of Sport and Exercise Physicians 123, 125
Australian Strength and Conditioning Association (ASCA) 22, 27

Beck, U. 109, 112
biology: biomedical 9; biophysical 3–4, 6–11, 13–15, 26–27, 31, 33, 42, 98, 105, 153, 169, 170, 172; neuro 68
biomechanics 7, 9, 11, 69, 82, 162, 164
biopsychosocial 61, 99, 112, 125, 137
Bos-de Vos, M. 107–108, 112
boundary: conflicts 108; crossing 9, 16, 103, 107, 110–112; protection 106; work 103, 108, 111
brokers 3, 9, 14, 111; brokering 9

certified strength and conditioning specialist (CSCS) 23–24
collaborate 104, 107, 110–111
collegiality 19, 88, 103, 105, 180, 183
Community of Practice (CoP) 36, 108–109
competence: behavioural 21–22, 25–27, 64, 125; cognitive 21–22, 25–27, 62–63, 125; cultural 22, 25–27, 29, 40–41, 44, 63–64, 87, 125; ethical 21–22, 25–27, 61, 64, 125, 184; functional 21–26, 34, 85–86, 125, 185; professional 6, 18–22, 25–28, 34–35, 40–41, 54, 57, 63–64, 81, 86, 88, 125, 135, 169, 182, 184
conditioning 15, 33, 50–53, 59, 63, 69, 76, 83, 85, 101, 104, 108, 115, 117, 119, 121–122, 124–125, 130, 134–136, 139–140, 142–143, 146–147, 153–154, 156–157, 159, 161, 167–168, 170–171, 179
conflict 16, 55, 85, 95, 97, 108, 111, 113, 148, 155, 161, 167–168, 175, 179, 183
critical thinking 5, 29–30, 41, 64, 76, 88, 90, 169
cultural relevance cycle 40
Cushion, C. 12, 16, 31–32, 43–44, 131–132, 139

data 33, 49–54, 69, 72–73, 75–78, 83, 87, 101, 129, 132, 135, 147; big 72, 75, 77
decision 14, 28, 31, 34, 37–40, 42, 63, 70, 72–74, 78, 81, 84, 87–88, 93, 95–96, 121, 144, 148, 158, 169, 171–176: modifiers 171; return-to-play (RTP) 166, 169, 171, 175
deliberate practice 117, 121, 135
development 10–12, 14–16, 20, 22, 27–28, 30, 36, 56, 63, 65–66, 74, 81–84, 87, 92, 95, 96, 101, 103, 117, 120–126, 128–139, 144–146, 148–149, 157, 159, 170, 179, 184, 186–187; position-sampling 124
dichotomy 39, 137
discussion 4, 6, 9–10, 13–15, 27, 29, 31, 36–39, 41, 57, 59, 74, 76, 84, 87–88, 106, 108, 111, 117, 121–122, 124, 131, 137, 146, 168, 172–173, 185; domain of work 19, 107–108; issues-based approach 14
diverse 15, 40, 64–65, 81, 85–88, 90–91, 96, 99, 102, 123
diversity 38, 40, 42, 86–87, 90–91, 94, 96, 98–102
drill 49, 71, 104, 118–120, 130, 142, 155, 167–168

elite sport 13, 15, 47, 52, 77–78, 112–113, 162, 171, 178, 180, 187
emotions 4, 35, 44, 76, 95, 97; emotional 13, 30, 35, 44, 94, 105, 121, 123, 183–184, 187; socio-emotional 108

Index

ethics 23, 27–29, 37–38, 43–44, 51, 53, 59, 87, 90, 162, 167–169, 173–176, 179; care ethics 39; caring for, caring about, caring why 12, 22, 33–35, 40, 54, 57, 106, 166, 170, 186; code of ethics 18–20, 22–24, 27, 107, 181; contractarian 37, 173; deontological 37, 39, 173–174; duty 24, 52, 123, 173; ethical code 106–107, 175; natural caring 40; normative 29, 37–39, 173; rule-based 167, 173–174; sport 44, 88, 169, 172, 175–176; utilitarian 174; value 3–4, 6–7, 11, 13, 19–27, 19, 32–33, 35–40, 42, 44, 49–50, 52–57, 60–61, 64, 67, 70–76, 84, 87–88, 92, 95, 104–106, 109–110, 121, 123–125, 131–132, 134–135, 146, 148, 154, 156, 167–170, 174–176, 180–185, 187; virtue 37–40, 43–44, 53, 87, 90, 174, 176

evidence-based 25, 31, 77, 85, 137, 162
exercise prescription 6
exercise specialist 7
Eys, M.A. 108, 112

female 5, 78, 81–82, 91–92, 94–98, 100–102, 139, 145, 163, 175, 187
fitness 43, 118–119, 126, 176; corporate fitness 6
Fletcher, D. and Wagstaff, C. 35, 43, 108, 112
friction 108
functional recovery 171

Gearity, B. 3–4, 7, 12 13, 16–17, 21, 27–28, 31, 43–44, 72, 74, 77–78, 91, 97–99, 101–102, 159, 163–164
gender 10, 43, 92, 94–95, 97, 100–102, 137, 176; gendered 91, 94–99, 101–102
generalisation 121
GPS 50–52, 54, 68–70, 74–75, 77–78, 147, 179

habitus 64, 143, 172–173, 175
health 8–9, 13, 15, 42, 44–45, 52, 60–65, 68, 73–74, 77, 82, 107, 112, 119, 123, 131, 135, 138, 151, 156, 158–159, 162–164, 168–169, 171–173, 176, 181, 183
heteronormativity 98
human movement 3, 4, 10–11, 15, 17

injury 5–6, 15, 33–34, 50–55, 60–61, 63–65, 73, 82, 85, 104–105, 108–110, 112, 124, 126, 129, 135, 141, 144, 147, 151, 153, 155–176, 180, 182–184, 186; risk 52, 54, 56, 59, 68, 71, 123, 156–158, 160–161, 165, 171, 175–176
institutional 24, 83, 98, 100, 110–111
instruction 11, 13, 16, 82, 98, 104, 130, 132; style 104
interdisciplinary 14–15, 75, 112
International Olympic Committee 124, 126, 163
International Society for Sport Psychology (ISSP) 123, 126

internship 20, 59, 81–84, 103–105, 140, 178–181
interpersonal 16, 21, 35, 39, 75, 95, 97, 110–111, 136, 144

job security 105, 174
Journal of Australian Strength and Conditioning 25
Journal of Strength and Conditioning Research 101–102, 126, 164, 186

kinesiology 20, 24, 66, 68, 82, 101, 154
knowledge: domain 36; knowing how 12, 19, 22, 34–35, 40, 54, 182; knowing that 12, 19, 22, 34–35, 54; knowing why 12, 34–35, 54, 57, 106; knowledge structures 36

Laskowski, K.D. 97, 99, 101
Lave, J. 35–36, 43, 108–109, 112
LaVoi, N.M. 94, 96, 98
Lawson, H.A. 19, 28, 33–35, 43, 51–56, 60, 65, 84–85, 90, 105–106, 112
leader 33, 53, 87, 96–97, 99, 105; leadership 36, 83, 94–96, 98, 100, 102, 144, 182, 186
learning 4, 6, 8, 11, 16–17, 20, 28, 33, 41–44, 55–56, 75, 82–85, 89, 119, 125, 127, 130, 132, 146–149, 180, 184; capability 9; in group 35–37; opportunity 9, 36 37, 124; styles 40; theory 31
legitimate peripheral participation 36, 43, 112

management 28, 43–44, 56, 68, 81, 88, 97, 100–101, 103–104, 106, 110, 113, 143, 147, 156, 162–163, 166–167, 172–176, 182, 186–187
measure 15, 26, 33, 49–55, 60, 63, 67–73, 77–78, 124, 127, 131, 133, 136–137, 145, 147, 154, 160
mentoring 7, 82–83, 88, 182
monitoring 15, 51, 53, 55–56, 67–68, 70–77, 147, 179; workload 62
morality 34, 43–44, 106, 176; challenge 111
motor: control 11, 124, 159; learning 24, 124, 159, 163
movement screen 34, 50–51, 54, 56, 175
multi-professional 106

Nancarrow, S. 106, 112
National Strength and Conditioning Association (NSCA) 7–8, 13, 22–28, 49, 107, 130, 138, 159, 181, 187
non-professional: sources 33, 53; staff 106
Norman, L. 39, 44, 97, 99, 101–102
NSCA Strength and Conditioning Professional Standards and Guidelines 107, 113
nutrition 24, 67, 70–71, 82, 155

Index

objectives 20, 52, 61, 108, 136, 166, 183
Occam's razor 43, 56, 73, 77
organisational 14, 24, 37, 52, 56, 75, 84–85, 87, 89, 100, 111, 180, 183; infrastructure 107; micro-politics 182, 185; values 175

parenting/parental 117, 120–121, 125–126, 163
parsimony 73
pedagogy: cases 4, 16, 22, 43, 49, 52, 55, 57, 63, 67, 70, 72–73, 75, 81, 84–88, 91, 96–97, 105–107, 117, 128, 135, 140, 146–147, 153, 157, 159, 162, 166, 169–173, 177, 180–182, 184–185; modest 4; pedagogical 3–4, 6, 8–16, 29, 31, 42–43, 49, 76, 81, 117, 137, 148, 182; signature 20
periodised 59–60, 62, 83, 147; periodisation 57, 61–62, 64–65
phronesis 16, 30
physical education 7, 9, 12, 15–17, 20, 28, 43–44, 56, 65, 84–85, 89–90, 100, 112–113, 120, 126–127, 134, 137
physiology 7, 9, 11, 43, 56, 65, 69, 77–78, 82, 136, 143–144, 147–149, 167
physiotherapy 104, 107, 111–112
plan 22, 27–28, 36, 50–51, 53, 55, 60, 62–63, 68–69, 71, 83, 87, 104, 121, 147, 175, 178, 181, 186; planning 7, 62, 65, 67, 104
position 50, 60, 65, 124, 126, 141, 155, 164, 170–171, 174, 185; paper 123, 126; statement 117, 123, 125, 138, 159
praxis 16, 29–30, 41, 101
prehabilitation 50, 53, 153–157, 164, 170, 176
privileges 34, 95, 106, 170
problem: framing 34–35, 37, 41, 54, 60, 84, 103, 105–108; naming 34–35, 37, 41, 54, 84, 105–108; setting 19, 28–29, 33, 37, 41–43, 51–56, 65, 67, 84, 90, 105, 112
problematising 53
profession: accreditations 24, 85, 106, 181; associations 27, 63, 85, 107; boundaries 23, 103, 107–108, 110–111; competition 106, 180; conduct 19; deprofessionalisation 33, 53, 55, 105; development 4, 13, 22, 24–25, 33, 36, 42, 50, 53, 81, 85, 87–88, 93, 96, 98–99, 107, 112, 140, 144, 147, 169, 179–182, 185–187; experiences 99, 102, 105, 144, 181; identity 19, 28, 106, 111, 113, 181, 183, 186–187; interprofessional 106–107, 111–113, 182, 184; knowledge 18, 20, 22, 25–26, 44, 56, 65, 74, 105; management structure 103–104; process based 52, 84; professional 4, 6–8, 10–13, 15–36, 40–45, 49–56, 59–65, 67, 73–76, 81–94, 96, 98–99, 101–113, 125, 131, 135–136, 140–145, 147, 156–158, 160–161, 166–167, 169–170, 175–187; professionalisation 52; professionality 21, 86–87; recognition 105;

respect 22–23, 30, 36, 59, 82, 104–105; responsibility 19, 107; services 107, 181; setting 22; socialisation 81, 84–85, 88; team 106–107, 111–112, 180, 182, 185; voice 15, 103–113
programming 44, 62, 83, 104
progression 30, 98, 104, 120–121, 132, 135, 146, 168
proprioception 63, 160, 171
psychology: sport 11, 17, 24, 27, 68, 83, 112, 123, 126
psychosocial: capabilities 147–148; readiness 171; skills 75–76

realist 4, 11
reflective: critical 12; practice 12; practitioner 12–13, 32–33, 159; premise 31; process 12–13, 31–32; reflexive 31–33; reflexivity 31–33
rehabilitation 6, 13, 68, 93, 107, 110, 112, 141, 156–157, 164, 168–170, 176
relational practice 18, 35, 43, 45
relationship: coach-athlete 52
research methods 82
rights 19, 34, 38, 96, 106, 111
role ambiguities 108

scaffold 10, 14, 20, 39, 136
Schön, D.A. 31, 33, 44, 51–52, 54, 56, 60, 65
science: exercise science 3–4, 7, 10–12, 20, 24–26, 30, 81–82, 91, 93, 124, 127, 169
scope of practice 24, 89, 104, 107, 161, 169, 185
self-presentation 52
sensorimotor 132, 159
sex: heterosexuality 98; sexist 95–96, 98; sexuality 98, 100
shared practices 32, 36
shared repertoire 36, 108
situatedness: situated learning 36, 43, 112; situated practice 21
social cohesion 108
socialisation 34, 53–55, 60, 81, 84–85, 88–89, 106; organizational socialisation 84–85, 89
sociocultural: sociocultural pedagogical approach 3
specialisation: early 117, 120–124, 129, 139
sporting ability 124, 136
sport: coaching staff 60, 132; organisation 78, 107, 111, 144; psychologist 16, 42, 113, 126, 131
sport coaching 7–8, 11, 16, 31, 35, 42–44, 60, 74, 95, 101–102, 111–112, 120, 132, 148
Sport New Zealand 129, 139
sport sociology 13, 17, 27–28, 78
squad 34, 54, 59, 63, 81–82, 103, 122, 143–144, 154, 158, 161, 167
staff 60, 63, 67–70, 72–76, 81, 83, 85, 88, 92, 99, 101, 103–108, 110–112, 132, 141

stakeholders 171, 173, 175
stereotypes 7, 35, 91, 94–99, 96–98, 132–133; stereotyping 94
strength and conditioning (S&C): colleague 19, 83, 105, 107, 111, 129, 178, 183; professional 8, 12–13, 15, 18, 22, 25–27, 33, 40, 53, 57, 61, 63, 81, 84–86, 91, 125, 131, 135, 140, 143, 147, 156–157, 160–161, 181, 183; sessions 12, 50, 58, 64, 68–70, 74–75, 82, 103–104, 123, 142, 147, 154
strength and conditioning coach (SCC) 4–5, 12, 17, 24, 49, 57, 92, 120, 166, 177–178: assistant 59, 68, 83, 179; head 12, 68, 83, 93, 100–101, 141, 154, 178–179
Strength and Conditioning Journal 4–5, 13, 15–17, 25, 27–28, 43–44, 56, 66, 78, 101–102, 138, 163–164, 176
structure 9, 14, 58, 85, 88, 103–105, 136, 148, 155–156, 182
surveillance 12–13, 28, 67, 70, 74–76, 78; survey 75, 97, 149
system 16, 56, 58, 72–73, 83, 96, 104, 112, 126, 134, 138, 145, 157, 160, 175, 187

talent: development 128, 133–135, 137–138; identification 15, 128–139; models 134

team: communication 104; dynamic 104, 144; environment 63, 105, 141–142; manager 103, 105; teammates 69, 118–119, 133, 141–142, 147, 154–155; teamwork 88, 108
technical 10, 11, 13, 23, 65, 123; efficiency 34, 52, 54, 106, 111; rational 54
tension 34, 37, 39, 97, 108–109, 159–160, 170
therapist: physical 57, 103–105, 107, 111; physio 110, 167–171, 175
training: environment 35, 40–41, 76, 85, 92, 184; integrative neuromuscular 135

United Kingdom Strength and Conditioning Association (UKSCA) 13, 16, 22–28, 91–92, 111

validity 33, 51, 53, 55, 72–73, 161–162

Wenger, E. 9, 17, 35–37, 43, 45, 108–109, 112–113
Wenger-Trayner, E. 17, 36–37, 45, 109, 113
Wilhelmsson, M. 107, 113
wisdom hierarchy 73, 78
women: athletes 95; coaches 35, 39, 44, 96, 99; diversity 97; sport 91, 97, 123; in strength and conditioning 91–102

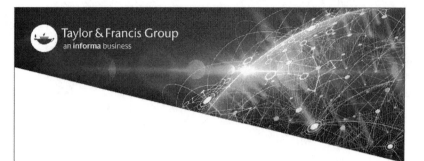